The War on Human Trafficking

The War on Human Trafficking

U.S. Policy Assessed

ANTHONY M. DESTEFANO

RUTGERS UNIVERSITY PRESS
New Brunswick, New Jersey

First paperback printing, 2008

Library of Congress Cataloging-in-Publication Data

DeStefano, Anthony M., 1946–
    The war on human trafficking : U.S. policy assessed / Anthony M. DeStefano.
        p. cm.
    Includes bibliographical references and index.
    ISBN-13: 978-0-8135-4059-7 (hardcover : alk. paper)
    ISBN-13: 978-0-8135-4418-2 (pbk : alk. paper)
1. Human trafficking—Government policy—United States.   2. Sex and law.
I. Title.

HQ125.U6D47 2007
364.1'3—dc22

2006031257

A British Cataloging-in-Publication record for this book is available from the
British Library.

Visit our Web site: http://rutgerspress.rutgers.edu

Manufactured in the United States of America

For Susan,
who got me started on this journey

Contents

Tables

Acknowledgments

On the morning of June 6, 1993, I was awakened by a telephone call from the morning editor at *New York Newsday*. Through the fog of sleep I learned that a decrepit freighter had run aground off Jacob Riis Park in Queens, New York. Hundreds of Chinese immigrants had been rounded up by federal agents and police. My job, I learned from my colleague, was to try to determine if Chinese organized-crime groups had been involved. It was an easy question to answer. Intelligence sources and police soon told me they suspected that the notorious Fuk Ching gang, led at the time by legendary leader Ah Kay, had been behind the smuggling operation, which became known as the Golden Venture.

For me, this telephone call began what turned into years of reporting on human smuggling and trafficking. By definition, the Golden Venture operation was a brazen, gang-led smuggling effort at a time when U.S. officials were overwhelmed by a constant flood of illegal immigrants. By boat, but more often by airplane and over land, immigrants seemed to be pouring into the country, raising alarms among law enforcement and politicians.

The smuggling transaction was fairly straightforward: immigrants paid people to get them into the United States illegally. Once the immigrants made it past immigration and the border patrol, they invariably never saw the smugglers again. But eventually a variation of smuggling, human trafficking, arose as another vexing problem. Investigators learned that immigrants were making onerous pacts with traffickers, a specialized breed of migration merchants who tricked, cajoled, forced, and otherwise compelled immigrants to undertake terrible jobs that often amounted to virtual slavery. The traffickers kept their hooks in the immigrants through an oppressive system of debt bondage and other forms of coercion.

The introduction to this book spells out in detail the kinds of stories I worked on when covering human trafficking, so I won't belabor the subject at this point. Suffice it to say that in the years I wrote about trafficking and immigration I interviewed numerous people, and what I learned from them has made it into this book. Some have asked to remain anonymous; therefore, I cannot acknowledge their help publicly. But they have earned my gratitude nonetheless.

In the time I spent as a journalist researching and writing about human trafficking, I was fortunate to have access to a number of experts: Sealing Cheng, Wellesley College; Ko-Lin Chin, Rutgers University; Helga Conrad, Organization for Security and Cooperation in Europe; Ann Jordan, director of the Initiative against Trafficking in Persons, Global Rights; Jane Manning of Equality Now; John Markey, formerly of the U.S. Department of State; Iana Matei of Reaching Out (Romania); Ambassador John Miller, senior advisor to the U.S. Secretary of State and director of the Office to Monitor and Combat Trafficking; James Puleo of the International Organization for Migration; Ambassador Richard Schifter; and Juhu Thukral, director of the Sex Workers Project at the Urban Justice Center. Assistant U.S. attorneys Dan Alonso and Pamela Chen of the Brooklyn U.S. Attorneys Office helped me understand some major trafficking cases prosecuted by their office.

I also want to thank David Burnham, co-director of the Transactional Records Access Clearinghouse, for his patience in guiding me through his organization's data collection process, which proved invaluable to me, particularly for my analysis in Chapter 12. Attorney Frank Bari of New York, a savvy street lawyer, gave me a special entrée to the world of Asian organized crime; and nobody knew the Asian crime scene better than he did. Iana Matei gets a special second mention because, for more than six years, she allowed me access to her work with trafficked women in Romania, giving me a unique vantage point on the problems and promises facing victims there. At the drop of a hat, Iana would pick me up and drive me to places she thought I should see. Iana has shown a tremendous amount of strength, courage, and sensitivity in dealing with people caught in terrible situations, sometimes placing herself in physical danger for their sake.

I made a number of research trips to Romania; and during one of those visits, in August 2000, I had the assistance of my good friend Virginia Farcas, who emigrated to the United States from the Transylvania region in 1991 and later became my neighbor. Virginia, her sister Laura, and the rest of their family offered hospitality and gave me advice that proved very helpful on my travels. Les Payne, my former editor (now retired) at *Newsday*, encouraged reporters to work on the newspaper's "Smuggled for Sex" series from 1999 to 2001 and allowed me to travel in Romania in the process. It was a wise move on Les's part and certainly paid off, not only in giving me the insight to write this book but also because it earned us an award for our stories from the New York Press Club in 2002.

Susan and our extraordinary poodle Oliver get a special thank you for putting up with my distractions and inattention while I was working on this book well as another about Mafia boss Joseph Massino. Of course, I also have to thank my editor at Rutgers University Press, Marlie Wasserman, for seeing the possibility of this book and for cracking the whip and getting me to focus when it was easy to lose my way.

Introduction

As a journalist, I realize that many good stories evolve from serendipity. That is what happened during my trip to Romania in the summer of 2000. July of that year happened to be particularly hot: temperatures rose higher than one hundred degrees Fahrenheit. Humidity was also high, and drought conditions persisted, making life in Bucharest uncomfortable. So on one particularly sweltering afternoon I retreated to the bar in the Sovitel Hotel and ordered a Coke to quench my thirst.

I had taken only a few sips of my drink when my cell phone chirped. The caller was Iana Matei, a Romanian woman whose name I had been given a few days earlier and who had learned I was looking for her. After introductions I told her that I was interested in the work she had been doing with women in Eastern Europe who had been employed as prostitutes. I explained that I was in the country on a working holiday to research for my newspaper, *Newsday,* a series of stories about the international smuggling of women for the sex industry. I thought her perspective and experience would prove important to the project, and I was correct.

In the city of Pitesti, located some seventy miles away from downtown Bucharest, Matei ran a hostel for women who had been prostitutes. Most, if not all, of the women living in her "Reaching Out" facility had left Romania at various times in search of work abroad, only to find themselves working in brothels or as topless dancers and hostesses in seedy bars. Some got as far as Italy and Turkey; but most wound up in other Balkan countries such as Albania, Macedonia, and Bosnia-Herzegovina.

Granted, some of the women, ranging in ages from sixteen to twenty-nine years old, knew they would wind up in the sex business. But many more, Matei explained, didn't expect what turned out to be numbing submission to an unanticipated number of sex partners each day. In the eyes of Matei and many other human rights activists, the women at the hostel had been tricked, inveigled, and coerced into lives as prostitutes. At the time, the average monthly wage in Romania was about one hundred dollars a month. Enticed by satellite television images of affluent western lifestyles, young Romanian women came to believe the entreaties of pimps, procurers, and assorted immigration merchants, who told them they could travel to better-paying jobs in places such as Italy, Greece, or Spain. Unfortunately, what awaited many of these women were not their promised restaurant, domestic, or factory jobs but lives as compelled prostitutes.

By 2000, the phenomenon of forced labor as described by Matei and other experts had become known as *trafficking*. Law enforcement often used the term to describe the movement of or commerce in illegal substances such as drugs. Journalists and some investigators had even described the smuggling of immigrants as a form of trafficking. But in the human rights lexicon the term was used to describe a particular form of illegal immigration involving fraud and coercion. As Matei explained, an immigrant was considered to be a victim of trafficking if the migration involved trickery, fraud, or coercion and ended with the migrant's forced labor in a job.

It was months before I returned to visit Matei and her shelter in Pitesti. But in the interim, thousands of miles away in Washington, D.C., American law enforcement officials and diplomats were grappling with the new trafficking phenomenon in their own way. There was no particular U.S. statute that defined trafficking. True, old U.S. peonage laws, written in the 1880s, covered the forcing of labor to liquidate a worker's debt. But trafficking as a particular immigration crime was not defined or penalized as a separate offense.

It turned out that the United States wasn't alone in having an ambiguous definition of human trafficking. Many other countries lacked laws dealing with the subject, and the United Nations began to feel compelled to act on what had become a global concern about the increase in human trafficking. The very summer that Matei and I had talked, negotiators from more than one hundred countries were meeting in Vienna to devise an international document that would attempt to eradicate the illicit commerce in humans by creating uniform national laws and cooperation in global law enforcement.

My conversations with Matei and my visit to her shelter sparked my continuing interest in the subject of human trafficking. One result was my contribution to a series of newspaper articles published in *Newsday* in March 2001. The stories dealt with the smuggling of immigrants for sex work into New York City. Our reportage, which encompassed two years of effort, was particularly relevant to the nation's largest metropolitan area because the city was a magnet for so many new immigrants and thus a coveted destination for women on the migrant sex-business circuit. Admittedly, we focused on the sex industry because it was a good subject for newspaper treatment.

Journalist, myself included, initially approached the subject of human trafficking as a law enforcement issue. After all, many of the publicized cases stemmed from the actions of federal immigration officials and local police who had discovered immigrant women working in brothels. But the deeper I dug into the subject of human trafficking, the more I learned that it went beyond being a story about criminals and victims. Human trafficking had become one of the major human rights issues of the late twentieth century; and as a news story, it had complex and multiple facets. As is often the case when advocates become energized about a subject, trafficking had become a political issue. It remains political to this day because it involves questions of morality and decisions about how the United States and the rest of the world address major deprivations of human rights.

Since politics and advocacy are intertwined with the subject of human trafficking, any public discourse is bound to be affected by the various arguments and emotions of those who are intimately involved. This can create problems in defining the dimensions of the trafficking problem and developing policies to deal with it. Researchers Anette Brunovskis and Guri Tyldum made this point when they stated in a review of studies on human trafficking that "uncritically using or publishing findings not based on sound methodologies may result in misinformation and hinder the creation of relevant policies."[1] For example, in late 1999 a study sponsored by the Central Intelligence Agency estimated that 50,000 trafficking victims entered the United States each year. For years, members of Congress and others in government assumed that estimate was accurate and relied on it to shape legislative responses to the problem. But over time the estimate was cut in half. By 2005, different methods of calculation had dropped the number to about 17,000.

Global estimates about the size of the human trafficking population also vary widely. I discovered that some sources put the number at 2 million while others believe that 700,000 is a more accurate figure. Questions also arise about what constitutes a trafficked person. Can we count a person who is in the process of migration? Or should that person already be working as a forced or coerced laborer? How should we account for former victims of trafficking who have since been rescued?

But one thing we do know is that the scope of global migration, be it illegal or legal, is large. By late 2005 U.N. estimates pegged the number of migrants worldwide at almost 200 million yearly. Almost half that number was comprised of women, and the United Nations believed that a growing number were migrating independently. So as I study the subject of human trafficking, it has become clear that it is not only a complex phenomenon but also part of a larger picture of human movement.[2]

Journalists know that much of their product is nothing more than what one pundit has called a first draft of history. Journalism is often done on the fly, quickly and with some imprecision, simply because events in the news are constantly evolving. Much of the reportage on the subject of human trafficking has followed this pattern, focusing on terrible cases of trafficked people in all sorts of bad straits. In the process, however, we have often ignored the more complicated long-term story of how trafficking policy has evolved. By their nature, policy stories deal with legislative and government affairs and are less compelling than the case studies of human problems they focus on; thus, it isn't surprising that the evolution of a U.S. trafficking policy has not been extensively covered. Nevertheless, because the development of U.S. government and law enforcement response to human trafficking has driven much of what has become the global reaction to this particular immigration issue, it's important to examine the evolution of U.S. policy so that we can gain an understanding of international trafficking issues. That is my reason for writing this book.

The work that you hold in your hands evolved from my years of reporting on human trafficking in the United States and abroad, when I came across scores of cases involving hundreds of trafficking victims and numerous immigrant cultures. In deciding which cases to deal with in this book, I chose to focus not only on sex trafficking cases, of which there were plenty, but also on labor trafficking cases, which in reality make up an equal, if not greater, number of cases. Because this is a work about the government's policy response, I also chose to include cases from criminal investigations that reflected the immigrant cultures in the United States: Latino, Asian, African, Middle Eastern, and Eastern European. Latino cultures are represented by cases dealing with trafficked Mexicans and Peruvians. Asian cultures are represented by Chinese, Korean, and Vietnamese cases. Eastern European cases involve immigrants from Russia and Ukraine. African victims in the United States included nationals from Cameroon, while Indonesian women were employed against their will in the U.S. households of Saudi nationals.

I chose some of the cases, such as the one involving the Cadena family and its Mexican prostitutes, not only because they so vividly show the terrors in store for trafficked victims in the United States but also because of how the particular incidents catalyzed policy initiatives. I examine others, such as the terrible labor exploitation suffered by Vietnamese migrants in American Samoa, because they illustrate how U.S. law enforcement officials could effectively work to deal with trafficking when the right resources and attention were brought to bear. Still other cases, such as those of the Peruvian day workers on Long Island, show that, despite beneficial changes in laws, trafficking remains a pernicious and perhaps intractable problem in this country.

But this book is more than just a series of case studies dealing with human trafficking. It also shows how U.S. policy on trafficking was created between the mid-1990s and mid-2006. I cover the formulation of the Victims of Trafficking and Violence Protection Act of 2000, the key foundation of U.S. policy. Known as the TVPA, the legislation was signed into law by President Bill Clinton on October 28, 2000, and was the culmination of the work of a number of senators and members of the House of Representatives, notably the late Senator Paul Wellstone of Wisconsin and Representative Chris Smith of New Jersey. The law was aimed at accomplishing what Clinton's administration called the "Three Ps": prosecution, protection, and prevention.

Prosecution is relatively self-explanatory; it holds traffickers accountable under criminal law and punishes them for their activities. *Protection* describes the various forms of assistance, ranging from housing and medical care to special immigration status, available to trafficking victims who want and need such help. *Prevention* relates to activities such as public education and job creation intended to keep potential victims out of the clutches of traffickers and away from exploitation. By warning potential victims about the dangers of submitting to traffickers and trying to develop viable economic alternatives to their desperate migration for work, this last goal gets closest to dealing with the root causes of trafficking. But it is also the most difficult goal to achieve because it relies on economic forces and changes in human behavior that may be impossible to influence. The vagaries of the global economy and the dislocation caused by war and disaster may be too powerful to overcome, even with the best laws a government can create. Added to those difficulties is the relatively small amount of funding that even the U. S. government has historically set aside for trafficking.

After passage of the TVPA an entirely new federal bureaucracy developed to deal with trafficking. The Department of State formed its Office to Monitor and Combat Trafficking in Persons to assess the anti-trafficking efforts of foreign nations and become something of a bully pulpit to promote the U.S. anti-trafficking message. Also created was the Human Smuggling and Trafficking Center, an interagency unit that coordinates efforts against alien smuggling, trafficking in persons, and terrorist travel and works as a liaison between U.S. diplomatic and law enforcement entities and foreign agencies. The Department of Health and Human Services and the Department of Labor created initiatives to help trafficking victims and disburse funding for local activities.

One of the aims of this book is to examine those efforts and come to a conclusion about their effectiveness. Thus, I not only have reviewed the U.S. government's self-assessments but have relied on independent data compiled by the nonprofit Transactional Records Access Clearinghouse (TRAC), which is affiliated with Syracuse University. Through persistent and creative use of the federal Freedom of Information Act, TRAC researchers have acquired amazing amounts of statistical information showing just how much work federal agencies have done in enforcing laws and gauging their effectiveness. Although I expound on the TRAC analysis later in the book, suffice it to say here that the data show that U.S. enforcement of the trafficking laws has been challenging and has not always resulted in outcomes desired by law enforcement agencies or policymakers. As often as American federal prosecutors bring criminal charges for trafficking, they have to decline to pursue cases because of problems that develop.

This book also deals with the 2000 creation of the U.N. Protocol to Prevent, Suppress, and Punish Trafficking in Women and Children. While not a U.S. government document, the protocol came into being a mere two months after President Clinton signed the TVPA and was clearly an American policy initiative. Understanding the protocol's background can help us identify the political forces that have affected U.S. policy debates on trafficking. For example, prostitution was a divisive issue in debates about the U.N. protocol. Some abolitionists wanted it to ban prostitution (a position that certain nations found unacceptable) and thus risked scuttling the negotiations. Even the U.S. delegation was pressured by domestic abolitionists, who thought the White House was too soft on prostitution; and this debate has continued to influence U.S. policy years after passage of the TVPA.

As I describe in this book, the U.N. trafficking protocol actually incorporated elements of the Three Ps and made international collaboration easier, allowing countries to rely on one another for extradition and mutual legal assistance without going through time-consuming bilateral negotiations. Yet ironically, while the Clinton administration was a driving force in creating the U.N. document, the United States was one of the last nations to ratify it, finally doing so in late-2005.

Following the momentous events of 2000, when the TVPA was passed and the U.N. trafficking protocol signed, American policy continued to evolve. As I will show, however, American response to human trafficking was affected by the events of September 11. The terrorist attacks caused a massive shift in U.S. law enforcement priorities, redirecting attention and resources in the war against terrorism. At least in the short term, reallocations of money and law enforcement personnel have affected the TVPA's implementation; and the start of the Iraq War in 2003, also a result of September 11, has affected federal spending priorities well into 2006.

After passage of the TVPA, legislators introduced a number of other changes that affected U.S. policy. Some changes were technical or minor.

But others were driven by the political agendas of those aligned with the religious right, who, like the abolitionists in the U.N. protocol debate, took aim at prostitution. Legislators on the right saw trafficking primarily as a phenomenon involving sex migration. Congressional hearings became forums for tales of women and children working as virtual sex slaves for pimps who had trafficked them throughout Europe and Southeast Asia. These horrors stories of sexual servitude turned the ensuing debate about trafficking into a platform for abolishing prostitution, the premise being that, if prostitution dries up, there will be no need for sex trafficking.

I believe the tendency to see human trafficking primarily as sex trafficking has muddled U.S. thinking about the intricacies of human migration. True, there are horrific stories about immigrant women forced into prostitution: the case of the Cadena smuggling ring in Florida, in which Mexican women were herded into trailers and compelled to have sex even during their menstrual cycles, rattled even veteran investigators. In many parts of the United States, prostitution has been illegal for decades; and most people have a visceral sense, because of religious or personal morality, about whether or not it is an appropriate profit-making activity. But as I have noted, trafficking is not just about sex work. Terrible cases have emerged involving trafficked immigrant laborers trapped in sweatshop industries ranging from garment manufacturing to farming to poultry processing. Other cases involve domestic workers kept as virtual indentured servants for employers, who sometimes are fellow countrymen.

But by focusing so much attention on sex work (though no one has provided reliable data on how large a proportion of trafficking cases involve such occupations), the U.S. debate about trafficking has become a way for anti-prostitution zealots to single out sex work as a particular evil. They have found ready allies in the Bush administration, which has advanced legislation and policies to conform to the anti-prostitution agenda while further polarizing human rights advocates working on the trafficking issue. Legislation advancing the anti-prostitution agenda includes the Trafficking Victims Protection Reauthorization Act of 2003, the HIV/AIDS act of 2003, and a 2006 revision of the TVPA aimed at reducing customer demand for prostitutes.

One aspect of the Trafficking Victims Protection Reauthorization Act has proved particularly controversial. The measure not only appropriates more money for anti-trafficking efforts but also prevents any federal money earmarked for anti-trafficking efforts from going to organizations that do not publicly affirm their opposition to the legalization or practice of prostitution. In 2005, this purity test also became a requirement for any U.S. group seeking federal funding for overseas HIV/AIDS programs. The aim of such pledges seems to be greater marginalization of prostitution—and, of course, prostitutes—by depriving them of assistance, particularly with AIDS treatment or prevention.

In early 2006, U.S. anti-prostitution forces succeeded in passing a TVPA revision intended to reduce demand for commercial sexual services. The law provides a series of modest grants to help local law enforcement officials arrest persons who pay for those services—what police call "Johns." According to some supporters of the legislation, these consumers include both men who solicit prostitutes and the pimps or procurers who control the women's activities; and one proponent has said that the government now equates prostitution with sex trafficking, a goal of the groups behind the agenda.[3]

By equating prostitution with trafficking, legislators have turned the precise targeting of an immigration crime that victimizes newcomers into a way of prohibiting and trying to abolish domestic prostitution. To generate support for such a position, proponents of the so-called "end demand" law of 2006 point to the worst-case scenarios of runaway-girls-turned-prostitutes and the physical and emotional deprivations suffered by those who work in street prostitution. These are powerful stories. But as other cases show, prostitution is a multifaceted industry with a proliferation of high-priced sex workers, including well-known pornography stars, fashion models, and aspiring actresses who voluntarily take part because it is lucrative. In 2005, a major federal prosecution in New York City disclosed that international call girls can make as much as 50,000 dollars in a weekend, hardly the pittance some immigrant sex workers earn.[4] High-end global prostitution attracts young women who want to make a lot of money. Thus, prohibition of prostitution risks not only ignorance of the fact that it can be a job preference but also the appearance of paternalism and even misogyny.

After years of reporting on the issue of trafficking, I felt that a serious book about the development of U.S. policy would reveal the various forces that have shaped the nation's response to the problem. Doing so would also allow me to take a more critical view (not easy in standard newspaper reporting) about the various policy responses and their effectiveness in a way that spanned several years of development. At the same time I would be able to weave into the story my experiences abroad, which also spanned several years, and show how the U.S. response to human trafficking has affected other parts of the world. Sometimes that impact has been positive; other times it has been troublesome.

Iana Matei's story is particularly relevant because it illustrates an important point in this book: U.S. policy initiatives concerning trafficking, particularly in the area of law enforcement assistance, have emboldened a wide variety of people to take significant action on the issue. In Matei's case,

American diplomats encouraged her activities with rescued women. The involvement of U.S. law enforcement officials in establishing a regional anti-crime organization in the Balkans meant that Matei and some of the women she was helping could assist in the apprehension, conviction, and punishment of a number of traffickers.

Because trafficking policy has evolved over time, I have structured the book chronologically. Central to the story are a number of cases that I learned about during my years spent reporting on the subject. Some are sex trafficking cases; others are labor trafficking cases. Each introduces and illustrates a specific point in the narrative. For instance, the Cadena case actually predated the passage of the TVPA. The degradation of the women and the brutal actions of their pimps and captors became modern versions of the stories of sexual captivity that had energized activists in Victorian England and pre-1930s America to fight prostitution.[5] The case mobilized Congress to see trafficking as a particular ill that had to be addressed by legislation.

Perhaps one of the most important labor cases I discuss involved scores of Vietnamese garment factory workers who were discovered living in American Samoa and working for a Korean businessman. "Sweatshop conditions" is too kind a phrase to describe the environment in which these workers toiled. They were deprived of good nourishment and decent housing and endured vicious physical abuse at the hands of their boss, Kil Soo Lee.[6] The American Samoa case is useful because it illustrates not only how in certain circumstances American law enforcement might adequately respond to trafficking but also how global economic forces and the relative ease of migration combine to put laborers in harm's way.

I also explore a case involving Mariluz Zavala and her associates, who smuggled more than eighty Peruvian immigrants into the New York City area, confiscated their passports, and then forced them to live in houses that Zavala owned. Between 2003 and 2004, she forced the immigrants to work, pay rent, and redeem their smuggling fees. The situation was a textbook case of labor trafficking and, like the Cadena case, involved revolting living conditions. Zavala was able to coerce and exploit the immigrants because of their anonymity as illegal aliens. Her case also illustrates the lengths to which migrants will go to work in the United States when they can't find employment in their countries of origin.[7]

Since enactment of the TVPA, sex-related trafficking cases have made up the majority of prosecutions initiated by federal officials. One case from the Chicago area illustrates the business arrangements set up to entice European women to come to the United States to work as dancers in strip clubs. According to federal court records, Michail Aronov, a Lithuanian citizen, set up a business called Beauty Search, Inc., which purported to import and manage women from Eastern Europe who wanted to work in strip clubs in southeastern Michigan. These women were impelled by reasons similar to those of some of Iana Matei's clients: they needed jobs. The Aronov case illustrates an extreme form of sex trafficking in which victims were loaded with enormous debts, forced to pay them off with sex work, kept in isolation, and psychologically and physically abused. But it also shows how the victims successfully sought out the help of federal officials: because of the TVPA's influence on both the legal apparatus and law enforcement priorities, two women were able to escape from Aronov's control and alert investigators to the trafficking ring and the other victims.[8]

Another case I discovered in 2005 had an interesting twist. It involved a woman known as Madam Jin but whose real name was Kong Sun Hernandez. Madam Jim was a federal informant for the U.S. Border Patrol and had been passing along reliable information about human smuggling activities on the U.S. and Canadian border. The problem was that she and her associates were also running a business on the side in which they imported women from South Korea to work in brothels. Because Canada doesn't have visa restrictions on Korean nationals, it has become a major trans-shipping point for immigrants who want to enter the United States. A significant portion of the Asian sex industry workers use Canada as a way to sneak across the border.[9]

Asian brothel businesses have long been a focus of police activity, particularly in New York, California, Georgia, and other states with large Asian populations. In Madam Jin's case, she smuggled women in through Washington State and on to Los Angeles, where they worked as call girls and paid off their smuggling debts through sex work. Although Madam Jin didn't plead guilty to sex trafficking, she did admit to human smuggling. Her case illustrates the dimensions of the immigrant sex industry and its surrounding ambiguous contractual relationships, which create difficulties for those enforcing the trafficking laws. A more substantial allegation of trafficking in the Asian sex industry surfaced in late 2005 with the results of a federal probe in San Francisco codenamed Operation Gilded Cage, which resulted in numerous arrests and the apprehension of scores of prostitutes from the Far East.[10]

Another Korean immigrant case related to forced labor has overtones of sexual abuse. It involved the Kangs, a Korean couple living in the New York City area, who owned a bar and nail salons in Queens. They recruited Korean women overseas who were interested in working as hostesses and explicitly promised the women that no prostitution was involved. That promise was a ruse. After the women immigrated to New York and found that they weren't making enough money to pay off immigration fees of more than 10,000 dollars,

Mr. Kang suggested that fast money could be made through prostitution, according to investigators. At first, the women resisted his recruitment; but then, officials said, he began to threaten them and abuse them physically. The Kangs plead guilty to human trafficking charges in late 2005. Their case illustrates, among other things, how the cooperation of victims can be vital in prosecuting traffickers.[11]

Domestic workers make up another class of trafficking victims and, for all anybody knows, may be as numerous as the victims of sex trafficking. They are used as cheap labor by families living in the United States and are deterred from complaining about their predicament because of their enforced isolation and unfamiliarity with American culture as well as fear of their employers. Consider the case of the Djoumessi family, who lived in Michigan and brought a domestic worker into the United States from Cameroon under false pretenses. The young woman, who was only age thirteen when she was first employed, was forced to care for the defendants' children and perform household chores without pay. The victim was beaten and forbidden to leave the home of her employer. Investigators determined that she had also been raped.[12]

Sometimes domestic trafficking cases have an element of sex trafficking. Two Nigerian nationals, Adaobi and George Udeozor, were charged with smuggling in a teenaged girl from their homeland and forcing her to work in their home and professional business in Maryland for no pay. The victim was sexually assaulted and regularly beaten. Adaobi Udeozor was convicted after a trial, but her co-defendant became a fugitive.[13]

Cases I discovered also occurred in places far from major metropolitan areas. In the towns of Albion and Kendall in western New York State, investigators discovered that migrant workers had been trafficked to work on farms. The victims were constantly monitored and threatened. Large deductions were taken from their pay to cover transportation, food, and housing charges accrued since they had been smuggled from Mexico into Arizona. In a sense, the trafficking victims were living in a "company town" situation, where their employers provided everything they needed but at a high cost that left them with virtually no money.

Another labor case shows that traffickers aren't all cruel Mafioso or Eastern European types. Some can be very respectable citizens. Such was the case of Johannes Du Preez, president of a substantial Atlanta business. A native of South Africa, Du Preez rose to local prominence in Georgia with a granite and marble company that specialized in supplying materials for home construction and renovation to reputable companies such as Home Depot.[14]

But in 2004, Du Preez, his wife, and others were indicted on charges they had smuggled in workers from South Africa and forced them to work in hard labor at the company. Allegedly, Du Preez brought in scores of South Africans, ostensibly to work as executives at his firm. The immigrants illegally entered under a special U.S. visa program reserved for foreign managers. The laborers then worked with heavy machinery to cut and polish stone, with their wages used to repay the cost of their visas and housing at an apartment complex. They were threatened, according to prosecutors, with the prospect of being reported to U.S. immigration officials if they complained. After a legal fight, Du Preez, his wife, and some of the other defendants pled guilty in a 2005 plea bargain arrangement.[15]

I have woven many trafficking cases into the narrative of this book to illustrate particular points. But it is important to keep in mind that this work is not meant to be a collection of stories, each more horrible than the last, about the victimization of trafficked persons. In my experience, much of the coverage of the issue has followed a predictable story line: vulnerable person meets criminal entrepreneur and is then tricked into a life of unspeakable servitude, finally to be freed by intrepid investigators. In a way, the formulaic approach to such stories isn't surprising: as Christopher Booker has noted in *The Seven Basic Plots: Why We Tell Stories*, overcoming the monster (in this case, the trafficker) is a standard plot line.[16] But I want this book to move beyond that formula; I want to look at the politicization of trafficking in the United States while assessing how the country has met some of the goals of the TVPA and its progeny.

Much has happened since my first telephone conversation with Iana Matei on that hot Romanian day in 2000. She is no longer a solitary figure fighting to get help for trafficking victims in her country. Romania, like many other countries, has acknowledged the problem of human trafficking with new laws, police units that specialize in trafficking, closer cooperation with neighboring countries, and a social service infrastructure to help victims. Many of these improvements have come about because the United States has used its own position as a bully pulpit and because of the carrot-and-stick methods of Washington diplomacy. In turn, the United States has been influential because the international community has come to recognize the trafficking issue as important.

As with drug trafficking, human trafficking depends on the existence of a ready supply of labor—in this case, people who are seeking economic salvation and will turn to migration entrepreneurs (traffickers) for help. Thus, there are substantial socioeconomic forces at work that make deterrence a difficult and perhaps impossible task. It is better, I think, to give victims places to turn to for help—refuges such as law enforcement protection, social services, and coveted green cards—rather than take on the hopeless task of mandating an end to sex work.

My review of American policy on trafficking encompasses roughly a five-year period between 2000 (when the TVPA was passed) and early 2006 (when Congress revised the law that dealt with demand for sex work). While brief, that period encompassed a great deal of legislative and law enforcement activity and a significant expenditure of government money. Since then, some members of Congress have become concerned that, despite those measures, trafficking seems to be increasing; and the Government Accountability Office has commenced an inquiry into the efficacy and effectiveness of U.S. government response to trafficking as well as the way in which it has interacted with international efforts (see Chapter 12).

Whatever politics surround the trafficking issue, it is clear that the phenomenon will attract nations' attention and energy for years to come. Human migration occurs on a vast scale globally; and even if only an infinitesimal portion of those 200 million migrants involves trafficked persons, the number of victims remains sizable. Powerful economic needs impel people to put themselves at risk by turning to traffickers. Only when governments address those needs will such risky behavior be reduced. In the meantime it is the next best thing for governments and human rights advocates to protect the victims who are caught up in the trafficking business so that they have a chance to live their lives in dignity.

The War on Human Trafficking

Chapter 1   The Barrio Girls

FOR THE YOUNG girls from Santiago Tuxtla, their journey to a personal hell invariably began when those big, fancy American cars drove into the little Mexican town some thirty miles south of the port city of Veracruz.

Santiago Tuxtla was not a beaming metropolis, but it wasn't the worst place in the world either. Its population of 51,000 lived in an area bordered on the west by green hills and on the east by the Gulf of Mexico. In the nice section of town, Hollywood stars Michael Douglas, Kathleen Turner, and Danny DeVito had once filmed scenes for their movie *Romancing the Stone*. An outdoor museum displayed the largest stone Olmec head to survive from the period before the Spanish Conquest. The Olmec had been a sophisticated ancient people who inhabited the area and were known for their elongated skulls, which they had artificially deformed as a sign of noble birth. They were clever mathematicians, artists, astronomers, and city planners.

Santiago Tuxtla also had a hardscrabble, poor neighborhood known as Barrio El Pilar. The lives of families from the barrio were circumscribed by monotony. This was particularly true for the women, who could count on only meager jobs in a tortilla factory or a belt-embroidering plant as well as the prospect of raising children who would face the same limited economic prospects.

The drivers of the fancy American cars were themselves from Barrio El Pilar, so they understood the residents' bleak futures. But they also offered hope. Lives didn't have to be consigned to obscure toil. Beyond Santiago Tuxtla, even beyond Veracruz—itself a city that seemed like Oz to the region's provincial population—there was money to be made. People could earn hundreds, even thousands, of dollars per week for honest work in the United States. Most persuasive of these drivers was a pleasant, well-dressed woman who told the young people that a better life was just a quick jump across the border.

Immigration to the United States had always been a way for Mexicans to climb the economic ladder and earn money to send back to their families and native villages. Mexicans were flooding north across the border at a rate that seemed unstoppable. Despite all the efforts of the U.S. Border Patrol, even with the help of fences, sophisticated surveillance devices, and posses of American civilians, the flow of Mexicans was escalating. By 2005 there would be an estimated 10 million Mexican immigrants living illegally in the United States. That number represented a decades-long stream of immigration. While many of those migrants chose to live in the southwestern United States, others traveled throughout the country; and according to the 2000 census, their communities were among the fastest-growing populations in New York City and other American metro areas.

In the late 1990s, when the fancy cars and smooth talkers arrived in Santiago Tuxtla, that river of migration was attracting the naïve and desperate young women of the barrio. They were captivated by the prospect of earning 400 dollars a week doing nothing more strenuous than waiting on tables in Florida restaurants. Those wages were certainly much higher than the 35 to 40 dollars a week the men earned as field hands tending to sugarcane, banana, and maize crops. It also wasn't back-breaking field labor or dreary, monotonous work in a tortilla factory.

The well-dressed lady in the fancy car told the girls that the trip north would cost about 2,000 dollars, including 25 dollars for the ticket to Matamoros, a town on the Mexico–U.S. border that was a common jumping-off point for would-be emigrants. Don't worry, she told the girls; the money they would earn in the United States would easily allow them to pay off the smuggling fee. Young women with names like Maria, Lorena, Inez, Rosa, and Erika were lured by her reassuring explanations as well as the patter of a male relative who was driving the lady's car in Santiago Tuxtla. Each woman heard the same story: the local Cadena family had a restaurant in Florida that needed waitresses. The family also needed nannies to care for the children of the restaurant owners.[1]

If they needed further proof of the affluence awaiting them in Florida, the girls had only to look at the big American cars the Cadena-Sosa family drove around town. Though some Tuxtla families were suspicious, many of the girls prevailed, convincing their relatives that a trip to Florida, where they could work for the Cadena businesses, was the best way to make financial headway.

"A lot of girls were going, to take care of children, wash dishes," the mother of one fourteen-year-old girl remembered. "So, she got excited. The truth is, we wouldn't let her, but she got excited and said, 'Mama, I'm going, so I can pull us up.'"[2]

After paying about twenty-five dollars each for a bus trip to Matamoros, the girls from Tuxtla were smuggled across the Rio Grande. Not every first-time smuggling attempt was successful. But the smugglers (known as "coyotes") persisted, and many of the young women were eventually able to enter the United States clandestinely. Then reality set in.

After a brief stay at a safe house in the Houston area, smugglers told the women the true story about the work they would be doing: they would be prostitutes. For the migrants, any lingering doubts must have evaporated when, on their first trips to American shopping malls and chain stores like K-Mart, smugglers began buying them sexy lingerie and provocative outfits. After a trip in a van from Houston to Florida and, for some, even as far north as Johns Island, South Carolina, the young women found themselves working as sexual machines in brothels. Men (known as *ticketeros*) charged each customer twenty dollars and gave him a single condom. After picking a woman, the customer had sex. Sometimes he used the condom, sometimes not. Each woman served as many as thirty customers a day, six days a week. The brothel owners—those sweet-talking men from the Cadena clan—skimmed ten dollars from each twenty-dollar fee. Seven dollars went toward reducing the woman's 2,000-dollar smuggling debt, leaving her three dollars earned after everyone else had taken a cut. The women had to turn in the opened condom wrappers at the end of each day to get credit for their sex work.[3]

True, a woman could pay off her smuggling debt in about two weeks if she kept to the pace of servicing thirty clients a day. But aside from the sex, her life was brutal. Brothel guards raped and beat the women. Pregnancies often led to abortions, the cost of which was added to the smuggling fee. Telephone calls home to Mexico were closely monitored, and the women had such limited contact with customers and Americans in general that they had little opportunity to break away. The brothel owners also had a habit of shifting the women from place to place, probably to keep them from developing contacts or friendships that could compromise the business.[4]

And the debts never seemed to disappear. Finding themselves endlessly bound to their bosses, the women drank whiskey to dull their shame and pain. "There seemed to be no end to my nightmare," a victim named Rosa later said at a deposition. "My debt continued to grow. The bosses did not pay me a percentage of money that they made from me, although I know other women were paid."[5]

Constantly short of funds, Rosa had to borrow more money from the bosses to buy food and call her family in Mexico. Each time, her debt increased.[6] This kind of debt bondage was one of the ways in which the bosses could keep a hold over their subjects. Although it was illegal under U.S. and international law, debt bondage was increasingly frequent in the sexual underworld of the immigrant communities. Some customers would take pity on the girls, pay them the twenty-dollar fee, and not have sex. But most expected to get what they came for in the Cadena-family trailers. Why else were the women there?

These sexual sweatshops would likely have continued to operate for many years had not something happened in late 1997: two teenaged Mexican girls walked to their country's consulate in Miami. Officials at the diplomatic office were disturbed by the stories the youngsters told and convinced them to talk with U.S. Border Patrol and Federal Bureau of Investigation (FBI) agents. The girls told the Americans that they had escaped from brothels outside the city. The establishments were in places like Boynton Beach, West Palm Beach, and elsewhere; and all were run by Mexicans. As described by the teenagers, the conditions were the closest thing to slavery the federal officials had ever come across. The condom wrappers took the place of time cards. "At the end of the night I turned in the condom wrappers," one of the young women said to investigators. "Each wrapper represented a supposed deduction to my smuggling fee. We tried to keep our own records but the bosses destroyed them. We were never sure what we owed."[7]

In November 1997 one girl took federal agents to some of the brothel locations. The establishments were essentially dilapidated trailers or duplexes near fields where migrant workers picked citrus fruit. FBI agent Alex Rivas later told a reporter that what they found in the brothels was shocking. "It was dirty, just plan dirty," Rivas recalled about the garbage-strewn rooms littered with condoms. "The bathrooms, I can't begin to tell you just how bad they were."[8]

Federal agents also discovered a number of women in the brothels and saw that they were intimidated by the law enforcement presence. Coming from small towns in Mexico where police were corrupt or lax in enforcing the laws, the women were understandably reticent about revealing their experiences. But as Rivas learned, their captors had warned the women that, if the police ever discovered them, they would go to jail for a long time, particularly if they talked.[9]

The women's silence could have prevented police from doing their job and would have kept the brothel owners from being held accountable. But over several months, federal agents, Rivas included, began to talk with the women and developed a sense of trust. Eventually, stories started to spill out: terrible tales of rape, coercion, and deception ultimately rooted in the oppressive Mexican backwaters the women called home.

After the raid the Cadena brothels were closed for good. Armed with information from the women, U.S. prosecutors began to build a case against the Cadena family, including Abel Cadena, Rogerio Cadena, Rafael Alberto Cadena, Camela Cadena, and Juan Luis Cadena. Their conduct had been too awful to overlook. But exactly what crimes could federal prosecutors charge them with? Clearly, the clandestine way in which the women had been transported into the United States fit the crime of alien smuggling, so prosecutors could easily apply that part of the immigration law. To address the women's working conditions, prosecutors turned to the Twelfth Amendment of the Constitution, which prohibits slavery and involuntary servitude. They could also have used old peonage laws, first written in the 1880s, which covered the use of forced labor to clear up debts. The women's descriptions of how the Cadenas had run the brothels, including their restrictions on movement and freedom, abysmal or nonexistent pay, and the endless shackles of debt, allowed prosecutors to fashion a theory that the women had been kept in conditions akin to slavery. To prosecutors, those conditions amounted to a violation of the women's civil rights. A conspiracy charge was also brought to cover the period between 1996 (when some of the women had been smuggled into the United States) and February 1998 (when the last of the brothels was closed).[10]

Following their arrest on the civil rights, alien smuggling, conspiracy, and prostitution charges, various members of the Cadena-Sosa ring pleaded guilty before trial, sparing the women the ordeal of testifying in open court. Seven members of the criminal enterprise pleaded guilty to civil rights conspiracy charges, among them Rogerio Cadena. But another seven suspects remained at large. Listed as fugitives were Hugo Cadena-Sosa, Juan Luis Cadena, Carmen Cadena, Rafael Alberto Cadena, Abel Cadena, Antonia Sosa, and Patricio Sosa.[11]

Had the Cadena case hit twenty years earlier, it might have gone unnoticed. But times had changed. By the mid- to late 1990s, the United States was acutely aware of the relentless economic pressure impelling a global migration from poor, economically weak countries to more affluent nations. The news media regularly featured stories of economic immigrants in all kinds of terrible straits, who had put themselves into situations of grave danger just to try to reach to American shores. A notable example was the June 1993 grounding of the Chinese smuggling ship the *Golden Venture* off New York City's harbor with a cargo of nearly three hundred illegal immigrants. At least six and perhaps ten of the passengers died while floundering in the bone-chilling surf. The country had seen many cases of immigrants placed in peril by smugglers and criminal syndicates anxious to make money from their sweat and blood. The voyage of the *Golden Venture* had become a metaphor for uncontrolled immigration.

Much as the *Golden Venture* symbolized the larger migration issues facing the United States, the Cadena women symbolized a new class of exploited persons: immigrants held in states of servitude and slavery, compelled to work under degrading and exploitative conditions to pay the price of their passage. Such exploitation wasn't unique to the United States. In Eastern Europe there were numerous reported cases of women who had been similarly forced into sex work. With large, floating populations of women seeking work outside of the troubled economies of former Iron Curtain nations, estimates of the numbers of persons migrating for sex work in Europe ran as high as 700,000, although that number is virtually impossible to verify.

And the issue wasn't limited to sex workers. Agricultural workers, domestic help, and factory employees were among those who had risked emigration and then found themselves bound and compelled to work in conditions of servitude. Some, particularly among the sex workers, agreed to the bargain and wanted to do the job. But others did not agree and were thus trapped in a life of unrelenting toil from which they saw no escape.

Such was the case of another group of Mexican immigrants, who found themselves in New York City at around the time that the Cadena women were suffering in Florida. On July 18, 1997, a desk sergeant at a police precinct in Corona, Queens, a section of the city with a large immigrant population, was approached by four Mexican immigrant men who handed him a note. The letter, written in poor English, asked for help. The men had trouble speaking and listening to the sergeant's questions for a very good reason: they were all deaf.[12]

Investigation of the boarding house where the men lived revealed more than forty other deaf Mexicans living in cramped apartments. The home had been illegally subdivided. But as officials soon discovered, building-code violations were the least of the problem. Questions from police, city, and immigration officials revealed that the immigrants had been brought to the city to sell trinkets on the subway system. Panhandlers and beggars are routine sights on the subways; but in this case, the immigrants had been brought to the United States illegally and, as further investigation revealed, forced to sell their wares for a dollar apiece. Yet even that paltry sum didn't go into the beggars' pockets. Instead, they turned it in to their handlers at the crowded rooming house.[13]

The destitute Mexican beggars also suffered in other ways. Allegations of exploitation, sexual assault, torture, and coercion surrounded the case, much as they did in the Cadena case. As federal officials probed further, they discovered that the ringleaders had connections to similar gangs in Chicago. Some of the immigrants said they had been given begging quotas and were sometimes sent back out, even late at night, if their take fell short. Eventually, twenty people were indicted on charges ranging from slavery to alien smuggling. All of the defendants pleaded guilty to various charges.[14]

Because of their illegal status, the immigrants remained under the control of the Immigration and Naturalization Service and were housed for several months in the Westway Motor Inn, a facility off the Grand Central Parkway. Their plight mobilized the government of New York City, which, under the leadership of pro-immigrant mayor Rudolph Giuliani, provided them with clothing, food, housing, and disability assistance. But because they were in the country illegally, the deaf Mexican migrants, like any other immigration detainees, were not able to leave the motel. The city, with prodding from the American Civil Liberties Union, finally intervened with immigration officials to get some of them special S-visas since they had cooperated with law enforcement in the prosecution of the gang's ringleaders.[15]

The *Golden Venture*, the Cadena brothel investigation, and the discovery of the deaf Mexicans in New York were the most prominent of a number of cases in the 1990s involving immigrants who had been exploited and put at risk in their search for jobs. Such incidents gave human rights advocates and government officials a new frame of reference in which to view the ramifications of illegal immigration. Though many migrants toiled in obscurity without any problems once they arrived in the United States, these high-profile cases showed that for many others their labor was forced, coerced in much the same way as any Mafia extortion victim might feel squeezed by threats of violence or economic harm.

The immigrants who illegally crossed international borders were generating billions of dollars for the migration merchants who supplied them with the means of transit. The clandestine nature of this human cargo business made it analogous to drug trafficking, given that the unauthorized residency status of the immigrants and their lives in the underground economies kept them in a state of perpetual illegality. In fact the term *trafficking* gained currency as a way of describing both immigrant smuggling in general and the particular coercion the migrants experienced from smugglers who wanted them to work in certain jobs.

Among human rights advocates around the world, this latter definition is an accurate description of what forced labor immigrants must endure, be they sex workers in Florida or panhandlers in New York City. Nevertheless, this conception of trafficking has not until recently been defined in the law. True, offenses to human dignity such as those I've discussed in this chapter were prosecuted under the mosaic of criminal laws that existed in the United States in 1997 and 1998. But no specific federal or state statute existed that dealt with trafficking as a discrete crime.

After state department official James Puleo picked up a copy of *Black's Law Dictionary* and found that historically the concept of trafficking has never applied to human beings as a commodity, a number of his colleagues at the department's Office of International Law Enforcement (INL) became curious about the absence of a human trafficking law. They were intrigued by the notion that there was room for the law to evolve to cover the crime of human trafficking. But since the state department and INL dealt mainly with foreign affairs, suggesting changes in U.S. domestic laws wasn't part of their mission. Any domestic legislative changes would have to come from other directions, particularly Congress or the White House.[16]

But trafficking in humans *had* become a major global human rights and law enforcement issue. In fact, by 1996 the United Nations had passed a resolution that signaled its concern about the problem. The passage of the resolution had the effect of slowly but inexorably starting the United Nations down a path that would eventually lead to action; and U.S. officials like Puleo and many others would play a role in shaping U.N. policy. Closer to home, the horrors experienced by the Cadena victims and other unfortunate immigrants were impelling change on Capitol Hill as well. It wouldn't take long for the evolving policies of the United Nations and Washington to converge.

Chapter 2   The Emerging Issue

By THE LATE 1990s, following the much-publicized Cadena and deaf-Mexican forced labor cases, American law enforcement officials had become acutely aware of other instances of immigrants in human trafficking situations. From the Northern Mariana Islands to Chicago, Bethesda, Maryland, New York, and other cities, investigators were discovering cases of migrants who had been forced or tricked into jobs that usually involved prostitution, although officials were finding instances of garment sweatshop labor as well.

In a number of publicized cases, the immigrants were women from Asia (primarily Korea, China, and Thailand) or Eastern Europe (usually the Czech Republic, Latvia, or Ukraine). Their stories basically involved the modus operandi in the Cadena case. The women claimed they had been recruited to take what they thought would be respectable, legitimate jobs in restaurants and nightclubs. Recruiters told them they would earn as much as 60,000 dollars, although they would have to pay back the cost of immigration travel. But once the women arrived at their U.S. destinations, the promised jobs didn't materialize. Instead, they were required to work as prostitutes or topless dancers in conditions ranging from bars in Chicago to underground Los Angeles brothels with twenty-four-hour surveillance. Reports of mistreatment and physical abuse were common.

Because the Northern Mariana Islands (a U.S. commonwealth) is more than 8,000 miles away from the U.S. mainland and close to Asia, it became a central location for some of these trafficking schemes. In one case, a gang of smugglers brought ethnic Chinese and Korean women from China to the islands with the promise of waitress jobs. But after arriving, the women were kept in a barracks-style apartment and told to work as prostitutes. The smugglers took the women's passports, airline tickets, and other documents and threatened to harm them if any tried to leave without paying their travel debts.[1]

In 1996, with a ready supply of young women anxious to leave Eastern Europe because of limited job opportunities, Alexander Mishulovich, an American of Russian ancestry, began recruiting Latvian women to work in what he said was a respectable nightclub. He told the women they would only be required to dance in bikinis, not in the nude. The women were instructed to lie to U.S. immigration officials when they applied for visas in Latvia. But once they arrived in the United States, they discovered that the dancing jobs required nudity; and like the Northern Mariana victims, they were kept in locked apartments. The women couldn't readily flee because Mishulovich had confiscated their passports. He told them that, if they wanted the documents back, they would have to pay him thousands of dollars. Beatings were routine. The only way for the women to earn their freedom was to pay off their smuggling debts.[2]

A similar case emerged in Bethesda, a Maryland city just a few miles from Washington, D.C. Like the Latvian women, a number of Ukrainian and Russian women had answered ads for waitress and maid jobs. But once in Maryland, they discovered they would be working as prostitutes. The brothel owners beat and traumatized the women. Asian women reported similar experiences, learning after their arrival in New York's Chinatown that they would have to sexually serve large numbers of brothel clients to pay off tens of thousands of dollars in smuggling fees. While many of the women in the Chinatown brothels may have known before traveling that they would work as prostitutes, probably they didn't know that the sex work would be so arduous or the living conditions so confining. Some reported that sadistic smugglers had burned them with cigarettes. In one case, mistreatment drove a young Chinese woman to escape through a window to report her abusive conditions to local police.

In each of these cases, law enforcement officials finally intervened. The Northern Mariana brothels were shut down and the ringleaders of the smuggling rings prosecuted under federal laws dealing with involuntary servitude, extortion, and transporting women in interstate commerce for prostitution.[3] Mishulovich was arrested with others on charges of peonage and obstruction of justice. He was convicted and sentenced to nine years in prison.[4] In the Bethesda case, the brothel owners were prosecuted and entered into a plea bargain that resulted in a fine and prohibition from running another business in the county.[5] In Manhattan, federal prosecutors convicted the Chinatown brothel operators, who were sentenced to prison terms of up to five years.[6]

Clearly, when American law enforcement focused attention and resources on trafficking issues, criminals could be successfully prosecuted. For immigrants, however, the outcomes were a mixed bag. Some of the Northern Mariana victims, like those in the Cadena case, were able to stay in U.S. territory with government assistance. But some of the women in the Bethesda case were deported back to Ukraine and Russia, as were some of the Chinese and Thai immigrants who worked in the New York City brothel.

As trafficking cases developed and gained publicity, the issue acquired more political traction. U.S. lawmakers and human rights advocates got involved. Each discovery of an immigrant brothel or sex club where the employees complained of mistreatment and coercion drew on news stories of monstrous traffickers and hopeful, innocent victims. Whether every case fit that precise mold was another question. Suffice it to say, however, that those basic stories instigated American legislators and other officials to see human trafficking as a modern form of slavery.

These growing and alarming news reports spawned another fundamental question: just how extensive was trafficking in the United States and around the world? Careful examination of the literature revealed that no one had a good answer. The reason was fairly simple. Trafficking was unlawful and, like any illegal activity, difficult to monitor. It existed in a world of covert deals and clandestine movements, making it hard to find and count victims. Officials hired to uncover and monitor such activities were sometimes complicit in them, either through bribery or as active members of conspiracies. Today, the situation is still difficult to track and categorize. Although, as of 2006, U.S. law and U.N. documents have developed more finely tuned legal definitions of trafficking, some degree of ambiguity remains.

Trafficking also involves victims who are related to the offense in varying degrees. For instance, there are people who are being trafficked across national borders and people who are currently working in labor situations involving coercion or fraud, two of the key elements of a trafficking offense. But there are also people who were former victims of trafficking and who have escaped or left their jobs. How should they be counted?

Time periods are also important in developing estimates. According to researchers Anette Brunovskis and Guri Tyldum, "if we wish to estimate the number of men and women who are current trafficking victims, it is necessary to specify for what time period the estimation is valid. The number of persons living under conditions that can be classified as trafficking at any given time may be significantly different from the number of persons trafficked for i.e. labour exploitation, organ removals, or prostitution every year. We need to know how long people in various groups stay in a particular stage, and how and when people move between stages, in order to understand and correctly interpret any number estimating the total amount of victims of trafficking."[7]

Complicating the picture of trafficking estimates in the United States is the fact that, by late 2005, some human rights advocates were expanding the kinds of persons defined as victims. No longer were they restricted to immigrants from other countries. Instead, advocates argued that there was a class of domestic trafficking victims: U.S. citizens and residents who traveled inside national borders as forced laborers—invariably, young people and children used for sex. As a result, prosecutors commenced a number of actions against brothel managers and assorted pimps who exerted psychological and physical control over sex workers. Finally, some advocates deemed that prostitution was inherently coercive and thus fell within the definition of trafficking. Such an interpretation would expand the number of victims to astronomical levels if the tens of thousands of prostitutes arrested each year were added to the list of victims.[8]

In the United States and internationally, growing numbers of organizations and government agencies began taking responsibility for dealing with trafficking and its victims. But despite the proliferation of involved organizations, some researchers found that these groups had no consistent way to gather data. In a study calling for better indicators of human trafficking, researchers Frank Laczko and Marco Gramegna highlighted the incompatibility of data collected by various law enforcement agencies and nongovernmental organizations (NGOs) as well as a lack of focus in the collection process: "Data are often based on the various trafficking definitions used by each individual agency and only cover those who have received certain types of assistance (e.g. persons participating in voluntary assisted return programs or those accommodated in shelters for victims of trafficking)." Some NGOs were better financed and more sophisticated in data collection than others, but in general few shared that information.[9]

Nevertheless, despite a history of inconsistent or nonexistent data collection, estimates proliferated about the dimensions of trafficking. In her April 2000 monograph "International Trafficking in Women to the United States: A Contemporary Manifestation of Slavery and Organized Crime," Amy O'Neill Richard made a notable attempt to quantify the problem. At the time Richard was an analyst with the State Department's Bureau of Intelligence and Research, and her monograph was written under the auspices of a branch of the Central Intelligence Agency (CIA). Based on information that was considered to be current through November 1999, her study became a point of reference for many subsequent policy developments in Washington. Yet even Richard was forced to admit that precisely estimating the scope of the trafficking problem were difficult, largely for reasons also noted by other researchers.[10] As she explained, "estimates of the trafficking problem in the United States vary, given differing definitions of what constitutes trafficking and research based on limited cases studies. At present, no one U.S. or international agency is compiling accurate statistics." Still, that didn't stop various researchers from taking a stab at estimation, and she noted that worldwide the numbers broadly ranged from 700,000 to 2 million trafficked women and children. That figure amounted to 45,000 to 50,000 women and children trafficked to the United States. Richard offered a regional breakdown of the source countries: about 30,000 from Southeast Asia; 10,000 from Latin America; 4,000 from Eastern Europe; and 1,000 from other areas, including Africa. A footnote cited her source as a CIA briefing on "Global Trafficking in Women and Children: Assessing the Magnitude," prepared in April 1999. Richard also noted that the figures didn't take into account internal trafficking wholly within national borders.[11]

By the time Richard was reporting the CIA-derived estimates, other sources were citing a wide range of figures for annual global trafficking. The numbers were widely divergent, ranging from slightly more than 500,000 (according to the U.S.–based Protection Project) to more than 1.25 million (claimed by participants at a conference on Southeast Asian women). After Richard published her monograph, other trafficking estimates continued to emerge and diverge. A later data comparison by the U.N.'s Educational, Scientific, and Cultural Organization (UNESCO) Trafficking Project showed a range of estimates: from 700,000 in a 2001 FBI report to nearly 4 million as cited in a U.N. study that same year.[12] As the UNESCO study concluded, "numbers take on a life of their own, gaining acceptance through repetition, often with little inquiry into their derivations. Journalists, bowing to the pressures of editors, demand numbers, any number. Organizations feel compelled to supply them, lending false precisions and spurious authority to many reports."[13]

Despite this numerical imprecision, horror stories about trafficking victims continued to capture public attention. And lawmakers did not remain oblivious. In the late 1990s, as lurid news stories of sex-slave brothels began to appear, members of Congress took note of an emerging and important human rights issue. One was Senator Paul Wellstone, a liberal Democrat from Wisconsin. The son of a Russian immigrant father and a mother born of Ukrainian parents and raised on Manhattan's Lower East Side, Wellstone had a working-class background, something he admitted being ashamed of as a youngster. But as he grew older, he came to appreciate his heritage and, through the experience and tutelage of his father, who fled persecution in Russia in the years before the revolution, was sensitized to the intolerance and cruelty behind so many human rights abuses. He exclaimed in his 2001 autobiography *The Conscience of a Liberal*, "Combined with my mother's passion for workers and for fighting for the underdog, you pretty much have the makings of a life and philosophy!"[14]

Wellstone's wife, Sheila, shared his passion for human rights and the optimism that wrongs could be righted; and in 1997 she took note when Bethesda police uncovered the case of the Ukrainian and Russian women who had been trafficked to a local brothel. Despite the arrests of the brothel managers and owners, she wasn't happy about how the victims were treated. Local officials in Montgomery County, Maryland, charged the women for their housing while they remained in the United States. After the brothel owners were prosecuted, the women were deported, sent back to homelands in no better shape and certainly with no better job prospects than they'd had when they'd left. For Sheila Wellstone, that outcome was grossly unfair, considering the relatively light penalty the brothel owners received. The plight of the Bethesda women, as well as that of girls in India and Nepal sold by their families to brothels for 1,000 dollars each, infuriated her. Their treatment was a form of violence, and Wellstone wanted her husband and others in Congress to do something about it.[15]

It didn't take long for Senator Wellstone to begin prodding his fellow lawmakers to take action on human trafficking. On March 10, 1998, International Women's Day, in what was the first significant congressional recognition of the issue, Wellstone introduced a resolution on the floor of the Senate denouncing international sex trafficking. Using maps of routes taken by emigrants from the former Soviet Union, Wellstone decried how the international community (by which he apparently meant individual nation-states and the United Nations) had ignored the problem.[16] "This resolution will effectively put Congress on record as opposing trafficking for forced prostitution and domestic servitude, and acting to check it before the lives of more women and girls are shattered," he said. "One of the fastest growing international trafficking businesses is the trade in women."[17]

Backed by Senate colleague Diane Feinstein, Wellstone went on to recount what had become a common theme in descriptions of trafficking: luring unsuspecting women and girls into lives of prostitution with promises of lucrative jobs. "Upon arrival in countries far from their homes, these women are often stripped of their passports, held against their will in slave-like conditions, and sexually abused," he said. "Rape, intimidation, and violence are commonly employed by traffickers to control their victims and to prevent them from seeking help."[18]

Wellstone continually hit upon the theme that the women were either naïve about what was in store for them or just desperate. The end result, he said, was that traffickers could easily exploit them. He recognized that domestic workers were also vulnerable to trafficking, but the theme of sex dominated his presentation; and he made a pointed note that younger women and girls were particularly sought-after commodities because they might be virgins and thus less likely to have AIDS. He even mentioned the 1997 Bethesda brothel incident as a way of underscoring the fact that the United States was now a destination for trafficking victims.[19]

Wellstone was disturbed that law enforcement, through either complacency or inadequate laws and practices, had made trafficking "a low risk business venture." He also criticized the international community for having "turned its gaze away" from trafficking.[20] His resolution, as well as a companion measure introduced in the House that same day by Representative Louise McIntosh Slaughter, asked the U.S. government to report on the issue to Congress. It required a focus on legal barriers that prevented effective governmental responses and on how to help victims. The measures did not propose any specific legislative action but did call on federal officials to continue working internationally to spread awareness of trafficking.[21]

The resolutions passed in both the Senate and the House. Those votes made it clear that human trafficking was now on the government's radar and could garner, when the time came, considerable political consensus. Internationally, trafficking was also recognized as an emerging law enforcement and human rights issue. It was a problem made more intractable because of the assumed involvement of organized crime. As experience had shown, national borders did not stop the illicit activities of the Mafia and similar organizations throughout the world. Any effort to confront the problems of organized crime required a concerted global effort. By the late 1990s the global challenge posed by transnational crime   and human trafficking was certainly one aspect—gave Washington, D.C., and the rest of the world a special opportunity to launch a number of unprecedented initiatives.

Chapter 3   The Global Response

AFTER CONCERTED EFFORT in the 1980s and 1990s, U.S. prosecutors succeeded in successfully attacking some forms of traditional organized crime, including La Cosa Nostra. The Five Families of the New York Mafia—Bonanno, Colombo, Gambino, Genovese, and Lucchese—were the focus of a number of prosecutions; and arrests and prison sentences thinned their leadership and culled their membership. American officials used potent enforcement tools such as racketeering laws, witness protection programs, and electronic surveillance to attack the Mob. These efforts didn't wipe out organized crime in the United States, but they certainly delivered some crippling blows, damaging the syndicates so heavily that some mobsters lamented that their familiar gangster life was over.

But globally the situation was much different. Other countries were ill-equipped to deal with criminal syndicates, lacking either laws, law enforcement capability, judicial experience, or the will to act. Although the migration of criminal organizers and a new swiftness in communication and banking meant that organized crime was now truly transnational, nations were many steps behind in dealing with various criminal combinations. This state of affairs troubled numbers of governments. By 1994, at the World Ministerial Conference on Organized Transnational Crime in Naples, several countries, including Argentina (which later drafted its own trafficking protocol), proposed the creation of a U.N. convention to deal with the problem.[1] During the next few years ministers and officials from the United States and scores of other countries held informal discussions about the feasibility of a wide-ranging global pact on organized crime. Progress was slow. According to a former U.S. diplomat involved in the policy discussions, the Italian government had pushed the issue of a global pact ever since the death of Giovanni Falcone, the famous anti-Mafia prosecutor who was assassinated in 1992. But despite Italy's pressure, other major powers felt little urgency about dealing with crime on a global scale.

In the mid-1990s, however, the U.S. Department of State began to develop international law enforcement standards covering a variety of criminal issues, including small-arms trafficking, money laundering, official corruption, and human smuggling and trafficking. According to the diplomat I have just mentioned, Washington had come to recognize that the major powers must be energized to collaborate if the world were to have any chance of negotiating international agreements on organized or transnational crime.[2] From that point until 1998, American officials met with counterparts in Russia and the G7 states (France, Germany, Italy, Japan, Great Britain, and Canada) to back the idea of a global summit on organized crime. The aim was to build a consensus for international treaties or agreements about organized crime.[3] The selling point was the criminal-syndicate trouble that most of these nations were dealing with on their own. Of course, Italy had had a long-standing struggle with the Mafia and was prepared from the first to act. Germany was coping with human smuggling and trafficking because its borders abutted Central and Eastern European countries that were experiencing upheaval and substantial emigration. In Canada, small-arms control was important. And gradually other nations, particularly those in the Organization of American States, which struggled with trafficking and immigration problems, came to support the idea of an international instrument dealing with organized crime.

After the United States had lined up support for the issue, the U.N.'s Commission of Crime Prevention and Criminal Justice and its Economic and Social Council took the reins.[4] Those bodies recommended in 1998 that the General Assembly adopt a special resolution that would form the basis for high-level diplomatic negotiations. The end result of those talks, according to the resolution, would be a "comprehensive international convention against transnational organized crime."[5]

In international law, a convention is an agreement between nations that is similar to a treaty or may serve as the basis for a treaty.[6] In an organization as large as the United Nations, drafting and approving a convention is a time-consuming process and can require many rounds of negotiations. Even before such negotiations take place, there are informal preparatory meetings; and a number of them took place in 1998 in anticipation of the high-level talks that would follow. During those early sessions, representatives from several countries proposed incorporating a series of additional international instruments called protocols. Each protocol would deal with a specific area of crime: illicit manufacturing and trafficking in firearms, illegal trafficking in migrants, and trafficking in women and children.[7]

Protocols are useful because they emphasize a problem and serve as models that national governments can follow when designing future legislative action. Nevertheless, they are not meant to be stand-alone items. Each protocol should be read in connection with the larger overarching convention, and each country is required to become a party to the convention in order to join any of the protocols. So in this case it was important to develop a signed convention on global organized crime; otherwise, there would be no international instrument covering human trafficking. Once the convention was signed, the various signatory nations would then be obligated to fulfill the requirements of the relevant protocols that they had also signed. As I will discuss later, it was fortuitous that the United States had started to focus on human trafficking just as the United Nations awoke to the problem; as a consequence, U.S. interest served as a catalyst for much of what happened in the international agreements.

In U.N. discussions on organized crime in 1998, Argentina proposed the drafting of a separate convention to deal with trafficking in minors, which some law enforcement officials thought had become a business of organized crime. But according to documents prepared by the U.N. Commission on Crime Prevention and Criminal Justice, a number of nations believed that the best and quickest way to address the problem was to develop a protocol for the larger crime convention.[8]

Many in Washington viewed the gathering impetus for a global pact on organized crime as an opportunity for the United States to propose a document that would address trafficking in women and children, two particularly vulnerable groups. James Puleo was a prime architect of the American position.[9] After Puleo left the federal immigration service in 1995, Jonathan Winer, deputy undersecretary of state for international law enforcement, asked him to frame a trafficking document. Winer had long expressed interest in establishing legal standards for dealing with international crime and knew that Puleo was well aware of the lack of any American law dealing specifically with human trafficking.[10]

The U.S. government's interest in crafting appropriate laws against trafficking had developed in tandem with rising international interest on the subject. Italy and Austria had already put together a protocol on human smuggling, but American officials believed it was not comprehensive enough to deal with the trafficking of persons.[11] As a result, with state department officials taking the lead, representatives of the major industrial countries signed a resolution in Vienna promising that all of the governments would work on a trafficking protocol to be included in the organized crime convention.[12]

By the end of 1998, American officials had outlined a trafficking protocol to guide U.N. deliberations. In March 1999, they introduced that proposal at an initial session of the Ad Hoc Committee on the Elaboration of the Convention against Transnational Organized Crime.[13] Then work on the convention and its protocols began in earnest, with negotiations continuing for almost two years in a series of meetings in Vienna. The ultimate aim was to finish the documents and have them ready for approval at a major international conference in the autumn of 2000.

Argentina and the United States presented a ten-page document titled "Revised Draft Protocol to Prevent, Suppress, and Punish Trafficking in Women and Children, Supplementing the United Nations Convention against Transnational Organized Crime" to the negotiators in Vienna. The document contained eighteen articles, or sections, intended as a framework for the negotiations and included a subtle emphasis that would ultimately shape the final product. Initially, Argentina had proposed a five-page document with eight articles that dealt with women and children. Meanwhile, the United States had submitted its own five-page document (with nine articles) emphasizing the more inclusive category of "persons." In the combined document, negotiators considered both options, realizing that at some point they would have to decide which categorization was appropriate.[14]

The preamble spelled out the belief that organized crime groups were profiting from international human trafficking.[15] Strictly speaking, that claim was true: trafficking was a crime that required organization; division of labor; handling of funds; and constant recruitment of new members, customers, and victims. But there was little or no evidence that western-based groups such as La Cosa Nostra or other Mafia syndicates had taken part in the trade. In fact, the 1930s conviction of New York Mob boss Charles "Lucky" Luciano for running a prostitution ring was the most recent instance in which a major Mafia figure had been linked to anything remotely resembling sex trafficking. By the late twentieth century, the American Mafia's only apparent involvement in the sex industry was as an entrepreneur in pornography distribution or a silent partner in strip clubs, although prostitution sometimes occurred on the premises. Rather, law enforcement suspected that emerging crime groups in Eastern Europe (the Mafiya, among others) and the Far East (such as the Japanese Yakuza and the Chinese Triads) were exploiting the drive for illegal immigration in areas of the former Soviet Union and Southeast Asia.[16] In light of this growing trend toward migration, trafficking had become an urgent problem for international law enforcement officials.

But while there had been plenty of news reports about Yakuza and Mafiya involvement in trafficking, that level of organized crime intervention didn't seem necessary for trafficking to proliferate. Instead, organized crime involvement often centered around a series of specialized smaller conspiracies, with various divisions of labor. One group of conspirators might move immigrants over international borders, while another might take command of the victims and send them to brothel or factory owners, who themselves operated yet another conspiracy, one more involved with labor exploitation. In other words, according to American investigators, the result was a set of connected small conspiracies that may have involved only a few participants in trafficking and were not necessarily under the control of a larger traditional criminal syndicate. Of course, in the end, the combination of the various conspiracies formed a particular kind of small-scale organized criminal activity.

The working proposal proposed promotion and facilitation of cooperation among nations to prevent, investigate, and punish trafficking for sexual exploitation or forced labor. Because it combined the initial work of Argentina and the United States, the proposal alternately defined victims as "persons" or "women and children." Achievement of its broad purposes depended on six undertakings that each signatory nation agreed to carry out. Simply stated, those measures included enactment of anti-trafficking laws, protection for victims, international cooperation on the problem, safe return of victims to their countries of origin, public information campaigns, and appropriate medical and legal help for victims. The early Argentinean and U.S. proposals had also included those broad goals, though Washington's document had offered more details.[17]

Deciding how to define trafficking was fundamentally important. As mentioned, the working proposal suggested two options: the State Department's broad category of "persons" or Argentina's focused categories of "women" and "children." Regarding the first option, the draft proposal defined *trafficking in persons* as the "recruitment, transportation, transfer, harbouring or receipt of persons: a) By the threat or use of kidnapping, force, fraud, deception or coercion, or b) By the giving or receiving of unlawful payment or benefits to achieve the consent of a person having control over another person, for the purpose of sexual exploitation or forced labor."[18]

The second option defined *trafficking in children* (that is, people under age eighteen) as any act by a criminal organization that involves "(i) Promoting, facilitating or coordinating the kidnapping, holding or hiding of a child, with or without his or her consent, for profit or otherwise, occasionally or repeatedly; or (ii) Offering, delivering or receiving a child in exchange for money or any other payment in kind, or serving as an intermediary in those acts."[19] Though the language was stilted, the definition was meant to cover any illicit purpose for which the child was used, including sexual or forced labor.

The goal was essentially the same in the definition of *trafficking in women*, but the draft protocol spelled out additional prohibited circumstances: the "illicit purpose" included slavery or servitude, forced labor, and prostitution. The sexual exploitation element covered prostitution carried out with a woman's consent as well as sexual tourism and pornography. One final "illicit purpose" spelled out in the Argentinean option was the removal of human body organs or tissues—the answer to years of rumors about organ brokers who were targeting children and the poor, convincing them to undergo surgery for removal of body parts that could fetch tens of thousands of dollars on the illicit organ trade.[20]

The protocol's essential purpose was to assure consensus among nations about the criminalization of trafficking—in other words, to make the activity a crime. Though the alleged depredations had been widely publicized, not all nations had criminal laws dealing with them. In some countries, the result was limited or nonexistent law enforcement, which, as U.N. crime experts emphasized, led to uneven or difficult international cooperation. The U.S. and Argentinean proposal thus stressed the obligation of signatory countries to criminalize trafficking and "impose penalties that take into account the grave nature" of the offense.[21]

Protection of victims was a major concern for U.S. negotiators. Experience, even in the United States, showed that trafficked persons were often treated like criminals, particularly in prostitution cases, when women sex workers frequently ended up in jail or were held as material witnesses with little concern for their well-being. Sometimes, according to victims' advocates, the women were deported after the criminal case against the trafficker was complete. Once back in their countries of origin, they were subject to the same conditions that had driven them to migrate in the first place: few jobs and low economic status. They also received little or no assistance from their home governments. For example, a young Mexican woman smuggled into the United States by the Cadena family told a journalist that she couldn't afford bus fare to travel with her daughter to testify at a legal proceeding in Mexico against one of the gang members. She also reported that another woman who had escaped from a Cadena brothel had been relegated to collecting cans in Miami to make a living. Such marginalization of victims angered human rights activists.[22]

To ameliorate the problems of victims and make their cooperation with law enforcement more likely, the United States proposed four separate articles to the trafficking protocol, each addressing a different aspect of victim assistance. Article 4 required governments to offer victims assistance with housing, education, and child care. It also required nations to assure victims' physical safety while they were on foreign soil and provide them with timely information about the progress of court or administrative proceedings. Although the article had originally required case confidentiality to protect victims' privacy, the United States inserted language that qualified that restriction, asking for confidentiality "in appropriate cases and to the extent possible under domestic law." Because any revision to American law that kept trafficking cases secret would not pass either constitutional muster or a First Amendment challenge, the United States felt that such qualifying language was also necessary in this case.[23]

Article 5 required nations to "consider" having immigration laws that permitted victims of trafficking to stay in the receiving state in "appropriate cases." This requirement would be useful in situations in which a victim had a valid asylum claim or if return to the country of origin would be dangerous, particularly if the person had cooperated with law enforcement in making a case against the trafficking network.[24]

The proposal in article 6 set up a reciprocal requirement for countries of origin (known as "sending" states), ordering them to accept "without delay" the return of a trafficking victim. Experience had shown that traffickers sometimes confiscated or destroyed victims' passports, creating problems with repatriation because lack of travel documents interfered with a person's ability to go home. The article proposed that countries should speedily verify the nationality of citizens and residents who had been victims of trafficking and issue "such travel documents or other authorization as may be necessary to enable the person to re-enter [their] territory."[25]

Article 7 required nations to provide means for victims to seek damage compensation from the traffickers. Such recompense might come from fines, assets forfeited from criminal enterprises, or restitution (the legal act of restoring something to a person). In addition, the article asked countries to consider measures and funding to help victims recover physically and psychologically.[26]

Because, to a large degree, trafficking involved immigration crimes, the draft protocol contained a number of articles dealing with law enforcement measures designed to thwart illegal migration. Similar measures were also laid out in a set of U.S. and Canadian proposals included in another protocol, which dealt with the smuggling of migrants by land and sea.[27] As the U.S. experience with Chinese migrants in the early 1990s had shown, smugglers often used boats to get their human cargo to a destination.[28] But while cases such as the *Golden Venture*'s were dramatic, smuggling more frequently involved air or overland travel.[29] Migrants traveling by air purchased fake passports and travel documents as part of a smuggling package provided by criminal organizations. Once en route to a destination, the immigrants would either destroy the documents or hope that immigration officials would not spot the ruse.[30]

Immigration schemes were numerous, and some cases showed that government officials had been complicit in the smuggling.[31]

Borrowing from the smuggling protocol, the trafficking protocol contained language that required law enforcement to cooperate more effectively with immigration agencies to spot trafficking schemes. It also called for measures to improve the security of immigration documents such as passports and visas as well as steps to deter forgery, and it required countries to give speedy assistance through international channels whenever they questioned the validity of a travel document.[32]

As I mentioned in the introduction, when the Clinton administration began to push for a U.S. position on trafficking, officials advanced the notion of the "Three Ps": protection, prosecution, and prevention.[33] Referring to the "prevention" aspect of that notion, article 12 of the proposed U.N. protocol called on nations to establish "social policies and programmes" to prevent trafficking. The specifics were vague but suggested cooperation between governments and NGOs and mentioned information programs that would "generate public awareness of the gravity of the offences relating to international trafficking." Such programs would offer information about the risks and dangers of trafficking, potential victims, and the causes and consequences of the activity.[34]

Other, more technical, articles in the working protocol dealt with ratification. Also included were provisions dealing with the document's applicability in light of previous international conventions on human rights and refugees and the need to apply the provisions of the organized crime convention to the trafficking document. Finally, the protocol noted that it would not legally bind nations unless the overarching organized crime convention also became binding.[35]

After the United States and Argentina proposed this skeleton protocol in March 1999, it spent nearly two years in Vienna under negotiation. Led by Undersecretary of State Winer, the United States fielded a team of seventeen lawyers, diplomats, and law enforcement officials, including James Puleo, to handle what was sometimes an arduous and contentious round of talks. As I will show, the protocol also had political repercussions in Washington, a clear indication of how emotionally charged the issue had become.

The Office of the U.N. High Commissioner for Human Rights raised the first major concerns about the draft protocol: the high commissioner wanted to ensure that some core rights of migrants already secured under international law would not be overlooked. While welcoming the protocol's general approach, High Commissioner Mary Robinson (in a so-called "informal note") took issue with what she saw as a limited class of persons under protection. Because trafficking purposes were constantly changing, the terms *sexual exploitation* and *forced labor* seemed inadequate to cover future developments.

According to the note, "a preferable and more accurate description of purposes would include reference to forced labor and/or bonded labor and/or
servitude." Inclusion of such phrases would keep the protocol consistent with
existing international laws and avoid undefined, imprecise, and emotive
terms such as *sexual exploitation*. As another consistency measure, the high
commissioner also recommended that a child be defined as anyone under the
age of eighteen.[36]

Perhaps the strongest criticism centered on the subject of assistance to
victims, a proposal the high commissioner called "very weak." She believed
that, as written in the draft, "victims of trafficking would appear to gain very
little from cooperating with national authorities in the prosecution of traffickers." Because trafficking victims were vulnerable and needed assistance and
protection, including adequate housing and health care, the protocol had to
incorporate those elements. The high commissioner also stressed that,
because victims invariably had illegal immigration status and were often prosecuted because of it, nations should be "directed" to refrain from prosecuting
them for such status-related offenses.[37]

Repatriation (returning victims to their home countries) also concerned
the high commissioner, who felt that "safe and, as far as possible, voluntary return
must be at the core of any credible protection strategy for trafficked persons."
Failing to include such a principle in the protocol "would amount to little
more than an endorsement of the forced deportation and repatriation of victims of trafficking," which was unacceptable in the context of organized crime.[38]

In addition, the high commissioner critiqued the protocol from the point
of view of asylum seekers. The international community had established procedures for dealing with people who feared returning to their homelands
because they believed they would be persecuted for their race, religion, or
political beliefs. Immigrants who might not have any other lawful right to
remain legally in a new homeland often claimed asylum. The new trafficking
protocol, as the high commissioner noted, actually covered migrants who could
also claim refugee or asylum status. But the draft didn't refer to the principle
in international law of *non-refoulement*, a basic tenet of refugee protection,
which provides that no one should be forced to return to a country where his
or her life or liberty is at risk. The high commissioner stressed that this oversight had to be remedied and suggested inserting a clause into the protocol
saying that "illegality of an individual's entry into a State will not be a factor
adversely affecting that person's claim for asylum."[39]

Throughout 1999 and into 2000, diplomatic teams met in Vienna for
numerous consultations, with the U.S. delegation functioning as a major source
of input and recommendations. Nations seemed unanimous in their belief in

the need for a trafficking protocol and had few disputes about its requirement that signatories enforce trafficking laws. The negotiations' most arduous task concerned the issue of assistance to victims and the concept of returning trafficked persons to their countries of origin (that is, those migrants who wanted to return).[40] In addition, U.S. negotiators had to fight a rear-guard action against certain domestic anti-prostitution advocates who had the ear of a number of conservative American politicians.

Abolitionists, as the anti-prostitution advocates were called, believed in essence that sex for sale was degrading and exploitative work for women and should be outlawed—never mind that prostitution was against the law in many of the involved jurisdictions, particularly in the United States. The abolitionists worked on numerous fronts to craft laws that would thwart the practice of sex work. Some feminist groups lobbied the U.S. Department of State, particularly Secretary of State Madeleine Albright, to push for tougher anti-prostitution language in the protocol. These groups even buttonholed a few members of Congress, complaining that the American negotiators were too lenient and were actually supporting prostitution.[41]

While like-minded people may see wisdom in advancing their cause, the reality is that, in the world of diplomacy, single-minded pursuit of a political agenda can make negotiations difficult. Such was the case with the anti-prostitution stance. Former U.S. government officials who took part in the negotiations recalled that pressure from the abolitionists complicated discussions about the definition of *trafficking in persons*. The original suggestion in the U.S. working protocol defined it as "the recruitment, transportation, transfer, harboring or receipt of persons, either by the threat or use of kidnapping, force, fraud, deception or coercion, or by the giving or receiving of unlawful payments or benefits to achieve the consent of a person having control over another person, for the purpose of sexual exploitation or forced labor." The U.S. proposal did not mention prostitution specifically as a form of sexual exploitation, a term that itself seems imprecise. Argentina's proposal further muddied the waters, defining *trafficking in women* and *trafficking in children* as activities carried out by "criminal organizations" for a variety of illicit purposes, including "the prostitution or other forms of sexual exploitation of a woman or child, even with the consent of that person."[42] The Argentine suggestion was much broader than Washington's in terms of explicating prohibited conduct and included a number of its own definitional problems, including exactly what constituted a criminal organization.

As the U.S. proposal for defining trafficking in persons gained favor among the Vienna delegations, the abolitionist lobby increased its pressure. The anti-prostitution posturing in Washington raised the hackles of a number of western countries, including Canada and the Netherlands. For nearly a year, according to the published account of Ann Jordan, a member of a human rights caucus that was part of the negotiation process, the concept of whether or not adult prostitution constituted trafficking divided the delegates. Eventually, several governments told U.S. negotiators that they would not sign the protocol if it called for the abolition of prostitution. Faced with the prospect of losing unanimity on the protocol, the American team forced the abolitionists to back off. The ensuing compromise among the Vienna negotiators was the definition that appeared in article 3 of the final document.[43]

> "Trafficking in persons" shall mean the recruitment, transportation, transfer, harbouring or receipt of persons, by means of the threat or use of force or other forms of coercion, of abduction, of fraud, of deception, of the abuse of power or of a position of vulnerability or of the giving or receiving of payments or benefits to achieve the consent of a person having control over another person, for the purpose of exploitation. Exploitation shall include, at a minimum, *the exploitation of the prostitution of others or other forms of sexual exploitation*, forced labour or services, slavery or practices similar to slavery, servitude or the removal of organs. [my emphasis][44]

This definition did not go far enough for the abolitionists. It did not say that prostitution was exploitative but that trafficking was an abuse of power that led to exploitation of a person's labor. Such exploitation could involve prostitution or sex work as well as other forms of forced labor. In other words, although prostitution was a form of work, it was not judged under the protocol as being exploitative per se. As made clear in the interpretive notes for officials' records of the protocol negotiations, the terms *exploitation of the prostitution of others* and *other forms of sexual exploitation* were not defined in the document. Thus, individual nations, not the United Nations, were responsible for addressing prostitution in their own domestic laws.[45]

Another diplomatic battle was fought over the concept of having trafficking victims returned to their countries of origin. Countries that were the target of illegal immigration often sent illegal immigrants back to their home countries. In the case of the *Golden Venture*, for example, more than one hundred passengers were returned to China.[46] Asylum seekers were, of course, granted rights and assurances under different international conventions and were allowed to seek formal entry into a country if they were credible victims of persecution or oppression. But among nations, customary law required most countries of residency to accept the return of their own nationals. According to an American official, a Pakistani official affirmed this point about customary law to the U.S. delegation. Yet the diplomat believed that putting the concept in writing, as article 8 of the protocol required, was quite another matter.[47]

Many sending nations agreed, among them not only Pakistan but China and India. During a session in Geneva, one diplomat from a developing nation told U.S. negotiators that return of his country's illegal migrants would cut off the flow of remittance money.[48] Such remittances (money that migrants send home from the countries where they are working) are clearly an important source of dollars and capital, and loss of such funding would create a hardship for families who have come to rely on the cash.

The Americans and other western diplomats from Europe and Canada believed that failure to include an article on repatriation of trafficking victims would sound the document's death knell. Faced with developing nations' reluctance to accept the concept of return, the U.S. delegation said it would not sign the protocol if repatriation were not included. That stance carried the day, and repatriation made it into the final version.[49]

In substance, article 8, "Repatriation of Victims of Trafficking in Persons," required a country whose national had been trafficked abroad to "facilitate and accept, with due regard for the safety of that person, the return of that person without undue or unreasonable delay." Repatriation could not contravene any of the person's rights in the receiving state, such as qualifying for asylum or being treated as a trafficking victim. It should "preferably be voluntary," and nations were obliged to provide necessary travel documents for persons without them.[50]

Once negotiations on the contentious article 8 were over, the trafficking protocol was essentially complete. In about two years, delegates from 125 countries had finalized not only the trafficking document but also a companion protocol on migrant smuggling and, most important, the overarching international convention against organized crime. The task, however, wasn't finished: the United Nations had to present the crime convention and the protocols to the international community for signature, and in November 2000 Italy's U.N. ambassador, Luigi Lauriola took that step. In an address to the General Assembly, he noted that there had been some opposition to the convention, with a number of nations opposed to even discussing an international agreement. But in the end, he said, those countries became the strongest supporters of the process.[51]

The ceremony for signing the convention and the two protocols was set for December 2000 in Palermo, Sicily. The symbolism of the setting was fitting. Sicily, and especially the city of Palermo, was the epicenter of the old Italian

Mafia, the most fabled and notorious criminal syndicate in the world. By signing a momentous international agreement against organized crime in Palermo, countries were invading the heartland of the traditional enemy.

Between December 12 and 15, delegates from more than 120 nations took over downtown Palermo for the signing conference. The event catered to the news media with a series of forums about transnational crime, including trafficking. There were several keynote speeches, among them one by U.S. Undersecretary of State for Global Affairs Frank Loy, who pinpointed the importance of the convention and the protocols: "[They] define—for the first time in binding international instruments—organized crime, migrant smuggling and trafficking in persons; and they require all parties to criminalize this defined conduct under their domestic law. But they permit individual countries to tailor the manner in which they implement their obligations to the particular needs of their system." The documents presented in Palermo made it easier to collaborate internationally on crime, he said. Instead of requiring nations to go through the time-consuming process of negotiating bilateral agreements, the convention and the protocols allowed countries to rely on each other for extradition and mutual legal assistance. Loy also highlighted the documents' "fundamental humanitarian aspects," particularly in the area of human trafficking and migrant smuggling; and the trafficking protocol, he pointed out, included far-reaching provisions for victims' services and protection. This element had been a main goal of the U.S. negotiation team, a fact that had been obscured in the political furor in Washington over prostitution, which had almost derailed the protocol. Nevertheless, the trafficking document called on states to provide not only witness protection but also, in appropriate cases, shelter, medical and legal assistance, and the possibility of permanent residence in the receiving country.[52]

By December 15, 2000, the Convention on Transnational Organized Crime had been signed by 121 nations, including the United States, Russia, China, France, Britain, Germany, and Japan. Eighty-one nations (including the European Union) signed the trafficking protocol. Notable abstainers were Pakistan, Japan, Egypt, China, Thailand, and Ukraine. These last three nations were major sources of illegal migration so were probably troubled by the protocol's provision requiring signatories to cooperate in accepting the return of their nationals. A total of seventy-nine countries signed the migrant smuggling protocol, with the major exceptions being the same countries that abstained from signing the trafficking protocol.[53]

But signing was only part of the process. For any of the documents to come into force or be legally binding, at least forty countries had to ratify the convention as a treaty. That threshold was crossed on September 29, 2003.

On December 25, 2003, the trafficking protocol entered into force; and on January 28, 2004, the migrant smuggling protocol also took effect.[54]

Passage of the trafficking protocol committed the global community to addressing human trafficking in concrete, affirmative ways. It required nations to criminalize trafficking and, when possible, to harmonize their domestic laws with the protocol to create something close to a universal legal standard. To monitor compliance, the United Nations carried out periodic assessments. Like the crime convention, the trafficking protocol was intended to promote action.

Chapter 4

"We Need This Bill"

IN THE EARLY summer of 2000, when Los Angeles police asked Shaefeli Akhtar her age, she couldn't answer them with certainty. She might have been twenty-eight years old, maybe twenty-nine. In Bangladesh her family didn't keep good records, and neither did that country's local authorities. But even if she had had access to her records, they wouldn't have done the young, bruised woman any good: she was illiterate. In any case Akhtar's age wasn't the most important thing about her. She had a more disturbing story to relate.[1]

Akhtar told police that she had arrived in southern California in July 1995, though she had no proof of lawful entrance. A married couple, Nur Alamin and Rabiya Akhter, had brought her there from Bangladesh using a fake passport and following a circuitous route through Saudi Arabia to Los Angeles. During her six years with the couple, they moved in and out of three homes. The pair seemed to be doing well: they owned the Great Star of India restaurant in a part of Los Angeles known as Koreatown, which in 1992 had been severely damaged in rioting following a controversial verdict in the case of Rodney King, a black driver beaten by several white police officers.[2]

But if Nur Alamin, his wife, and their two children were living well, Shaefeli Akhtar was not. She told police that she had been forced to work as a housekeeper and take care of the couple's sons with little or no pay. After spending her days cooking and cleaning, she was forced to sleep on the kitchen floor or behind a sofa. If she complained, she said, the couple threatened her, beat her with a broom, and warned her that her family in Bangladesh would be harmed if she stopped working or tried to leave. She also said that Alamin had sexually assaulted her. On June 30, 2000, finally fed up after another beating, Akhtar escaped from the house and went to police.[3]

What she described to authorities was a story of compelled labor that had become all too familiar to federal investigators at the U.S. Department of Justice. Within that agency a special unit, the National Worker Exploitation Task Force, had been set up to deal with increasing complaints about people (often, but not exclusively, immigrants) who had been subjected to slave-like working conditions and coerced into such labor through debt bondage or extortion. It was a classic trafficking scenario, and agents had seen it before in prostitution cases. But now the work had little to do with sex. It was a particularly ugly version of forced labor, often involving victims who were illegal immigrants and thus afraid of complaining to authorities.

In the 1950s television newsman Edward R. Morrow produced the documentary *Harvest of Shame*, which dealt with the plight of migrant farm workers. A subsequent series of reforms, sparked in part by the United Farm Workers union, helped improve working and living conditions and increased political awareness of the many migrants who had entered the United States, both legally and illegally, from Mexico. But despite those improvements, farm workers continued to be exploited. Sometimes the victims weren't immigrants, and sometimes the exploiters didn't fit the classic trafficker mold.

Consider, for example, the case of Michael Allen Lee, who lived in Florida in a major citrus-growing area with a constant demand for seasonal workers to pick crops. Fruit growers used him as a middleman to procure workers quickly. But Lee didn't need immigrants to fill the growers' labor quotas: plenty of homeless black men in the Fort Pierce area jumped at the jobs he offered. As an extra enticement, he told them they could live in one of the houses he owned. With a pay rate of thirty-five to fifty dollars a day, Lee had no trouble finding takers. But given what happened next, the men might have been better off living on the street.[4]

Lee not only recruited workers but gave them short-term loans to cover rental space in his homes as well as food, cigarettes, and in some cases crack cocaine. After deducting all those costs, the men brought home, on average, less than ten dollars per day. Rent for space to sleep on the floor was thirty dollars a week, and for that price they received only floor mats as beds. Awakened before five o'clock in the morning, the men were crammed into vans and driven to the groves, where they spent twelve hours a day picking fruit. Lee had, in essence, developed his own version of a company store: a worker who was able to earn 400 dollars a week might end up with only 150 after Lee deducted charges. If the men complained or wanted to quit, they risked being beaten.[5]

Experts believed that there were thousands upon thousands of agricultural workers in states such as Florida who had been coerced to work and live in outrageous conditions. Other workers, like Shaefeli Akhtar, found themselves

enslaved in domestic drudgery, exploited by former countrymen who had trans-
planted their traditional but cruel labor standards and expectations to the
United States, which perceived such treatment as a violation of human rights
and dignity. Although Akhtar, the Fort Pierce citrus workers, and countless others in similar situations didn't consider themselves to be trafficked persons, some
people in powerful places had recognized their plight and were attempting to
prevent such abuses from ever happening again in the United States.

Since 1998, Senator Paul Wellstone, encouraged by his wife Sheila, had
been exhorting his colleagues in the U.S. Senate to address human trafficking in
a substantial way. That year he introduced a resolution condemning trafficking
and calling on the state department and other agencies to investigate and take
action against international sex traffickers. The measure passed, but a more
ambitious effort in March 1999—his proposed International Trafficking of
Women and Children Victim Protection Act—didn't fare as well. In essence,
the measure called for the creation of an interagency task force to evaluate how
governments were responding to trafficking and helping victims. In addition,
U.S. immigration officials would have been required to give trafficking victims
special consideration so they could pursue asylum or seek redress in court.
Despite its modest aims, the bill died in committee.[6]

But suddenly everything changed. By April 2000, Amy O'Neill Richard's
report, "International Trafficking in Women to the United States: A
Contemporary Manifestation of Slavery and Organized Crime," had received
wide publicity. Now Americans and Congress were facing what law enforcers
had known for a long time: trafficking in persons, particularly in women and
children, was significant on nearly every continent; and the United States had
become a destination for trafficked persons working in the sex, agricultural, and
garment industries as well as in domestic settings. Although she admitted the
absence of accurate statistical assessments, Richard repeated government and
NGO estimates claiming that between 700,000 and 2 million women and children were trafficked around the world each year. Of those, 45,000 to 50,000
were trafficked to the United States.[7]

As later studies showed, those estimates were too high.[8] But her report gave
the public at least a general sense of the pervasiveness of trafficking. It also concluded that several measures, including new legislation, must be implemented.
In addition to new trafficking laws, the Department of Justice would benefit
from a unified task force approach. In Richard's words, "currently, the U.S.
Attorneys' offices appear to be understaffed and overburdened, making investigations of potential trafficking cases difficult. Moreover, at present, many U.S.
Attorneys do not have a sufficient number of victim witness coordinators capable of working effectively with the victims."[9]

According to Richard, victim advocates believed that federal, state, and local law enforcement officials should have specialized training to identify and respond to trafficking victims. Consular officials abroad should also learn to identify instances in which front companies recruit and transport victims to the United States. She concluded, "Without implementation of these proposals, trafficking in women—this modern-day form of slavery in the United States—will not only continue but also will grow," adding that it was only a matter of time until organized crime groups involved in trafficking overseas began to target the United States. "Lastly, providing shelter and services for trafficking victims will not only provide law enforcement with invaluable witnesses in their criminal cases against traffickers, but also will exemplify the humanitarian ideals of respect and dignity for the individual on which U.S. law is based."[10]

The Richard report set the stage for more concerted congressional action. On April 12, 2000, backed by Republican senator Sam Brownback of Kansas and Democratic senator Diane Feinstein of California, Wellstone introduced the Trafficking Victims Protection Act, which he later described as "one of my proudest accomplishments."[11] In his address to the Senate, he acknowledged that the trafficking problem seemed to have become intractable:

> The long and the short of it, colleagues, is though, it is hard to believe, in the year 2000 there are maybe 50,000 women and children trafficked to our country, maybe as many as 2 million worldwide.... Despite increasing governmental and international interest, trafficking in persons continues to be one of the darkest aspects of globalization of the world economy, becoming more insidious and more widespread everyday.... Trafficking in human beings is not just some problem over there—it's a problem over here. We too must do our part. We need this bill enacted into law this year.[12]

In introducing the measure to his colleagues, Wellstone pointed out several specific features:

1. The bill would criminalize all forms of trafficking in persons and establish a system of punishment ranging up to life in prison for offenders involved in trafficking children.
2. It would revamp immigration procedures so that victims would be allowed to remain in the United States to testify in criminal cases. This provision would allow immigration officials to circumvent laws requiring them to deport illegal immigrants.
3. It would establish programs and skills training to integrate trafficking victims into their communities.
4. It would establish mental and physical health programs for victims.[13]

Wellstone's trafficking bill addressed a number of long-standing concerns among advocates and human rights experts. Provisions dealing with immigration status, health concerns, and long-term benefits clearly broke new ground, recognizing that trafficked persons should be thought of as victims rather than conspirators in league with the traffickers. Similar concerns were being addressed in Vienna during diplomatic negotiations over the U.N. trafficking protocol (though at this date the final protocol would not be finished or signed for another ten months), and the United States was maintaining a consistent stance on both fronts.

Wellstone's domestic measure was designed to have an international impact. Some foreign governments, because of lack of interest, insufficient resources, differing national priorities, or outright corruption, had done little to address trafficking. In response, the proposed bill required the state department's annual country reports on human rights practices to now include "a separate list of countries of origin, transit or destination for a significant number of trafficking victims which are not meeting minimum standards for the elimination of trafficking." If those standards were not met, the United States had the option of imposing sanctions. The bill would also allow the secretary of state to list foreign persons involved in trafficking and the president to take "tough action" against anyone on the list.[14] Wellstone had pushed this reporting aspect in his failed International Trafficking of Women and Children Victim Protection Act of 1999, which had also called for limited sanctions: nations could lose their eligibility for police assistance (that is, U.S. aid or training for foreign law enforcement officials).[15]

But in 2000, not everyone agreed about including more expansive foreign sanction provisions. According to Wellstone, Senator Brownback wanted a system of mandatory sanctions; but Wellstone himself believed the discretionary approach was the better route. Mandatory penalties, he said, were not useful. Apparently, he'd had a change of heart since 1999, when his bill had explicitly stated that nations "shall not" be eligible for police assistance.[16]

> Trafficking exploits poor women and booms in societies undergoing severe economic distress. To impose economic sanctions in trafficking legislation that cuts off a broad range of bilateral and multilateral assistance programs designed to improve the economy of specific nations is to cause harm to the very people who might be helped by the legislation. For example, I don't believe we can justify cutting off funding designed to foster economic reform so that those most susceptible to trafficking such as women and children, can find work; or cutting off funding for programs that increase professionalism and independence in the judicial system so that traffickers can be held accountable; or even cutting off programs designed to provide training

and technical assistance to countries which are generally making an effort to combat trafficking.[17]

By creating a list of offending countries, the United States would give those nations notice that they risked sanctions. This would put the president into a better position to "impose specific, targeted, and workable sanctions against trafficking countries," an approach Wellstone preferred to mandatory penalties.[18]

State department officials also were wary of mandatory sanctions and said as much to Wellstone and other senators in the days before the bill was introduced. In a prepared statement, Frank Loy said, "Sanctions would be profoundly counterproductive" and would not help build an international effort to combat the transnational nature of trafficking.[19] He listed four reasons:

- Economic sanctions would exacerbate the causes of trafficking in certain poor countries where people did not have many economic opportunities.
- They would not punish traffickers or organized crime but governments and people.
- Countries facing sanctions might downplay the seriousness of trafficking and thus hurt international cooperation.
- Local government might see the anti-trafficking work of human rights groups and NGOs as a threat and cease collaboration.[20]

Wellstone clearly had key support for the less punitive and non-mandatory sanctions proposal that became part of his bill.

Because of his years of involvement with the anti-trafficking issue as well as his outspokenness, Wellstone is often viewed as its most active congressional advocate in the late 1990s and early 2000s. But Congressman Chris Smith, a Republican from New Jersey, was also involved and proposed significant trafficking legislation in 1999, the same year that Wellstone introduced a forerunner of his 2000 proposal. On November 8, 1999, Smith introduced in the House his own Trafficking Victims Protection Act of 1999, which had thirty-seven bipartisan sponsors. A comparison of Smith's 1999 bill with Wellstone's 1999 pilot proposal shows many similarities. Smith's bill actually foreshadowed what Wellstone would introduce five months later in the Senate and, as it turned out, became the true framework for the country's first comprehensive trafficking legislation. Smith's bill also explicitly condemned sex trafficking, which conservative Republicans seemed to equate with the trafficking phenomenon in general.

Let's look at the details. Wellstone's 1999 bill proposed an interagency task force of U.S. government officials who would evaluate progress in the United States and abroad in the areas of trafficking prevention, protection and assistance of victims, and prosecution of traffickers. It also included the carrot-and-stick sanction approach. The president would be authorized to withhold not just police assistance but a wide assortment of foreign aid, technology exports, and other assistance to foreign governments that were making little or no progress in reducing trafficking or helping victims. Wellstone's bill would have modified immigration laws to help trafficking victims and required the Department of Health and Human Services and other agencies to offer trafficking victims physical and mental health services and shelter. Finally, the bill addressed gaps in American laws that covered trafficking, proposing a revision of the federal criminal code. For the first time human trafficking would be defined in the code. In addition, it called for prison sentences of up to twenty years or even life if death, kidnapping, or aggravated sexual abuse were involved.[21]

Specifically, the Wellstone measure defined as a *human trafficker* anyone who "recruits, harbors, provides, transports, employs, purchases, sells or secures, by any means, any person, knowing or having reason to know that person is or will be subjected to involuntary servitude or peonage or to unlawfully exploitive labor conditions as described in subsection (b) of this section." The term *exploitive labor conditions* was defined as covering instances in which "the labor or services of a person are obtained or maintained through any scheme or artifice to defraud, or by means of any plan or pattern, including but not limited to false and fraudulent pretenses and misrepresentations, such that the person reasonably believes that he has no viable alternative but to perform the labor or services."[22]

Smith's 1999 bill generally followed the same format and also called for the establishment of an interagency task force to monitor and combat trafficking. But unlike Wellstone, Smith wanted the task force to study international "sex tourism" and make recommendations on how to deal with it. He also wanted the task force to list countries that were origin, transit, or destination points for significant numbers of victims of "severe forms of trafficking"—essentially defined as sex trafficking involving a person under the age of eighteen.[23]

Smith envisioned revisions of the federal criminal code along the lines that Wellstone had recommended, but he wanted to revise it specifically to deal with sex trafficking of children. His proposed penalty for that offense was life in prison if the victim were under the age of fourteen or up to twenty years in jail if the victim were between the ages of fourteen and eighteen.[24]

Smith's measure also spelled out particular topics that the task force on trafficking would cover in its reports. Unlike Wellstone, he wanted countries to meet specific minimum standards for eliminating trafficking. Among them were laws prohibiting and punishing severe forms of trafficking (child sex trafficking) and efforts to deter such activity. Failure to meet these minimum standards could result in U.S. withholding of non-humanitarian aid and U.S. pressure on institutions such as the World Bank to deny loans or other funds to offending countries.[25]

The Clinton administration had a number of reservations about Smith's measure. Most troublesome for the White House was the bill's broad sanction provision, which, as Loy had mentioned, would be counterproductive in the fight against trafficking and undermine the work of NGOs abroad. The administration also had concerns about the T-visa requirements of the House measure, which the White House saw as too restrictive. The reporting requirements envisioned by Smith also seemed to duplicate what the State Department was already doing in its annual country reports on human rights practices.[26]

Though both Wellstone and Smith were eager to fight human trafficking, their key philosophical differences revolved around the issue of sex. Wellstone had always acknowledged that traffickers force victims to perform labor or services such as prostitution and sexual servitude, possibly exposing them to deadly diseases such as HIV/AIDS. But his 1999 legislation did not isolate sex trafficking because he saw it as a particular component of a wider trafficking problem. Smith, in contrast, was very disturbed about the sexual exploitation of trafficking victims under age eighteen, and his concerns influenced much of what appeared in his legislative proposal. Wellstone didn't appreciate the conservative Republican's seeming preoccupation with sex and trafficking, said one of his former aides. He saw trafficking as slavery and thought that the "sex as sin" angle pervading the debate was misplaced.[27]

Wellstone made a point during the Senate hearings to remind listeners that trafficking was not just about sex and not only about women and mentioned as an example the case of the deaf Mexicans. He didn't believe the estimated 50,000 trafficking victims brought into the country yearly took into statistical account the men in forced labor situations. Questioned by Wellstone, a State Department official agreed.[28]

But it should not have surprised anyone that sex trafficking had become the main reference point for policy discussions and debates about human trafficking in general. Since the mid-1990s the news media had related numerous stories about enslaved women who were forced into sexual servitude. Despite publicized cases of other kinds of trafficking and forced labor situations, these stories of sex slaves became emblematic of the issue and were sure to catch readers' attention. The tales had definite victims and villains as well as a neat moral that was easy to comprehend, especially if you were an overworked news editor.

Interestingly, this wasn't the first time the news media had popularized stories of unwitting women captured by devious, exploitative men and sold into sexual bondage. According to Gretchen Soderlund and Emma Grant, they were also rampant in the 1910s, a period in American history known as the

Progressive Era. At that time, the frozen rhetoric surrounding those lurid tales (and reflected later in the trafficking discussions) served as "a smokescreen for the creation of harsh and ultimately moralistic laws preventing the mobility of sex workers" and created difficulties for sex workers who performed such work of their own free will.[29]

Many victims advocates emphasized that trafficked persons had been forced to engage in sex. But critics such as Soderlund and Grant disagreed, claiming that some sex workers had used their status as victims to take advantage of immigration authorities.[30] There is no way to know which sex workers were exploiting their presumed status as trafficking victims, yet even the possibility that migrants might abuse immigration laws became a major point of contention in congressional debates. As I will discuss later, those worries led Congress to set limits on the number of trafficking victims allowed to apply for special visas to remain in the country.

The stories of sex trafficking victims also figured into the rhetoric of Wellstone and others who proposed legislation in 1999 and 2000. Even in 1998, when Wellstone first began to speak out on the issue, he emphasized that "sex traffickers use violence and intimidation, holding women in slave-like conditions and sexually exploiting them for economic gain."[31] To be fair, he noted in the same breath that thousands of immigrants who were trafficked ended up in domestic servitude and forced labor. Yet his most powerful and emotional images referred to women who had allegedly been forced into prostitution.

During Senate hearings in early 2000, speakers introduced numerous stories that contained the same basic elements: vulnerable young women, some barely in their teens, were tricked into thinking they were going to work in regular jobs, only to find themselves working as prostitutes. One of those speakers was Dr. Laura Lederer, then director of the Protection Project, a program of the Kennedy School of Government at Harvard University. Part of her work involved compiling a compendium of trafficking and prostitution-related laws around the world. In the process, she came across a number of stories related by trafficked women, and during her Senate testimony she told one about a girl named Lydia. As Lederer explained, Lydia's tale was really a composite of several stories told by women and children who had been trafficked in Eastern Europe. The character known as Lydia was sixteen years old and represented one of many similar young girls in "any of the sender countries in Eastern Europe, the Ukraine, Russia, Romania, Lithuania, the Czech Republic, Latvia."[32]

In Lederer's retelling, a beautifully dressed woman approached Lydia, took the girl and some friends out to dinner, and then invited them home for a drink. "Taking that drink is the last thing that Lydia remembers. The woman drugged her, handed her and her friends over to another agent who drove them, unconscious, across the borders and into—and here you can fill in any of the other countries that are receiver countries, Germany, the Netherlands, Italy, any of the Middle Eastern countries, as far as Japan, Canada and the United States."[33]

Lederer's testimony then assumed a familiar note: Lydia woke up in a "strange room" and learned from a man she had never met that he owned her and that she would work for him. With no passport and unable to speak the country's language, she was a captive who had to work in a brothel, servicing up to twenty men a day so that she could pay her captor 35,000 dollars in smuggling and transit fees. "For the next six months she was held in virtual confinement. She was forced to prostitute herself. She received no money. She had no hope of escape." Finally rescued in a police raid on the brothel, Lydia endured more hardship when she, as an illegal immigrant, was transferred to a prison cell to await deportation. Her life was filled with fear as well as physical distress and illness, while the trafficker was able to buy his way out of trouble.[34]

As Lederer readily admitted, Lydia's tale was a composite but also emblematic of a major problem, including what the speaker alleged to be roughly 1 million children forced into prostitution in Southeast Asia.[35] But a young Mexican woman identified only as Inez related a more concrete story to the committee. She was a survivor of the infamous Cadena sex ring, which federal and state officials had broken up in Florida in the late 1990s.

"My story begins in the fall of 1997, in Veracruz, Mexico," said Inez, recalling how a friend had approached her with tales of vast opportunities for work in the United States. "She told me she worked in the United States at a restaurant and had made good money. At the time I was eager to assist my family financially, so I decided to learn more about this job opportunity. My friend set up a meeting with two men who confirmed the job openings for women like myself at American restaurants. They told me they would take care of my immigration papers, and that I would be free to change jobs if I did not like working at the restaurant."[36]

Inez said she crossed the border at Brownsville, Texas, in September 1997 (presumably with the help of a smuggler) and eventually made her way to Houston. There she met a man named Rogerio Cadena, who drove her and some other women to a trailer in Avon Park, Florida. "This is when I was told my fate," she said. "I would not be working in a restaurant. Instead, I was told I owed a smuggling fee of $2,500, and had to pay it off selling my body to men."[37]

Inez testified in detail about the conditions of the Cadena brothels and the demands of the sex work she was required to perform. If she or any of the other women declined a customer's request for special sex acts (and many of those customers, she said, were drunk or high on drugs), they were beaten. Any girl who got pregnant was forced to have an abortion, and the medical costs were added to her smuggling bill.[38]

News accounts of the Cadena brothels and the prosecutions of brothel managers and family clan members had already publicized the experiences of Inez and the other victims. But Inez's firsthand testimony clearly evoked sympathy from members of the Senate subcommittee. Senator Brownback told her, "We are deeply grateful to you for being willing to subject yourself to this and the fear that goes with what you have been through, and God bless you for doing that, because you are speaking out for millions of women around the world that this has happened to them as well."[39]

But aside from recounting an all-too-familiar litany of details about sexual servitude, Inez's testimony raised an additional point. She mentioned that, after federal immigration investigators and the FBI had raided the brothels, they sent the women to a detention center for many months. Thus, Inez and some of the other women began to believe that the Cadena gang had been right about one thing: "We thought we would be in prison for the rest of our lives." Finally, thanks to the efforts of a number of attorneys, including several from the Florida Advocacy Immigrant Center, the women were released to the custody of a women's domestic violence center, where they got medical and psychological help.[40]

Wellstone picked up on this theme of social services for trafficking victims, noting that it was important to assure victims that their cooperation with law enforcement would not have adverse repercussions: "There are several things you have said that are very important to take note of. One is that when women are put in this situation, as happened to you, they are not going to be able to step forward if what they have to worry about is either being deported or put in detention camp, and that is one thing we have to make sure that does not happen." As his legislation made clear, Wellstone believed that trafficking victims should receive medical services, counseling, and other help. He also pointed out that some women could not cooperate with investigators because they feared for the lives of family members in their country of origin, and Congress needed to consider this issue when drafting the legislation.[41]

Because there were no comparable hearings in the House, the Senate hearings on trafficking (which took place before the Subcommittee on Near Eastern and South Asian Affairs of the Committee on Foreign Relations) were the only forum in Congress for public testimony on the issue. But clearly a viable coalition of liberal Democrats and more conservative Republicans was committed to doing something about the trafficking problem. The next step was to craft viable versions of the bills introduced into the House and Senate. In other words, the issue had moved into the realm of political bargaining and gamesmanship.

As the Senate hearings showed, the Clinton administration was concerned about the use of sanctions; and negotiations over the legislation would have to grapple with that point. Also contentious, particularly in the House, were T-visas. As I've mentioned, this special category of immigration documents would permit victims to remain in the United States while they helped law enforcement officials prosecute trafficking conspiracies. The concept of a T-visa was incorporated into both the Senate and the House versions of the legislation, but members of Congress differed on the issue: some believed the visa category should be unlimited, while others believed it should be capped at a certain level.

The Senate bill had no T-visa limit. But in the House, the Committee on the Judiciary reported a version of Smith's legislation that set a 5,000-person limit on T-visas, prompting a debate about whether that level was reasonable, given the extent of reported trafficking into the United States. Some believed the limit was set to satisfy an "unrealistic concern" about abuse of the law: that is, fear that people who wanted to obtain legal immigration status would falsely claim they were victims of involuntary servitude or sex trafficking. Representative Melvin Watt of North Carolina argued against this concern during a House debate on the legislation: "Most significantly, the bill unnecessarily caps at 5,000 per year the number of victims who can receive a con-immigrant visa and caps at 5,000 per year the number of victims who can become permanent [U.S.] residents." It seemed unfair and arbitrary, he said, to not offer protection to the 5,001st or 5,002nd victim of trafficking: "We have no arbitrary limit on the number of refugees who can enter this country. We have no arbitrary limit on the number of [asylum seekers] who can enter this country and, in my judgment, it is beneath our dignity as a nation to use an arbitrary cap to shut our doors to victims of slavery and sex trafficking."[42]

Watt wanted the House to accept the Senate decision not to cap the visas. But in opposition Representative Charles Canady of Florida said the cap proposed by the House was based on reasonable estimates of the potential numbers of trafficking victims who might be eligible to take advantage of the visa benefit. "The original estimates were substantially below the 5,000 cap that is included in the bill, so I believe that it is unlikely, extremely unlikely, that this cap would have any practical impact," he said.[43]

Zoe Lofgren, a representative from California, thought the figure of 5,000 might actually be too low based on the CIA's 1999 report (compiled by a non-CIA researcher), which estimated that as many as 50,000 women and children were trafficked into the country each year. Though the CIA's figure was later disputed, it had nevertheless driven the trafficking debate until this point and was used to justify more liberal visa levels. Anything less, Representative John Conyers of Michigan said, does a "good disservice to our international image as a country concerned with human rights."[44]

Ultimately, House members voted in mid-September 2000 to have its eight conferees (including Smith) meet with six senators (including Wellstone) to come up with a compromise that addressed the visa cap as well as a number of other inconsistencies and differences in the two trafficking bills. The conference work took the better part of a month, and on October 5, 2000, the committee spelled out the final form of what would become the federal trafficking statute in a joint statement to the House and Senate. The statement, which was printed in the *Congressional Record*, first enumerated the various sections of the bill and the Senate's and House's separate versions and then stated which legislative house's version made the final cut.[45] Often both versions of the different provisions were nearly identical, and the committee's choice of one over the other needed little elaboration; but a few sections merited longer discussion to explain why one version had prevailed.

The provisions concerning T-visas, sanctions, and punishment of traffickers required lengthy explanations, an indication of both their legal and political importance. As I have discussed, the House and Senate bills had each contained a T-visa provision that allowed trafficking victims to stay temporarily in the United States under certain circumstances. Eligibility was limited to persons who (1) were victims of a severe form of trafficking; (2) were no older than age fourteen or had been induced to participate in sex work or slave-like labor by force, fraud, coercion, or deception; (3) had complied with reasonable law enforcement requests for assistance in any investigation; and (4) had a well-founded fear of retribution if removed from the United States or would suffer extreme hardship if deported. The bills also allowed the attorney general to give the holder of a T-visa the right to permanently stay in the United States.

The House version contained the controversial annual cap of 5,000 on T-visas, while the Senate version contained no such limit. The conference report generally adopted the House version and specifically kept the 5,000 limit, believing that the number allotted was sufficient. But it added a provision requiring U.S. immigration officials to report each year if any legitimate applicants had been denied T-visas because of the limit. If necessary, Congress would then consider raising it.[46]

The conference report acknowledged that some persons might falsely claim to be trafficking victims when in fact they had agreed to work to pay off a smuggling fee. If that were true, they wouldn't be eligible for a T-visa. An exception was a victim of a "severe form" of trafficking, defined as sex trafficking of a person under age eighteen or the transportation of a person for labor by force, fraud, or coercion that then led to involuntary servitude, peonage, debt bondage, or slavery.[47]

Regarding sanctions, the Clinton administration was concerned about draconian requirements that would force the United States to withhold certain kinds of aid to nations that didn't meet certain minimum standards for combating trafficking. The House version of the bill said that the president "shall" withhold non-humanitarian foreign assistance or waive the requirement if such assistance was in the "national interest" of the United States. The Senate version stated that the president "may" take any number of steps, including withholding foreign assistance, instructing U.S. executive directors of multilateral lending institutions to vote against loans or other assistance to offending countries, as well as prohibiting arms sales and other exports.[48]

The conference report noted that the agreed-upon legislation gave the president the freedom to take no action against countries that had not been doing enough to combat trafficking but were now making "significant efforts" to comply with legal standards. In cases of egregious offending nations, the president had the ability to withhold "non-humanitarian" and "non-trade-related" assistance. Apparently, the conferees did not want to hurt countries' ability to meet their citizens' basic needs, a situation that might backfire on the United States by forcing more economic migration and human trafficking.[49]

The conference report also dealt with changes in federal criminal laws aimed at the prosecution and punishment of traffickers. Some of those changes were similar in both the House and the Senate versions of the bill, such as increasing the penalty for involuntary servitude, peonage, and other violations from ten to twenty years and to a maximum sentence of life in prison in cases of kidnapping, death, or sexual abuse. But conferees made one change related to a subtle form of coercion involving threats to a third person. This would allow prosecutors to address cases in which individuals were trafficked into domestic service because of threats directed at their families living abroad.[50]

Now that the conferees had come to an agreement, their report needed to pass both houses of Congress. While the measures had a great deal of support in Congress, passage was not necessarily a sure thing. In *The Conscience of a Liberal*, Wellstone recalled that he and his supporters needed unanimous consent to pass the conference report without much debate. "Otherwise, the majority leader would pull the bill from the floor. There was very little time left in the session, and he needed the floor open for other legislation."[51]

According to Wellstone, smooth sailing in the Senate became choppy waters when his friend Senator Tom Harkin said he would not let any other bills move until the Senate had voted on the nomination of a candidate for the U.S. Court of Appeals. Trading on his friendship with Harkin, Wellstone convinced his fellow senator to let the trafficking measure be heard first. But Senator John McCain was angered by a move to block another measure he was backing and wanted to "shut the Senate down" and hamstring any unanimous-consent agreement. Wellstone pleaded with McCain, who relented. "If Tom Harkin and John McCain had not helped a friend, the trafficking legislation would not have passed," he said.[52]

On October 6, 2000, the report resoundingly passed in the House by a vote of 371 to 1, despite the fact that it had been packaged with some unrelated measures that members found annoying. On October 11, the Senate voted 95 to 0 to pass the conference report, effectively approving the trafficking bill. On October 19, the measure was sent to the White House; and on October 28, President Bill Clinton signed into law the Victims of Trafficking and Violence Protection Act of 2000.[53] Following are the main provisions of the law:

- It amends the federal criminal code in a number of ways, increasing penalties for the crimes of peonage, enticement into slavery, and sale into involuntary servitude from ten to twenty years, with life imprisonment possible in crimes involving death, kidnapping, aggravated sexual abuse, or attempted homicide. It also defines the crimes of forced labor, trafficking, and sexual trafficking of children or others by force; penalties for all can be life imprisonment.
- It prohibits document destruction, particularly when related to travel or immigration in a trafficking situation.
- It requires convicted traffickers to make restitution to their victims and permits courts to forfeit the property of any convicted trafficker if it was used in or derived from the offense.
- Victims of trafficking in the United States are eligible for certain immigration benefits. Most important is the T-visa, which permits a victim to remain in the country if he or she has helped law enforcement *and* would suffer extreme hardship if expelled from the country. Spouses, children, and parents of such victims can also receive T-visas; but there is an annual limit of 5,000. If a victim has been in the United States for three years, has been of good moral character, and has answered reasonable law enforcement requests for assistance, he or she may change a T-visa to a permanent resident green card.
- Victims of trafficking in the United States can benefit from programs of the Department of Health and Human Services, the Legal Services Corporation, and other federal agencies. Immigrants who are trafficking victims are eligible for the same benefits and services that are granted to refugees. They are given access to appropriate medical care and other services and cannot be detained in a way that is inappropriate to their status as crime victims.
- The secretary of state is required to include information in reports on human rights and security assistance that detail a country's status as a point of origin, transit, or destination for victims of trafficking.

- The president must establish an interagency task force to monitor and combat trafficking, and the secretary of state must set up a special office to monitor and combat trafficking. This latter office will help the secretary of state compile a report assessing nations' progress in eliminating "severe forms" of trafficking.
- Countries that do not comply with minimum standards for the elimination of trafficking or do not make efforts to comply with those standards may be denied non-humanitarian, non-trade-related foreign assistance from the United States.
- The bill authorizes the appropriation of money from a number of agencies to carry out the purposes of the act. The departments of Health and Human Services, Labor, Justice, and State are each authorized to contribute 5 million dollars in fiscal year 2001 and 10 million dollars in fiscal year 2002. The bill also authorizes a total of 4.5 million dollars to fund the interagency trafficking task force. Total authorization of appropriation comes to 93.8 million dollars over the two fiscal years.

Strictly speaking, the Victims of Trafficking and Violence Protection Act of 2000 predated the signing of the U.N. trafficking protocol in Palermo by a good two months. But by passing a domestic trafficking measure, the United States was jumping ahead and bringing itself into conformity with the U.N. measure's requirement that nations take action to adopt their own legal systems to deal with the phenomenon.

Like the protocol, the American anti-trafficking law dealt primarily with law enforcement issues. It amplified and redefined statutes already on the books, added new immigration enforcement measures, and set up a system for evaluating the trafficking actions of other nations. But human rights advocates believed that the American legislation did more than the protocol to advance and protect the rights of trafficking victims. Ann Jordan, an attorney with Global Rights, a human rights organization formerly known as the International Human Rights Law Group, has said that, while the protocol sections dealing with victim protection and assistance use weak and tentative language, the Trafficking Victims Protection Act is more assertive.[54] Instead of phrases like "shall consider" and "in appropriate cases," which appear in the protocol section dealing with victims, the American law states that victims "shall" have various forms of assistance from federal agencies.[55] Such language is clearly more forceful.

By passing the trafficking law, the United States did what the protocol required. But in one of the diplomatic oddities of this period, the United States did not ratify the U.N. measure until 2005. Practically speaking, lack of ratification had no legal effect; but it embarrassed American diplomats.

Chapter 5   The Learning Curve

W ITH THE PASSAGE of the Trafficking Victims Protection Act (TVPA), American law enforcement officials had, by the beginning of 2001, more legal clout and better tools to deal with human trafficking. Not only did the statute codify the offense of trafficking and related crimes, but it also increased the penalties for those convicted. And the U.N. protocol, while not an American statute, nevertheless validated trafficking's priority as a federal concern. The U.N. document also set the stage for the steady legislative changes in other nations that complemented the Washington initiatives.

The FBI focused closely on human trafficking, and bureau officials were well aware of various news media accounts about the experiences of trafficked women in Eastern Europe.[1] With so many migrants from the former Soviet Union and surrounding Balkan and Baltic nations arriving in the United States, the FBI paid close attention to those immigrant communities for signs of trafficking, particularly for sex work.[2] But at least in the early stages, what was happening abroad did not seem to be happening in the United States. One high-ranking FBI organized crime expert said that, although the agency was on the lookout for large-scale sex trafficking operations that brought European women into American cities, investigators weren't finding such cases. Either they didn't exist at the level portrayed in news accounts, or the alleged victims were keeping silent about their travails.[3]

Privately, American police officers as agreed with their FBI counterparts: trafficking, particularly in the area of prostitution, wasn't showing up at the level Congress had expected. Their skepticism continued well into 2004, when police officials in New York City were creating a special unit to investigate trafficking. At the time those officials questioned the need for such a unit because they had no clear sense of the size and significance of the problem. As a result, the unit was subsumed within a larger organized crime bureau.[4]

But despite a lower-than-expected rate of trafficking offenses in the United States, law enforcement uncovered several cases not long after passage of the TVPA. The first prosecution under the new law was initiated in January 2001 and involved Russian women and a strip club in Alaska. The case showed the federal government that it would need some time to learn to use the provisions of the anti-trafficking statute.

The Alaska case involved four defendants charged with conspiring to lure six Russian women and girls to Alaska to, as the Department of Justice said, "enslave them." The actual charge in the superseding indictment filed in Anchorage's federal district court was forced labor as defined under the new law. Federal prosecutors said the defendants tried to coerce the victims to perform in a strip club by using threats and by confiscating their passports and return plane tickets. Indicted were Victor Virchenko, a Russian national; Pavel Agafonov, a naturalized U.S. citizen; and Tony and Rachel Kennard, both U.S. citizens living in Anchorage.[5]

Part of the alleged scheme, according to federal prosecutors, involved false representations to immigration officials that the Russian women were coming to the United States for a cultural exchange program in which they would perform Russian folk dances. In reality, officials charged, the Russian migrants would work as strippers in the Crazy Horse Saloon nightclub run by the Kennards. The indictment was a result of work by the National Worker Exploitation Task Force, a federal interagency unit set up to handle trafficking cases. The Department of Justice's Civil Rights Division and federal prosecutors in Anchorage handled the actual prosecution of the case.[6]

But trouble developed fairly early; and although federal prosecutors had promoted the case as the first prosecution under the new trafficking law, they quickly decided to drop the charges related to kidnapping and forced labor. According to federal district judge James K. Singleton, Jr., who handled the matter, the prosecution emphasized that the case, in essence, concerned "child sexual abuse and exploitation," an attempt to have it designated as a matter of "special public importance" and thus receive preference in trial scheduling. But in Singleton's review of the case record, he concluded that "this is a mischaracterization of the case." Allegations that the some of the dancers were younger than age sixteen was only a small part of the case; primarily, it concerned immigration fraud.[7]

At the time federal prosecutors wouldn't comment on why they had decided to drop the trafficking charges, although sometimes prosecutors take such a step if they believe they lack proof. But the government didn't come away empty-handed. As a result of a plea bargain, defendants Tony Kennard, Victor Virchenko, and Pavel Agafonov pleaded guilty to charges of visa fraud and violations of the Mann Act, which prohibits the interstate transportation of women for sexual purposes. Charges against Kennard's wife, Rachel, were dismissed. A Department of Justice spokesman said the pleas amounted to a "just result."[8] In August 2001, Virchenko, Agafonov, and Tony Kennard received sentences of up to thirty months in prison. Kennard tried to challenge the sentence on appeal but was unsuccessful.[9]

Federal officials told *Newsday* that organized crime syndicates were trafficking women into U.S. cities, and Singleton agreed that Alaska should not become a conduit for women traveling from Eastern Europe to the United States for purposes of prostitution and sexual exploitation. But "that concern is best addressed by enhanced surveillance by customs and immigration officials, not by turning a fraud case into a sex case," he said.[10]

Federal prosecutors had more success with two other cases initiated in early 2001: one concerning sex work with non-immigrant prostitutes, another concerning a domestic worker who had emigrated from Cameroon. The sex case involved charges of involuntary servitude lodged against fifteen pimps accused of recruiting prostitutes, some of them juveniles, in the Atlanta area. The trial was an interesting exposé of life and society among Atlanta pimps; and as a result, the lead defendant, Charles Floyd Pipkins, was convicted of racketeering, involuntary servitude, enticing minors to engage in prostitution, violating the Mann Act, and other charges. Although he was sentenced to forty years in prison, in early 2005 the U.S. Supreme Court granted him the right to be resentenced because the federal sentencing guidelines, which had been in effect for nearly twenty years, had been ruled unconstitutional in an earlier case.[11]

In the domestic worker case, a man and a woman were charged with holding a teenage Cameroonian girl in involuntary servitude in the Baltimore area. Prosecutors said the couple, Louisa Satia and Kevin Waton Nanji, recruited the girl with the false promise that she would go to school in America. But once the youngster arrived, she was forced by threats and physical violence to work as a domestic servant. Trial evidence showed that she had been assaulted repeatedly and may have been sexually abused in the three years she worked for the couple. In December 2001, Satia and Nanji were convicted of involuntary servitude, conspiracy to harbor, and a related charge. They each received nearly ten-year prison sentences and were ordered to pay their victim 105,306 dollars in restitution.[12]

These early successes showed that the trafficking law could be applied in both immigration and non-immigration cases, in both sex and non-sex cases.

Department of Justice officials trumpeted these and subsequent victories in glowing news releases that often ended with a statement about the department's resolve to pursue traffickers. In later years, the department's annual reports related a steadily increasing number of prosecutions initiated against traffickers and a parallel increase in convictions. But if we consider the statistics for 2001 (the first full year in which the TVPA provisions were enforced) in a wider context, we see that the cases presented a number of difficulties for investigators.

The TVPA contained several key criminal provisions related to the offenses of trafficking: 18 U.S.C. 1583 (enticement into slavery), 18 U.S.C. 1589 (forced labor), 18 U.S.C. 1590 (trafficking with respect to peonage, slavery, involuntary servitude, or forced labor), and 18 U.S.C. 1591 (sex trafficking of children by force, fraud, or coercion). In addition, investigators could also use laws predating the TVPA that pertained to slavery and involuntary servitude (18 U.S.C. 2421 and 18 U.S.C. 2422). Taking these various laws into account, Department of Justice officials reported that in 2001 they started sixty-three investigations that resulted in ten filed criminal cases, four of which involved sex trafficking. A total of thirty-eight defendants were charged, of whom twenty-three were convicted—a conviction rate of 60 percent, which is below average for federal prosecutors, who usually convict 80 to 90 percent of indicted defendants. The disparity between the conviction rate in trafficking cases and the general conviction rate indicates the existence of special problems with these prosecutions. But what were the problems? The government report released in 2005 doesn't explain. But if we examine other government data not usually released to the public, some of the problems in trafficking cases are illuminated.[13]

These data were compiled by the Department of Justice and obtained by the Transactional Records Access Clearinghouse (TRAC), a nonprofit group affiliated with Syracuse University (see my preview of TRAC in the introduction). With help from lawsuits as well as the federal Freedom of Information Act, TRAC has created a vast statistical data base of federal law enforcement and court information, compiled those data, and made them available to the public and subscribers. Thus, anyone can examine the year-to-year work results of the various agencies, including federal prosecutors. The TRAC data base permits searches of criminal investigations, which can be keyed to specific parts of the criminal code as used by various U.S. attorneys' offices. The results demonstrate not only how many investigations were started and went to conviction but also why cases were dropped or discontinued.

TRAC's analysis (at my request) of pertinent trafficking laws showed the problems federal prosecutors faced in 2001, when they were building their first

Table 5.1
Reasons for Nonprosecution of Human Trafficking Cases
(under 18 U.S.C. 1584, 89, 90, 91), Fiscal Year 2001

Reason	Number
Civil, administrative, or other alternatives	1
Lack of evidence of criminal intent	2
Minimal federal interest	1
No federal crime evident	2
Suspect to be prosecuted by other authorities	2
Weak or insufficient admissible evidence	5
Total Dispositions	13

SOURCE: TRAC analysis of Department of Justice data.

cases under the TVPA. For instance, a data search centered on four TVPA sections (18 U.S.C. 1584, 89, 90, 91) found that thirteen trafficking cases had been disposed (that is, thrown out or prosecuted) in that period. The data show that ten of those thirteen cases, or 77 percent, did not go to trial or conviction, for a variety of reasons (see table 5.1).[14]

There were different results when TRAC analyzed data for offenses involving charges of slavery and involuntary servitude. In 2001, prosecutors disposed twenty cases and began seventeen prosecutions (85 percent), a marked difference from the 77 percent of TVPA cases that did not go to trial. Although there were five convictions under the slavery/involuntary servitude law, that doesn't mean that the conviction rate for those cases was only 29 percent because a case commenced in one year may not necessarily be completed by a finding of guilt or acquittal in the same year. We would have to track each case individually to find the results and then compute a conviction rate.[15]

Prosecutors in 2001 were not limited to filing charges against trafficking suspects under the TVPA or slavery laws. They could also use money laundering, interstate prostitution, and alien smuggling laws. But since those laws can cover a wide variety of offenses having nothing to do with trafficking, it is virtually impossible to extract trafficking-related offenses that might have been prosecuted under those criminal code provisions. As a result, it's difficult to use the TRAC data to check the sixty-three trafficking investigations reported by the Department of Justice in 2001.

But prosecutors' lists of reasons for dispositions show that the trafficking law provisions did not give them a blank check to make cases. In that first year of activity under the TVPA, they had no track record to speak of and certainly no appellate rulings to consult. Unfamiliar with the law, they were cautious. The Bush administration had taken over the White House and was setting its law enforcement priorities. While the administration later pushed trafficking as a key issue, it had no clear direction in 2001.

There were also budget constraints. Although Congress can authorize the expenditure of certain funds, it requires the necessary legislation to appropriate the money so that it can be spent. There are many competing priorities for such funds and only a finite amount of cash to divide among them. As a result, not every program or policy gets the money it has been promised, which was the case in regard to the money authorized by the TVPA. A review of the appropriation bills passed for fiscal year 2001 and signed into law shows that Congress actually approved and committed for disbursement only about 7 million dollars of the nearly 32 million dollars authorized for anti-trafficking programs.[16]

Something else happened in 2001 that had a significant impact not only on trafficking cases but on all federal, state, and local law enforcement activities: the terror attacks of September 11. Overnight, law enforcement priorities radically shifted. Federal agencies directed their immediate attention to the attacks and their aftermath. This was dramatically apparent in New York City, where FBI agents of all stripes, some of whom may have been working on organized crime and labor racketeering cases, were suddenly detailed to search the smoldering World Trade Center wreckage for the crucial black boxes of the jetliners used as suicide weapons. The destruction of the towers obliterated the offices of a number of investigative agencies (the FBI was housed a few blocks away in a different site) and destroyed evidence and files in many pending cases.

With all agencies involved for the foreseeable future in terrorism-related investigations, other problems took a back seat. Nascent investigations into other crimes were placed on hold, and trafficking became a lower priority, as illustrated by the experiences of the Human Smuggling and Trafficking Center. Even though the federal government had announced creation of the center in December 2000 as way of looking comprehensively at trafficking, alien smuggling, and terrorism, the organization languished. The events of September 11 diverted resources and staff so completely that it took until 2004 for the trafficking center to become operational at even half-strength.[17]

Chapter 6   The Lady from Pitesti

Aᴏ SEPTEMBER 11 the United States realized that it needed the sustained cooperation of law enforcement in other countries to make any headway against terrorism. This meant that American officials had to build relationships with their counterparts abroad and in some cases provide funding and technical assistance to beef up their law enforcement and intelligence capabilities—not only in anti-terrorism investigations but in other areas of law enforcement, particularly human trafficking.

As I have discussed, trafficking is an element of global migration; and problems that propel emigrants to either seek out human smugglers or fall victim to a trafficker have ramifications beyond national borders. By 2001, nations were spending billions of dollars annually to cope with the flow of immigrants, both legal and illegal. Law enforcement actions aimed at smugglers, traffickers, and their human commodities added to the financial toll. Although global trafficking garnered an estimated 7 to 10 billion dollars per year, the costs to individual countries were undoubtedly larger. Dealing with the problem required both local and international initiatives, as the U.N. protocol had made clear. If doubters remained, September 11 took care of them.

Trafficking affected all regions of the world. But the travails of victims in Eastern Europe caught the attention of American lawmakers in the late 1990s, when Wellstone first proposed legislation to deal with the problem. As I've mentioned, I experienced firsthand the effects of trafficking in Eastern Europe when I met activist Iana Matei of Romania, who had established a shelter for women north of Bucharest. Unlike its Warsaw Pact allies, Romania suffered badly after communism ended in Eastern Europe. The nation regressed economically, and the Communist apparatchiks continued to hold power in a system rife with corruption. At one time Matei saw so little promise in her nation's future that she became a refugee and moved to Australia. With a college degree in historic preservation that had no apparent use in that relatively young country, Matei continued her studies and became a psychologist.[1]

The overthrow of dictator Nicolae Ceauşescu finally revealed to the world the depth of Romania's dysfunction and social ills. Among them was the tragedy of the tens of thousands of orphans, many of them AIDS-infected, who had been warehoused for years in grim state institutions. The plight of those abandoned children drew Matei and her son Stefan back home in 1998. Matei felt she had a responsibility to redeem a lost generation, but she had no plan to assume responsibility for prostitutes—nor did she particularly care about the issue.[2]

But one night she received an unexpected telephone call from beleaguered Romanian police, who had just arrested a number of young prostitutes. Knowing that Matei was working with orphans and abandoned children, police believed she was the best person to handle the arrested women, many of whom needed baths, food, and places to live. This one-night stopgap effort eventually led Matei into a new calling that that became an unsettling foray into the world of crime and suffering and was often financially precarious.[3]

By the time I met Matei, however, she was dovetailing her work with the resurgence in international law enforcement and diplomatic cooperation that were so vital for U.S. anti-trafficking efforts. The timing of her entry into this sphere was fortuitous. Events brought her to high places where diplomats, politicians, and law enforcement officials asked her for advice and guidance. Although she could never have predicted such a future, Matei's work, like that of countless other social workers and human rights activists, became intertwined with Washington politics. In her experience, the American policy response to trafficking illustrated some of the best and worst that the U.S. government had to offer.

I met Iana Matei after she had obtained a three-room shelter in Pitesti for trafficked women. From that modest facility, she had an excellent view of the shifting trends in the human trafficking story. Because of her contacts with Romanian government agencies, she became familiar with the intractable nature of government bureaucracy. When International Organization for Migration (IOM) staff in other countries rescued young Romanian and Moldovan women who wanted to return home, those women often arrived at Matei's shelter because there as no other comparable facility in the country. By mid-2000 the Romanian government had still not provided funding for shelters for trafficking victims. Thanks to the generosity of the California-based Lift

Foundation, Matei's refuge, known as Reaching Out, was the only option in town.[4]

By July 2000, the Reaching Out facility in Pitesti had dealt with fifty-three young women, some as young as thirteen years old, offering them therapy and training in basic skills that would give them a chance at self-reliance and keep them away from traffickers and prostitution. In conversation with a visitor, Matei said that all but two of the women who had passed through her shelter had been able to avoid returning to prostitution.[5]

But the prevalence of trafficking in the Balkan region meant that, as soon as she had moved one group of women out of the shelter, others arrived to take their places. In a report released in 2001 (based on data collected in 1999 and 2000), the IOM found that the Balkans were major transit zones for trafficked persons moving from Eastern to Western Europe. As reasons, the organization cited regional armed conflicts in Kosovo, Albania, and the former Yugoslavia, which had broken down "social, political and legal structures." Nevertheless, the IOM didn't attempt to estimate the scope of the problem because the data were fragmented and unreliable: "The clandestine nature of trafficking, combined with victims' fears of traffickers, complicates and hinders data collection." Problems also existed in how governments and NGOs differentiated between smuggling, trafficking, and so-called irregular migration; and some countries continued to classify trafficking information and thus limit its distribution.[6]

Though the IOM's report was admittedly not comprehensive, it did illustrate the point that Iana Matei had been making all along: many of the nearly seven hundred women assisted by the IOM in Europe in 2000 came from either Moldova (46 percent) or Romania (25 percent). Because Matei received many of her referrals from the IOM, women from those countries arrived steadily in Pitesti. A map reproduced in the organization's report was crisscrossed with arrows and lines showing the various trafficking routes through the Balkans; and Romania appeared to be a major transit point linked to Serbia, Bulgaria, Hungary, Moldova, and Ukraine.[7]

In the summer of 2000, despite significant efforts by NGOs and some European governments and official agencies, as well as the publicity surrounding the U.N. protocol, trafficking persisted on the continent. And not only women from the Balkans were caught in the trafficking stream: the IOM study showed that European law enforcement agencies and NGOs were also seeing trafficked women and children from Nigeria and Colombia.[8]

Iana Matei recognized that police in Romania had attitudes that fostered the traditional view of prostitutes as petty criminals who deserved to spend time in jail. When sex workers were arrested, they were invariably locked up and prosecuted. Those who had entered the country illegally were deported. Pimps and smugglers were generally not prosecuted unless police had caught them red-handed. The idea that a woman—or a child, for that matter—could be a victim of coercion was an alien notion. Police believed that all prostitutes chose to follow the business, which was undoubtedly true in some cases. But trafficking and the concept of sex work as forced labor had not gained much credence among Romanian law enforcement by the summer of 2000.[9]

In fact, many law enforcement officials in the Balkans were corrupt and willing participants in prostitution operations and, by extension, human trafficking.[10] Matei told shelter visitors that police in any number of Romanian cities were not only clients of some of the trafficked women but also took money from pimps in return for protecting brothels or their stable of prostitutes.[11] Allegations even surfaced that some members of the international peace-keeping force in Bosnia and Kosovo were clients of these women. Although Matei had tried to interest Romanian officials in reports of police and military corruption, the country was mired in economic trouble under the stagnant presidency of Emil Constantinescu. She got little help.

But human trafficking had become a key human rights and law enforcement issue in the United States, and officials in Washington were working on a number of fronts that would affect the situation in Romania—and Matei in particular. One involved a special organization set up in 1996 as an economic recovery vehicle for the Balkans but that was also a law enforcement venture. Known as the Southeast Europe Cooperative Initiative (SECI), it was the brainchild of U.S. diplomat Richard Schifter.[12] A one-time advisor on human rights to President Ronald Reagan, Schifter supported the 1992 presidential campaign of Bill Clinton and was rewarded with a post in the Clinton administration as a special assistant to the president for national security affairs.[13]

In a Department of State television interview, Schifter said the idea for SECI resulted from a conversation in 1994 with an Albanian professor in Tirana about whether the southern part of that country should become part of Greece. That issue had been raised after a period of strife in which some ethnic Greek leaders in Albania had been arrested. According to Schifter, the professor was against drawing more borders in the region: "Let's take a look at what has happened in Western Europe in these last 50 years. The borders have become less and less important. There has been cooperation across borders. And that is what we need for our region."[14]

Back in Washington, Schifter proposed that the Balkan nations and others in southeastern Europe form a cooperative venture of the sort organized after World War II in Western Europe, which eventually led to the European Union. The aim, Schifter said, was to give the region a "stepping stone" for eventual integration into the European Union.[15] Thus, SECI formed in late 1996 and set up programs in which twelve nations (Albania, Bosnia, Herzegovina, Bulgaria, Croatia, Greece, Hungary, Moldova, Romania, Slovenia, Macedonia, and Turkey) worked to harmonize customs and trade laws as well as promote private investment.[16]

It quickly became clear to SECI member states as well as to Schifter that organized crime in the region needed to be addressed. "The region cannot possibly thrive economically unless there is a significant step up in foreign investment," he said. "Foreign investment in turn needs to be attracted, not discouraged. Organized crime—the operations of organized crime discourage foreign investment." He believed that solving the problem required coopera-tion among law enforcement agencies, much as trade and customs bureaucra-cies cooperated through SECI. The result was the formation of SECI's Regional Center for Combating Transborder Crime.[17]

The SECI crime center was housed in Bucharest's parliament building, built by order of egomaniac ex-dictator Ceauşescu. Reputed to be the second-largest building in the world (the Pentagon is the largest), it sits on top of a hill; and everything about it is immense. The building required 700,000 tons of steel and brass and 1 million cubic meters of marble, and it kept seven hundred architects and tens of thousands of Romanian workers busy for years. Its stone staircases were larger than even the grandest Hollywood set, and the hallways were long enough for footraces. But although Ceauşescu planned for a "palace of the people," after he was deposed, the new government thought it was too large to be useful. Thus, it had plenty of room to house the SECI crime center.

To work properly, the crime center needed to be a mini-Interpol—that is, a smaller version of the international police agency known as one of the world's most sophisticated law enforcement operations. But Balkan nations had only just overthrown their communist governments, which for decades had encour-aged police agencies to operate as fiefdoms of the rulers. As a result, Balkan cops had deep-seated suspicions of their foreign counterparts, especially their Eastern European neighbors; and some law enforcement observers were not optimistic that SECI could work as an intelligence-gathering outfit.[18]

Nevertheless, it had significant sponsors in the United States. With Schifter pushing the idea, the center got underway in October 2000. Liaison officers from the member nations each had space in the center's operations area, and observer nations such as the United States and Italy also had personnel there. The only American financial help was a few hundred thousand dollars' worth of communications equipment. Perhaps more important were the U.S. law enforcement advisors detailed to SECI. Among them were at least three FBI agents as well liaison officers from the Drug Enforcement Administration and the Immigration and Naturalization Service. In Washington, John Markey, who was technically under the command of the Customs Service but had been detailed to the Department of State, worked as the overall U.S. advisor.[19]

After traveling to Romania and talking with both American and European law enforcement officials about organized crime, Schifter began to see the scope of the region's trafficking problem. Experience in two White House administrations had made him well aware of the issue in general. But now he felt compelled to raise the issue with the Romania government.[20]

His first approach drew a quizzical response. An advisor to President Constantinescu thought he was proposing a ban on prostitution. Explaining that he was simply talking about women who were held against their will, Schifter, with help from the U.S. embassy staff in Bucharest, told Romanian officials that law enforcement's traditional approach—to ignore trafficking and just arrest prostitutes—had to change. He also emphasized that trafficking was tied to official corruption. In light of Schifter's argument, Constantinescu committed his administration to address the trafficking situation. Although he took no immediate action, the mere fact that the Romanian government had committed itself to Washington in such a way was a sign of change in a country known as a trafficker' paradise.[21]

In Pitesti, American activity had a tangible effect. By late August 2000, U.S. personnel in Romania and Washington had heard about Matei's program, and FBI officials invited her to visit them in Washington. They were trying to gauge the accuracy of reports that women from Eastern Europe and the former Soviet Union were illegally immigrating to the United States to work as prostitutes. Because Matei had a ground-floor view of the state of trafficking in the Balkans, they wanted to talk with her to gather leads, intelligence, and perspective.[22]

Given what she had seen of FBI agents in Romania, Matei had been impressed with their early efforts against trafficking. Officials at the American embassy had sifted through intelligence reports of their Romanian counterparts to learn about trafficking gangs, leaders, and routes. They seemed to be serious; and for Matei, who had grown pessimistic about local police efforts, their presence was encouraging. So during a trip to California in September 2000 to visit with her sponsoring agency, she took a detour to meet agents in Washington. She also met with Schifter, who was then preparing for the October 2000 inauguration of the SECI crime center. The two talked in his office about the trafficking situation; and the diplomat, she remembered, was optimistic: big things were planned, he said, for Romania and the rest of the Balkans.[23]

By 2001, as federal prosecutors were investigating the first American cases under the TVPA, Iana Matei had become an unofficial clearinghouse in

Romania for information about trafficking networks. Her primary sources were the women who came to her shelter, either in transit back to their families or to figure out the next step in their lives. Aware of Washington's priorities, Romanian police were no longer turning a blind eye to the traffickers and had been making arrests. A few of the women from Matei's shelter had also provided information to investigators who were putting together cases involving a Macedonian network.

But Matei had noticed a lack of consistency among the police: while some eagerly tracked smugglers and traffickers, others did not seem engaged with the problem. Observers from NGOs also noted the variability in police response, and in April 2001 they scheduled a series of meetings in the cities of Sinaia and Campineau to draft a trafficking strategy that they intended to pass along to the government in Bucharest. Protocols were needed, Matei said, so that NGO advisors could train Romanian police to recognize victims as well as to keep officers on the job who had developed expertise in trafficking issues, thus providing continuity and an institutional memory that would help future investigations.[24]

While Matei was not entirely pleased with the content or the pace of the meetings, she conceded that change was indeed taking place. NGOs in Romania were networking more closely, and government officials seemed more open and cooperative—for good reason.[25] The SECI crime center in Bucharest had become, with U.S. assistance and prodding, a force for cohesive effort against organized crime in the region.

By May 2001, with trafficking firmly established as a serious international issue, the SECI nations convened a conference in Bucharest on trafficking in human beings and illegal migration. The aim was to discuss and devise "practical measures" to deal with trafficking or, as a Romanian government news release stated, "to strengthen national capabilities and practices against trafficking" as well as make use of the SECI operation.[26] FBI director Louis Freeh was a keynote speaker; and Washington also sent eight other officials, including SECI liaison John Markey. By inviting Freeh to speak, the Romanian government said it hoped to stimulate action against trafficking. The government also called on all Balkan nations to adopt model anti-trafficking legislation and ratify the U.N. protocol. In short, they were acknowledging the U.S. strong interest in trafficking and expertise in law enforcement, which was becoming increasingly important to the SECI operation.

Opening the conference, Romanian prime minister Adrian Nastase acknowledged that the country's Ministry of Interior had developed "an excellent teamwork with the Federal Bureau of Investigation" as part of the SECI operation and profusely thanked Freeh. He also singled out Iana

Matei, who was working at the Pitesti shelter and was unable to attend the meeting, for her work of "profound humanism."[27]

When Freeh spoke, he told the delegates that their countries needed greater unity in dealing with trafficking: "We have to direct our efforts to protect the most vulnerable. We will only succeed if we collaborate police officer to police officer, government to government." His remarks were tailor-made to enhance the status of SECI as well as European trafficking initiatives developed under the aegis of the Stability Pact, an organization within the Organization for Security and Cooperation in Europe (OCSE). Credible law enforcement efforts, he said, required these initiatives to cooperate and share intelligence because organized crime required an organized police response.[28]

As a result of the Bucharest conclave, the Balkan governments were forced to acknowledge "an inadequate degree of alignment of the legislation in the area of trafficking in human beings," which in plain English meant that some nations had laws while others either lacked them or had weaker versions.[29] If allowed to persist, such inconsistency would be a critical flaw in the whole notion of a regional crime initiative. The SECI model was based on information sharing among member nations and a unified clearinghouse for trafficking intelligence. This was the same idea embodied in the TVPA, which called for a unit to coordinate U.S.-based federal law enforcement agencies. But while the United States now had a federal statute designed to pull together various agencies in efforts against trafficking, the Balkan states still had major differences in trafficking laws. For instance, Romania's national proposal was far advanced in the legislative process. But Albania, a hotbed for traffickers, had no legislation and wouldn't for another three years. Thus, law enforcement intelligence passed on to SECI by a Bulgarian police officer might prove useful to a Romanian investigator but relatively useless to an Albanian one.[30]

Nevertheless, in light of Washington's interest in the trafficking issue, the Balkan states realized that they also had to demonstrate concern. After the May 2001 Bucharest conference, the SECI countries began, with U.S. help, to adopt model trafficking laws, using the U.N. protocol for guidance.[31] But the change didn't happen overnight. Even Romania took time to adopt laws and even more time to instigate actual criminal investigations. Ultimately, the nations required both Iana Matei's persistence as well as U.S. assistance and prodding to put together one of the Balkans' biggest trafficking cases.

Chapter 7   Finding Leku

In THE DAYS immediately after September 11, I met with three men in the nearly deserted lobby of the 1930s-vintage Lido Hotel in Bucharest. All were police officials from Macedonia, but only one—a tall man I will call Peter—was able to speak competent English.[1] Drinks were served, and the Macedonians lit their ubiquitous cigarettes. The whole scene looked like the setting of an espionage movie.

The men had traveled to the hotel to talk about terrorism and trafficking. Traditionally, law enforcement had not connected those problems. But since trafficking involved illegal immigration, it was logical to believe that terrorists could use these same smuggling networks to move secretly over international borders.

At this moment, the world's attention was focused on the horrid events that had just occurred 5,000 miles away in the United States. But the Macedonians told me they had been having their own problems with terrorism, fueled by ethnic rivalries between their country's large Albanian minority population and the ruling Macedonians. The Albanians saw their struggle as a fight for freedom and liberation. To the Macedonians, however, the bombings and shootings were organized crime. And as Peter explained, with his colleagues silently looking on, rampant human smuggling in the Balkans was helping the Albanian rebels.[2]

Peter was in contact with the SECI crime center in Bucharest, and he was well aware of the information passing through the U.S.-backed operation. By this time, the SECI center had become operational and had organized itself around task forces investigating trafficking, drugs, and auto theft. Although every Balkan country dealt with such crimes, Macedonia, a relatively small nation hemmed in by Bulgaria, Albania, Greece, Kosovo, and Serbia, had porous borders and areas of relative lawlessness that made it seem like the Balkan answer to America's Wild West. Brothels had sprouted up, particularly in border areas surrounding Lake Struga and Lake Ohrid, with a constant supply of young women to staff them. Reports had filtered into Bucharest that Macedonian officials were involved in the flesh trade, a suspicion borne out over the years by a number of arrests.

According to Peter, one man was not only controlling a large portion of Macedonia's trade in trafficked women but also suspected of paying proceeds to Albanian political officials. That money, Peter alleged, was financing what he called Albanian terrorism. Referring briefly to his colleagues, Peter said the trafficker's name was Dilaver Bojku, although he was known by the street name "Leku." To make sure I understood the name, Peter scribbled it down on paper.[3]

In 2001 the political situation in Macedonia was extremely tense. Ethnic conflict between Macedonians and Albanians had been exacerbated by the country's new constitution, which had reduced the Albanians' status in the republic and made them feel like second-class citizens. Fighting erupted; and two Albanian groups—the National Liberation Army (NLA) and the Ushtria Clirimtare Kombetare (UCK)—launched attacks against Macedonian security forces, clashes in which more than fifty people were killed and scores wounded. Although the populace already possessed tens of thousands of firearms, arms trafficking and smuggling increased existing security problems.[4]

But Leku seemed to thrive. Working primarily out of the Hotel Bern in the town of Veleshta, he portrayed himself publicly as a businessman who ran legal cabarets, bars, and restaurants. He lived well, traveled in a new Audi, and was accompanied by three women reputed to be his wives as well as by various other consorts. He also had business interests outside Macedonia, mainly involving nightclubs in neighboring Kosovo. In an interview with journalist Preston Mendenhall of MSNBC, Leku dismissed critics' concerns about the women who worked for him, showing the reporter documents indicating that his clubs (which had names such as "Kiss Me") were legitimate businesses employing legal immigrants, not trafficking victims forced to work as dancers or prostitutes.[5]

Leku's notoriety, however, coincided with Macedonia's ethnic fighting and SECI's growing involvement, with U.S. backing, in regional anti-trafficking efforts. Since the fighting was fueled in part by the proliferation of weapons and resources among armed Albanian groups, Peter and other officials believed that suspected traffickers such as Leku were involved. As one study had found, human trafficking for brothels went "hand-in-hand with gun running."[6]

With trafficking high on the SECI agenda, the United States prodded member states to take action; and Leku's public bravado and arrogance had made him a key target. FBI special agent Anibal Torres, sent from the United States to work on trafficking with SECI, became involved as the organization gathered intelligence about the suspected pimp and smuggler. Strictly speaking, SECI had no operational mandate to make arrests: that job was reserved for police officials of the member nations. But in Washington, John Markey kept pressuring SECI and the Macedonians to do something about Leku. In the opinion of American officials, he had become a symbol of Balkan lawlessness and must be stopped.

Even with Washington cracking the whip, pursuit of Leku would not be easy. As the MSNBC interview made clear, Leku was portraying himself as legitimate, claiming that his women employees were working freely and that Macedonia was rife with corruption.[7] He himself traveled without restriction around the region, crossing at will into Albania, Kosovo, and Montenegro. He also seemed immune to prosecution. Although he was arrested in 2000 after officials raided and closed one of his brothels near Kosovo's Pristina airport, he spent only two weeks in jail and was never forced to account for his conduct.[8] To make a case against him, Macedonian officials needed women to testify that he had forced them into prostitution. In short, they needed help from Iana Matei.

Because of her work in the region and her ties to SECI and Agent Torres, Matei was well aware of the reputation of Veleshta, the town where Leku had his headquarters. It had at least a dozen bars and brothels; and an estimated two hundred women from Romania, Moldova, and Bulgaria worked there. That number, Matei learned, did not take into account women from Russia and Albania, who were also in Veleshta. She had also learned that Albanian terror organizations were collecting money from the bars and that those groups might be working with Muslims to fight the Macedonians.

Romanian women who had been trafficked in the region and then repatriated usually spent some time in Matei's shelter. Marianella and Michaele were two such women: they had been rescued in Macedonia after working in Veleshta. In Pitesti, they confided to Matei about their experiences as prostitutes. Matei had a delicate task in such situations. She had to support and sympathize with the women in her care. To keep their trust, she had to avoid appearing to be either the source of any trouble for the women or an arm of the police. Yet dealing with trafficking required a meaningful police effort, and cooperation from the trafficked women was important.[9]

Romanian police and SECI officials knew that the two women had been involved with Leku and were eager to hear them talk. Over several months in 2002 and 2003, Matei carefully guided Marianella and Michaele through a series of meetings with the police in which they discussed Leku's operation and their experiences with him. Both women proved eager to help police and were willing to testify against Leku should the need arise.[10] By early 2003 Macedonian officials had acquired enough evidence to bring charges against him on prostitution-related offenses.[11]

Naturally, the Romanian women were anxious about their cooperation, and that anxiety increased when a bomb detonated in a courthouse in Struga, damaging the building but causing no casualties. A communiquè from the Albanian National Army claimed responsibility and said the group was trying to deter Macedonians from encroaching on the Albanian people and arresting them. Police believed, however, that the blast was retaliation for Leku's arrest.[12]

Despite the explosion, his trial began as scheduled; and in March 2003, Marianella testified in Skopje, accompanied by Matei, who drove her there.[13] But Michaele decided against making the trip. According to Matei, Romanian officials had asked her (as well as another potential witness) to fly to Skopje by a circuitous route that would have left them for nearly thirteen hours in a Hungarian airport waiting room without armed police protection.

Like major Mafia trials in the United States, the trial required a great deal of witness security and protection. Armed escorts accompanied them during court appearances and when they traveled in Macedonia. Nevertheless, since he was a powerful regional crime figure, Leku had support from a number of associates, who appeared in court and applauded him. As one official later noted, some of their actions seemed designed to intimidate both the witnesses and OSCE observers. Several Macedonian newspaper reports said that Leku wanted members of the news media removed from the courtroom, alleging bias.[14]

In their testimony, the women told of being sold a number of times down the trafficking chain until they finally wound up in Leku's bar. One woman stated that a Macedonian cab driver who had transported her was working in tandem with the bar. Another woman, a Romanian national named Juliana Sherban, offered particularly compelling testimony. She stated that Leku brought her to one of his bars in Veleshta in September 2001 and forced her to work as a prostitute for about six months. She also accused him of beating her when she refused to have sex.[15]

Despite the bravado of Leku and his supporters, the court found him guilty of what the press called "pimping" or "mediating in prostitution." Before the verdict, he had told reporters he would go on a hunger strike if convicted; and after the guilty verdict was announced, he gave way to depression and anxiety and had to be hospitalized. Denied bail, he was sent to jail in Struga.[16]

Leku's conviction was a modest victory: he faced only a six-month prison term. Yet officials hailed it as an important step in convincing corruption-prone Macedonia to deal with human trafficking. And Washington was optimistic, particularly in light of SECI's success at facilitating cross-border cooperation among Balkan police agencies.[17] Matei was pleased that SECI and Romanian police had devoted resources and security to ensure that the witnesses could provide useful information. Though the women were worried about testifying, they did so anyway and were protected by law enforcement. Still, police had failed to properly handle Michaela and physically get her into the courtroom to testify, which Matei blamed on professional jealousy within the ranks.[18]

But then disaster struck. On June 20, 2003, as Leku was being transferred from the Struga prison to a higher-security facility for "corrective labour activities," he escaped. The incident was not dramatic: Leku, who reportedly was not handcuffed, simply pushed aside the guards who were walking with him and ran toward some nearby houses, where he eluded pursuing officers. He then got into a black van and was driven away.[19]

In the fight against organized crime, the incident made the Balkan police look like the Keystone Kops. And there was plenty of finger pointing in Macedonia. A spokesperson for the Ministry of Justice said prison officials should have taken more "serious measures" to secure Leku during his transfer. She also cast aspersions on the judiciary, presumably because she believed that Leku's relatively light sentence had frustrated law enforcement efforts to deal with trafficking.[20]

In Washington, news of Leku's escape came as an embarrassing jolt. Not only had Macedonia just received the highest-possible rank in the state department's mandated annual report on trafficking, but the entire SECI operation was scheduled for assessment in August. The timing couldn't have been worse. According to one American official, Washington even discussed placing a hold on law enforcement assistance money earmarked for Macedonia. But John Markey jumped into action, setting aside extra funds for expenses incurred by Balkan officials in the search for Leku.[21] While reports claimed that he had authorized a 10,000-dollar reward for Leku's capture, Markey later denied offering any bounty.[22]

Markey's actions reignited the enthusiasm of his Balkan colleagues. On July 4, 2003, just before midnight, Montenegrin police, along with officials from the Macedonian Ministry of the Interior, arrested the fugitive at a cafè in the city of Ulcin. Reportedly, Leku, who been hiding for days in a basement in Veleshta, was planning to leave for Brazil with a forged passport.[23]

In early August, SECI and the Macedonian anti-trafficking effort were assessed as scheduled at the U.S. state department. Diplomats and law enforcement officials, both Balkan and American, were in attendance. With Leku recaptured, the meeting opened on a positive note. But according to one participant, the fact that he had escaped at all highlighted an obvious problem: corruption was endemic in the Balkans. While SECI had been able to handle intelligence collection and dissemination, the Leku episode showed that member nations still had law enforcement deficiencies, which had to be addressed immediately if trafficking efforts were to succeed.[24]

In the years before the fall of communism, lingering suspicions and the paranoia of the authoritarian regimes prevented Balkan police from taking part in any sustained regional anti-crime initiatives. Assessment of the SECI operation took this history into account. But as one American official said, by initiating and supporting the concept of regional cooperation, Washington was allowing Balkan law enforcement to develop a latent competency that allowed police to tackle difficult problems like trafficking, narcotics, and even weapons of mass destruction.[25]

Moreover, through SECI, Balkan women such as Matei's clients could play a meaningful role in the apprehension, prosecution, and punishment of traffickers. This, in turn, allowed member nations to appropriately incorporate victims' views and testimony into criminal cases, an aim stated in article 6 of the U.N. protocol. The SECI apparatus allowed activists and victims' advocates to connect law enforcement with victims and thus build a credible response to trafficking.

Washington insisted on further assessments of SECI, with the goal of helping the organization find out what it was doing wrong and right and, in the process, adjust anti-trafficking programs in ways beneficial to the region. In September 2002, with U.S. guidance, SECI initiated a week-long regional anti-trafficking operation, code-named Operation Mirage. Law enforcement agencies from the twelve member states as well as some NGOs took part in a series of border stops and interdictions aimed at uncovering traffickers and their human cargo. The aim was to find out if SECI states could carry out such a regional task and gather intelligence.[26]

SECI's required evaluation report was a bare-bones document, heavy on statistics but light on analysis. For instance, the report noted that agents carried out more than 20,000 inspections of nightclubs, restaurants, and border-crossing points. In the process they identified 237 victims of trafficking, of whom 23 (or 9 percent) were referred to NGOs for help, a number that some critics found unacceptably low. A total of 293 "criminal procedures" were started against "responsible criminals." The report didn't detail the results of those criminal cases, so there was no way to assess conviction rates or penalties. Still, SECI officials called the operation a success.[27]

A second Operation Mirage was held in 2003; and the statistical results showed a higher rate of criminal cases commenced (319) and victims identified (463), of whom 70 (or 15 percent) were referred to NGOs for help. Most victims came from Ukraine (134) and Romania (127). The overwhelming majority of suspected traffickers, numbering 125, were citizens of Albania.[28]

Like the report for the first Operation Mirage, the 2003 study was skimpy on details about the outcomes of the criminal cases. But at Washington's insistence, it did include some critical assessments, including one glaring problem: intelligence and police agencies needed to break out of the nine-to-five working mode and become capable of processing intelligence around the clock. This would likely incur "better operational results" and lead to the discovery of more trafficking victims because the SECI countries would have speedy access to criminal and identification records.[29]

The SECI countries had hoped to pinpoint trafficking cases with regional ties; but as the assessment indicated, such action "did not seem to meet the expected level."[30] In other words, the 2003 operation highlighted the need for coordination of criminal intelligence analysis, more specialized law enforcement training on trafficking, and cooperation with NGOs such as the IOM. Still, the experience proved that member countries wanted to take part in more regional law enforcement projects. American officials privately expressed satisfaction with the fact that those nations were recognizing the value of working together to stop trafficking.

In July 2004, the IOM published a report that dealt specifically with changing patterns and trends in Balkan trafficking. The report underscored the persistent evolution of the problem and the need for a sophisticated regional response such as SECI's. It stated that organized crime groups involved in trafficking—for either sex work or other kinds of forced labor—were in a state of "continuous expansion, evolution and specialization." The report did not define those crime groups but said they were operating throughout the region with relative ease. According to the IOM, a younger and more managerial type of trafficker was able to open up "dangerous channels of corruption at all levels" and change operations radically.[31]

Although observers had known for years that poverty and unemployment are major reasons for migration and trafficking, the IOM study showed that victims continued to come from "low socio-economic situations and grim personal circumstances [like] those which have driven victims to leave their home countries in the past." In other words, life hadn't changed enough in the Balkans to deter economic migrants from relying on traffickers. Most victims were still unaware they would be forced into prostitution; even those who did took the risk anyway because they felt they had no other choice.[32] The report's implications were clear: despite dramatic diplomatic action and U.S. involvement in regional law enforcement initiatives, trafficking was a persistent problem. Economic migration was still a major factor in the movement of trafficking victims, and the poor underbelly of the Balkans—Albania, Moldova, Romania, Ukraine, and Bulgaria—remained a primary source.

The IOM study also stressed that the traffickers were adapting their tactics to deal with new law enforcement strategies and found that agencies "have been unable to identify fully the new modes of trafficking, or to adjust their response to changes in the modus operandi of criminal groups." In other words, Balkan law enforcement was not able to cope with the traffickers. The reasons centered on corruption, lack of intelligence capability, and lack of regional cooperation.[33] This was a much more pessimistic view than SECI's.

But small successes sometimes breed progress. By the summer of 2005, with continued U.S. assistance and oversight, the SECI nations appeared to be building on previous cooperation and addressing some of the IOM criticisms. An internal assessment done at U.S. request (I received a copy in August 2005) described several cases that had achieved "very good results" and built "excellent professional relations" among regional law enforcement.[34] The report also noted that U.S. establishment of a prosecutorial working group in the Balkans had allowed SECI investigators to work better with regional prosecutors in making trafficking cases.

U.S. law enforcement funding had financed four cases coordinated by SECI and Romanian officials, which led to the arrests of twenty-one traffickers and the repatriation of forty-eight Romanian victims. The two-to-one ratio of victims to suspected traffickers indicates that the smuggling operations were moving small groups of victims as a way of deflecting police attention.[35]

Separate FBI funding, the report stated, had supported Operation Nistru. ("Nistru" is the Romanian name for the Dniester River separating Moldova and the volatile Transnistra region.) That particular operation had involved SECI and prosecutors' offices in Moldova, Romania, and Hungary and had focused on traffickers in Central Europe. The effort resulted in the arrests of sixty-five suspected traffickers, including fifty-two in Austria, which was not a SECI nation but participated nonetheless.

U.S. financial and logistical assistance also allowed witnesses to participate in court proceedings against a number of traffickers arrested in SECI operations. The most notable innovation, the report stated, was a video-conference system, which FBI financial and technical support made possible. The new system permitted a woman in Moldova to testify against a suspect in Macedonia. While video links were standard fare in the American criminal justice system, use of such technology in the Balkans was a major breakthrough in trafficking investigations, allowing victims to testify against their alleged abusers and traffickers without the need to travel great distances or worry about security problems and intimidation.

Yet even without teleconferencing, SECI officials reported success in getting victims to testify against traffickers. A total of thirteen witnesses from Moldova, Romania, and Bulgaria testified against traffickers in the region. Unfortunately, the data did not indicate the results of those proceedings, including information about convictions. The significant factor was that witnesses throughout the Balkans now felt comfortable enough with regional law enforcement to cooperate with authorities.

The story of SECI's quick development and maturity illustrates the Department of Justice's ability to implement President George W. Bush's directive requiring all federal agencies to help foreign states abolish human trafficking. While SECI didn't receive much from the 50-million-dollar funding initiative proposed to fight trafficking, it did receive significant collaboration and training from U.S. law enforcement. But by early 2006 some U.S. officials were privately complaining that SECI was losing its edge because of state department inattention. Markey had left to work for an organization affiliated with the Department of Homeland Security. With no one person dedicated to keeping SECI focused on human trafficking, the organization began to focus more on drug and cigarette smuggling.[36]

Chapter 8   Sweat, Toil, and Tears

ONE COMPLAINT RAISED about the state department's annual trafficking reports was that they emphasized sex trafficking cases and thus paid too little attention to other kinds of servitude, especially those involving labor exploitation. In the three years after the TVPA's enactment, federal prosecutions were also heavily weighted toward sex cases. But traffickers were clearly exploiting an even greater number of workers in a variety of other industries, as well as household employees toiling anonymously in seemingly respectable homes.

One of the largest forced labor cases ever to come to federal attention occurred in the group of islands known as American Samoa, an incorporated territory lying about 2,300 miles south of Honolulu. Because it is located so far from the mainland, American Samoa is a relatively safe place for smugglers, traffickers, and unscrupulous businesspeople to work. That's why Kil Soo Lee chose it.

A Korean businessman, Lee ran Daewoosa Samoa, Ltd., a garment manufacture. He had purchased the struggling business in the late 1990s on the basis of an ingenious plan: because American Samoa was a U.S. possession, he could label goods as "made in America" and sell them to large retailers such as J. C. Penny and Target. In other words, he could claim that not only was the clothing made stateside but it was also ostensibly manufactured according to American labor standards.[1]

By 1999, American Samoa had a population of about 55,000, and factory workers were in demand. To supply his labor needs, Lee decided to bring in workers (mostly women) from Vietnam and China, assuring them they would have steady work and wages of four hundred dollars a month, a munificent sum since many Vietnamese were earning an average of two hundred dollars a year. He recruited the women through labor export companies in Vietnam, which charged them fees of up to 6,000 dollars for the jobs. Some borrowed those fees from relatives, while others turned to Vietnamese loan sharks.[2]

Many of the workers had never left their country before and, when they arrived in American Samoa, were shocked at their oppressive living and working conditions. The seamstresses were housed in crowded dormitories with wooden walls and metal roofs. Up to eighteen workers were assigned to each room, which was also crowded with clothes strung on lines between bunk beds. "It looked like a barn or warehouse that they just stuffed people in," one Vietnamese worker later told an American journalist. "I felt like I was going to jail."[3] For these women, who had flown thousands of miles from home in hopes of making money for their families, their living conditions were only the beginning of the horror show. For a start, pay was sporadic and only a fraction of what Lee had promised. Workers later recalled that the meals he provided were usually limited to cabbage broth or an occasional chicken casserole. Sometimes he only served rice. Added to the terrible physical conditions, as some seamstresses later told federal investigators, were Lee's demands for sexual favors.[4]

The desperate conditions required workers' desperate actions. During an escorted visit outside the factory compound, one employee threw what the FBI later called an "S.O.S note" out of a company car. The document was passed along to the U.S. Department of Labor, which launched a civil investigation and ordered Lee to pay hundreds of thousands of dollars in back wages and fines. Financially strapped, Lee couldn't make the full payment; so the Department of Labor had to write the checks.[5]

In November 2000, according to the FBI, Lee ordered his guards to beat or kill any worker who didn't produce clothing fast enough. Investigators said there were many beatings and that some of the workers were severely injured. According to victims, heavy-set American Samoan men rushed at the workers and struck them with plastic pipes. One worker lost an eye; others were bloodied and lost teeth.[6]

The beatings were the beginning of the end. FBI agents in Honolulu heard leaked stories of the attacks and launched a large-scale investigation. They began gathering evidence, including business records, computers, and photographs, and conducted interviews, working fast enough to arrest Lee before he had a chance to flee. The FBI then started pooling resources from other offices and spread its search for evidence into South Korea and Thailand as well as to the U.S. mainland.[7] As a result of the investigation, attorneys with the Civil Rights Division of the Department of Justice empanelled a grand jury in Honolulu, which indicted Kil Soo Lee and two of his factory managers on assorted charges of human trafficking. They also accused Lee of extortion and money laundering. By the time he was indicted, Lee was effectively out of the factory business.

In February 2003, a federal jury in Honolulu convicted Lee in what was at that time the largest human trafficking case ever prosecuted by the

U.S. government. He was convicted of involuntary servitude, extortion, and money laundering. One of his factory managers and a Samoan garment worker had earlier plead guilty to trafficking charges. Lee received a sentence of forty years in prison, one of the longest ever given under the trafficking laws, while the two other defendants received sentences of fifty-one to seventy months in prison. At his sentencing Lee claimed he had been convicted on lies and insisted he was innocent. (He filed a notice of appeal in the case.) But a number of his workers gave victim impact statements to the court describing their physical and psychological trauma, and the sentencing judge told Lee he had displayed contempt for American laws.[8]

After the prosecution, another element of the Trafficking Victims Protection Act came into play: the T-visa provision. According to the FBI, two hundred of the Daewoosa Samoa workers opted to take advantage of the flexible visa law and try to make a new life in the United States.[9] T-visa applications in this case alone showed that the number of victims involved in labor trafficking cases could exceed anything yet seen in sex trafficking situations, which so far had ranged from a handful of victims to as many as two dozen. Granted, the American Samoa factory case was an anomaly in that it had occurred in a remote location not easily monitored by federal law enforcement; and given the episode's notoriety and local officials' increased sensitivity, a similar situation is not likely to reoccur there. But even in the mainland United States, law enforcement didn't have to look far to find cases of labor exploitation.

Johannes Du Preez, a native of South Africa, was a standout in the Atlanta business community. Within twenty years, he had carved out a successful niche in the granite industry. His company, Newton Granite & Marble, Inc., produced beautiful polished countertops for kitchen and bathroom construction. In Newton's factory, located in an industrial district near the airport, workers fabricated stone into products readily sold to contractors and building supply companies such as Home Depot. Du Preez's company was a family affair: his wife Franciska was a co-owner and another South African émigré, Stanley Fur, worked as an accountant and helped to hire workers.[10]

And it was here, in the area of labor, where things got troublesome for Du Preez and his associates. Stonework requires employees who can put in long hours and do considerable amounts of heavy lifting. To get the staff he needed, Du Preez brought hundreds of white South Africans as well as some Britons and Zimbabwe blacks into the United States under a special visa program reserved for managers and executives. Although the workers may have been skilled in polishing and cutting stone, they certainly weren't corporate managers, despite assertions to the contrary in the falsified paperwork provided to U.S. immigration officials.[11]

Allegations of falsified immigration documents signaled serious trouble for Du Preez because they served as the basis for a federal felony charge. But the situation was worse than document fraud. As investigators discovered, the workers had to repay Du Preez not only for the cost of their immigration documents but also for the expense of their housing at a nearby apartment complex. If workers didn't cooperate with these conditions of employment, owners threatened to turn them over to immigration authorities.[12]

The alleged threats against immigrant workers turned the situation into a trafficking case. A three-year federal investigation led to the August 2004 arrest of Du Preez, his wife, his accountant Fur, and others on charges of conspiracy, fraud, harboring aliens, and other crimes. Though not originally indicted under the provisions of the TVPA, the Du Preez defendants were in essence accused of behavior that fit the trafficking label; and a revised indictment did allege violation of the trafficking act.[13]

The superseding indictment accused the defendants of an immigration scheme involving a shell company in South Africa that was formed in 1990 and later sold to Du Preez, who allegedly purchased it with the intent of tricking U.S. immigration officials into believing that it was an operational quarry that needed special visas to transfer managerial employees to the United States for valid business reasons. The American subsidiary was identified in the indictment as Newton Granite. The indictment charged that the immigrants involved in the scheme weren't working for the South African company but were employed by Newton, which paid to lodge them in apartments it had leased in the Atlanta area. Workers' spouses were also encouraged to work at Newton Granite for cash or a credit against the cost of their rent, furniture, and immigration documents. Du Preez and his wife were accused of abusing or threatening to abuse "the immigration and other legal processes" to obtain the labor and services of the migrants.[14]

Fortified by evidence from number of the immigrants, U.S. officials in Georgia constructed a strong case against the Du Preez defendants. The allegations were not as severe as those involving the brutality in the American Samoa situation, but they were still quite serious, particularly since they involved large-scale abuse of the immigrant visa program. In November 2005, Du Preez pleaded guilty to charges of conspiracy and harboring aliens. Although he faced a maximum of fifteen years at the time of his planned sentencing in March 2006, he has since become a fugitive.[15]

The middle and northern regions of New York State have a long history of dairy, fruit and vegetable farming; and like Florida, Texas, and California, New York requires a fair share of temporary and migrant farm workers during harvest periods. Some of those workers have entered the

United States legally; others have not. Maria Garcia understood their situations very well.

Garcia was an American of Mexican heritage and had lived for a time in Texas. In the late 1990s, she had settled in New York State as a farm labor contractor and was registered as such with state officials as well as the U.S. Department of Labor. Her business was to recruit workers for farms in Orleans and Genesee counties. To do this, Garcia and her son, Elias Botello, went to Arizona and promised false documents those who needed them to work in the United States. The pair then transported recruits to the town of Albion, New York. Positioned in the middle of rural Orleans County, Albion is a shipping point for crops such as cabbage, apples, and beans. The town has a population of about 8,000, more than 70 percent of whom are white, and is located very close to a state prison for women.[16]

Garcia told the workers to expect to earn at least the minimum wage of $5.15 a hour and possibly more. To pay their traveling expenses to New York, however, the workers owed her 1,000 to 1,800 dollars, which Garcia said she would deduct from their paychecks until they had paid off the full amount. Also added to their debts were charges for food, housing, electricity, and daily van rides to the fields from camps in Albion and nearby Kendall, a village half the size of Albion with a population that was almost entirely white.

Isolated in upstate New York, the farm workers had little else to do but work. But even if they had wanted to run away, Garcia made sure they wouldn't. Investigators later found that she had warned workers that they couldn't leave until they had paid off all their debts. After one group of workers left anyway, Garcia spoke of them disparagingly and warned the remaining men not to talk to strangers. If they ventured outside the confines of the camp, they would be caught and deported, she said.[17]

Some workers complained to Garcia and her son about the conditions of the trailer accommodations in the camps. The response was sometimes hostile and abusive. One migrant worker, Francisco Santiago, thought the trailer housing was terrible, particularly for his pregnant wife and five-year-old daughter, who had to share housing with five other migrant workers. As Santiago complained to Garcia, they might make only fifteen dollars a week after deductions, but they still needed heat, electricity, and hot water. The next day Garcia's son confronted Santiago and beat him up with brass knuckles. Santiago was hurt badly enough to have to go to a clinic for treatment.[18]

As word of such abuses spread, federal officials began investigating Garcia and her labor contracting business. The result was a federal indictment in June 2002, which charged Garcia, her son, and others with forced labor offenses under the TVPA, the first use of the law in an involuntary servitude case in the continental United States. The indictment charged the defendants with various immigration and trafficking offenses. Faced with the prospect that several immigrant farm workers would testify in court as government witnesses, Garcia, her son, and two other men pleaded guilty in December 2004 to trafficking-related charges.[19]

At sentencing time, federal prosecutors decided to invoke the section of the TVPA requiring traffickers to pay restitution to victims. The court would calculate the amount owed. Although Garcia argued in court papers that the benefits the victims had received from the government (immigration status, travel assistance, and cash payments) should reduce the restitution award, the court didn't agree. She was ordered to pay 250 dollars to each victim, not a large sum but a symbolic award. She was also sentenced to forty-six months in prison, her son to fourteen months.[20]

Though the Garcia case was the first labor trafficking case made on the mainland, it certainly wasn't the biggest. Two brothers, Juan and Ramiro Ramos of Florida, worked in the farm labor contracting business much the way Maria Garcia did. After immigrating to the United States in the 1980s, they themselves had been citrus pickers before starting their contracting business.

Working under the company name R & A Harvesting, Inc., the Ramos brothers recruited Mexican migrant farm workers in Arizona and transported them to Florida farms in the Okeechobee County area to pick the citrus crop. The scheme involved more than seven hundred workers, most of them undocumented. They were invariably poor: in Mexico some had lived in one-room homes built of straw or cardboard, making a miserable five dollars a day as farmhands. With no prospect of economic advancement, many had borrowed 250 dollars to pay a coyote to escort them across the U.S. border, where they waited in an abandoned trailer for a week before a recruiter took them in a van to Lake Placid, Florida, and sold them to the Ramos brothers for 1,000 dollars apiece.[21]

As in the New York State case, the migrant workers were each assessed a 1,000-dollar transportation fee. But rather than relying on psychological coercion, as Maria Garcia had, the Ramos brothers and their confederates used firearms, twenty-four-hour surveillance, beatings, and other forms of coercion to compel the migrants to work until they had paid their debts. Investigators found that even the drivers of the unlicensed vans used to transport the workers were threatened at gunpoint.

Members of the Coalition for Imokalee Workers, a group that looked after the interests of migrant farm workers, heard reports of these various abuses and started its own undercover investigation, which revealed the men's living conditions. Six workers were assigned to each converted room in an old bar. When payday came around, they were docked for transportation, living space, food, and even a check-cashing fee—and were left with virtually no money. The coalition helped three farmhands escape and passed along information about the Ramos operation to the FBI.[22]

The resulting federal investigation led to the indictment of the Ramos brothers on charges of conspiracy to hold workers in involuntary servitude, extortion, and other crimes. But because the conspiracy began before the TVPA had been passed, the criminal cases against the brothers and their conspirators were prosecuted under old laws. On a practical level this didn't matter much: both brothers received substantial prison sentences in November 2002—twelve years and three months for each. A Ramos cousin received ten years, and the government seized more than 3 million dollars in property found to be proceeds of the criminal enterprise.[23]

All the worker exploitation cases described so far in this chapter involved labor-intensive industries requiring large numbers of workers. Another constant was the use of illegal immigrants, whose vulnerability meant that employers could control them by threatening exposure to government officials. This deterred some immigrants from complaining about their employment conditions. To make matters worse, employers kept the migrants isolated from the mainstream population, both spatially and language-wise: since the immigrants didn't speak English or spend time with outsiders who spoke their own language, they could not communicate with anyone beyond their own group.

But some labor trafficking cases didn't involve immigrants at all. One case that came to light in Florida's agricultural industry involved a labor contractor who preyed on homeless people of African-American ancestry, an ironic situation because the suspect involved, Michael Allen Lee, was himself a descendant of African slaves. But although he did not prey on illegal migrants, his scheme did employ methods that investigators had grown familiar with.

Lee recruited homeless men around the Fort Pierce, Florida, area to pick oranges for local growers. The workers succumbed to a promising pitch: good wages and a comfortable place to live. But though the men nominally earned thirty-five to fifty dollars a day (itself a pittance), they rarely brought home more than ten dollars—primarily, it seems, because "home" was floor space in a house that Lee owned, which he charged the pickers thirty dollars a week to rent. Lee created his own company-store situation, giving the men loans to cover rent, food, cigarettes, and cocaine. Their indebtedness, according to investigators, allowed him to coerce them to keep picking fruit and in one instance beat a worker to prevent him from leaving.[24]

Things began to unravel for Lee in April 1997, when a man named George Williams approached a local sheriff's deputy to say he had escaped from a nearby house in Fort Pierce, where he had been beaten and held against his will. The resulting investigation uncovered the servitude situation and the workers' exploitation, complete with tales of how Lee charged his workers forty dollars for wine. Lee was arrested in late 2000 and in February 2001 pleaded guilty to a charge of involuntary servitude. Since his offense predated the effective date of the TVPA, he was sentenced under the older laws and received four years in prison.[25]

Domestics and housekeepers belonged to another group of trafficking victims that for years existed outside the view of law enforcement and society. The jobs "maid" and "nanny" might conjure up benign images and associations. But the TVPA helped increase law enforcement's sensitivity to the possibility that household workers were being trafficked and exploited. It didn't take long for investigators to uncover some egregious cases.

In Arlington, Massachusetts, the neighbors of the well-to-do Saudi couple living on Mystic Street noticed that the household always seemed to have lots of domestic help. Three or four maids, apparently ethnic Indonesians, always seemed to be around the house. And homeowner, Hana Al Jader, wife of Prince Mohammad Al-Saud of Saudi Arabia, seemed to change her maids every six months. At least that's what the situation looked like in early 2004. In reality some of those domestics had been with Al Jader for years, having come from Saudi Arabia as far back as February 2000.[26]

Al Jader was partial to South Asian maids and by many accounts had used a number of them at her home in Saudi Arabia. Some of the maids were recruited for the trip to the United States with the promise that they would be paid five hundred dollars a month. One who made the trip was Veronica Pedroza, a Philippines national, who arrived in the United States legally with a temporary visa that expired in May 2000. At least two other women, both Indonesians, also entered the country with Pedroza and were taken with her to the Mystic Street dwelling.[27]

Pedroza and the other women were expected to work and be on call twenty-four hours a day. Cooking and cleaning were only part of their duties: the prince was disabled and required substantial care. As soon as the women arrived at the Al-Jader home, Hana confiscated their passports and visas and locked them in a metal cabinet in her bedroom. This was the first level of control she exercised over the women: telling them that if they left the house without their papers, the police would find them and put them in jail. Fear of the police was not the only factor in keeping the arrangement secret. Another was to bar the women from making telephone calls without permission. When calls were made, Al-Jader dialed the telephone herself to make sure she knew who the servant was contacting.[28]

The situation at the Al-Jader home fast developed into exploitation. The women were told that if they quit, they had to pay back the cost of their travel to the United States. Moreover, the promised wages never materialized, so the women were kept in a state of impoverishment. Pedroza later told investigators that, in the five months she worked for the Saudi family, she only saw two hundred dollars. Desperate for a way out, Pedroza fled the house. The Coalition to Abolish Slavery and Trafficking, a nongovernmental group that had developed expertise in helping trafficking victims, spoke with her and put her in touch with the FBI. After Special Agent Christa Snyder took a statement from the woman, other federal agents began an investigation, which uncovered that the Al Jader family had moved to another home in nearby Winchester. On November 16, 2004, the FBI executed a search warrant on both homes used by the family, finding two Indonesian servants in the Winchester dwelling who told the agents they hadn't been paid any money of consequence and wanted to leave. Questioned by agents, Hana Al Jader opened a safe in her bedroom and turned over passports and unused airline tickets to Saudi Arabia for the two domestic workers. Within weeks she was arrested on charges of involuntary servitude. In September 2006 Al Jader pleaded guilty to federal visa fraud and charges of harboring an alien. As of this writing, her sentence is pending.[29]

About six months after Al Jader was arrested in Massachusetts, federal investigators came across another well-to-do Saudi family with a preference for Indonesian domestic help. Homaiden Al-Turki and his wife Sarah Khonaizan had four children—three girls and a teenage boy—and needed household help in their Colorado home. For that they turned to Sitzulaikan Warsito Alib, who in 2000, at the age of seventeen or eighteen, was brought by the family from Saudi Arabia. The young woman was constantly on call, with her normal work day beginning at six o'clock in the morning, when she prepared breakfast for the entire family. After that, the day was filled with cleaning duties, more cooking, and laundry. She also did yard work, car washing, and other tasks. Alib didn't leave the house unescorted except perhaps to retrieve mail.[30]

The domestic drudgery mirrored what the Indonesian domestics had experienced in Al Jader's household. But for Alib, there was one terrifying difference. Ms. Khonaizan spent part of the summer in Saudi Arabia with her children. As investigators discovered, that was the cue for her husband to start allegedly taking sexual liberties with Alib. In court papers later filed in the U.S. District Court for Colorado, federal prosecutors alleged that Al-Turki fondled and assaulted the young woman. He told her that, if she tried to run away, her expired visa would get her into trouble. Al-Turki was convicted in June 2006 on state charges of unlawful sexual contact with force, theft of services, and extortion. He was sentenced in August to twenty years to life in prison; and as a result, federal prosecutors dropped their trafficking charges. Sarah Khonaizan pleaded guilty in May 2006 to federal charges of harboring aliens and received a five-month jail sentence.[31]

After a neighborhood woman befriended Alib and listened to her allegations of sexual abuse, police and federal investigators were contacted. The result was the June 2005 indictment of Al-Turki and his wife on charges of involuntary servitude. Investigators found that the money paid to Alib for her years of work amounted to a pittance. In court papers filed in federal court by the U.S. Department of Labor in 2005, the government charged that she had been paid so little that she was owed more than 62,000 dollars in back wages. The FBI estimated that she had been paid about $1.91 *a day* at a time when the federal minimum wage was $5.15 *an hour*.[32]

Publicized trafficking cases such as those involving the Al-Turki and Al Jader families led some observers to believe that Saudi nationals had a propensity for abusing domestic workers, and several websites used these and other cases as opportunities to spew ethnic diatribes. But under the authority of the TVPA, investigators came across numerous cases involving abuse of foreign domestic workers by both immigrant families and native-born Americans.

For instance, in early 2005, a Michigan couple named Joseph and Evelyn Djoumessi were accused of bringing a thirteen-year-old girl from the couple's native Cameroon into the United States to work as a domestic. Investigators determined that the victim had been tricked into making the trip with the promise of getting an American education in exchange for household work. Federal prosecutors charged in court papers filed in Detroit that Evelyn Djoumessi had falsely identified the girl as her daughter in order to speed up the youngster's entry into the United States. The child wasn't permitted to attend school but was forced to clean the Djoumessi home, prepare meals, and take care of the family's three children. Like men in similar cases, Joseph Djoumessi allegedly raped her and threatened her with jail if she reported her abuse to authorities.[33]

The alleged mistreatment went on for more than three years but finally stopped when the young girl began surreptitiously visiting the next-door neighbors and eventually revealed what was happening. After local police were notified, they arrested both Djoumessis, who were subsequently convicted in state court for crimes stemming from sexual misconduct. Joseph was sentenced to a maximum of fifteen years in prison, while Evelyn (convicted of third-degree child abuse, a misdemeanor) received three years of probation with a special condition that seemed rather fitting under the circumstances: she had to clean her own house for those three years.[34]

These actions didn't end the couple's legal problems. Both were indicted in February 2005 for the federal crimes of involuntary servitude. The charges included violations of the TVPA as well as harboring a child. At the time I wrote this chapter, the case was still pending.

As you have seen, many labor trafficking cases involved workers who were directly abused by those responsible for the wrongdoing. But a case uncovered on Long Island, New York, in 2004 showed that trafficking offenses could extend well beyond those who worked directly for the traffickers. Many immigrants made pacts with traffickers to gain entry into the United States and then tap into the American economy. But no matter how understanding and solicitous the immigration merchants might be, the immigrants were still trapped in the kind of coercive conditions that had become the hallmark of labor exploiters.

In their native Peru, Mariluz Zavala and her common-law husband Jose Ibanez had a reputation for working immigration magic for other Peruvians. Apparently, they had such extensive connections at the U.S. embassy in Lima that prospective immigrants simply had to pay 7,500 dollars to receive a visa that would allow them to travel to the United States. They were never interviewed by consular officials or otherwise screened. Those who could only pay 6,000 dollars did have to go through the embassy screening process to get a visa, but Zavala was still willing to help them travel to the United States. After the embassy issued the visa, each prospective migrant gave Zavala a 1,000-dollar down payment and later an additional 1,000 dollars, thus securing the promise of a place to live, a job, and transportation to New York. Whatever remaining money they owed for their journey and travel arrangements would be paid in the United States.[35]

As the embassy-screening situation shows, Zavala had connections among the consular employees in Lima. One immigrant later told investigators that Zavala gave her a set of sample questions that would be asked at the screening interview and coached her on the correct responses. Zavala also gave the woman a fake marriage license to support the claim that she had a husband staying in Peru to whom she planned to return. Another immigrant said that he gave some passport-size photos and his Peruvian passport to Zavala, who returned it with a visa stamp although he had never been interviewed or screened at the embassy. The simplicity of the visa scheme raised obvious questions about the system's vulnerability to exploitation by terrorists or other criminals.[36]

Zavala's connections in the United States also helped her trafficking operation work smoothly. According to investigators, once the immigrants arrived from Peru, they were taken to one of a number of homes that Zavala owned in the Long Island towns of Amityville, Brentwood, and Coram. At that point, the situation began to show the earmarks of other trafficking operations.

The immigrants were told to turn over their passports to Zavala or others in her family. Their paychecks went to Zavala's husband Ibanez or her daughter Evelyn, who deducted travel and living expenses.[37]

Jobs did exist for the migrants at a cleaning company and a factory. So that workers could show proper documentation, they were taken to Queens to get fake Social Security cards and fake resident alien (green) cards, another instance of how easily such documents could be obtained fraudulently. The workers earned 370 dollars or more per week; but once Ibanez deducted travel and living expenses, they were left on average with 50 dollars per week, hardly enough to live on, let alone save for themselves or their families in Peru. In an attempt to make ends meet, sometimes the immigrants worked at two jobs. To assure prompt payments, Zavala and her family held house meetings where they reminded the aliens of their obligations and threatened to report them to law enforcement. One immigrant told investigators he believed that if he didn't cooperate, his family in Peru "would suffer the consequences."[38]

Federal court records show that at least two of these Peruvian immigrants began to cooperate with U.S. immigration investigators. In one case, an informant, identified only as "CI-2" (short for "confidential informant 2"), taped Zavala arranging a U.S. trip for the witness's relative at a price of 12,000 dollars, which she said she would raise to 13,000 dollars if the person took a less direct route through Mexico. Agents with the federal Bureau of Immigration and Customs Enforcement (ICE) set up surveillance of Zavala's homes and discovered that numerous adults were entering and exiting the premises. A single house in Amityville seemed to have fifteen residents, said an ICE agent.[39]

Those details were enough for ICE officials to get a search warrant; and on June 21, 2004, federal agents executed raids on the three Long Island residences owned by Zavala and her husband. What the agents found turned their stomachs. In affidavit filed after the searches, Brooklyn assistant U.S. attorney Bonnie Klapper said that "one of the agents reported to me today that in all of her years as an agent, including having searched homes in Chinatown, she has never seen more horrific living conditions then the conditions maintained by these defendants." Instead of fifteen people in the Amityville home, agents found a total of thirty-four residents (seventeen men, eight women, and nine children) in a single-family house that had been subdivided into fifteen bedrooms, some with only one or two mattresses as furniture. Wherever agents looked, they found unrefrigerated food, flies, and other signs of squalor. The Brentwood home was only marginally better, with twenty-seven residents, including three children, living in nine bedrooms. People even lived in the garage and garden shed, officials said. Only eight people, including a nine-month-old infant, were found in the Coram dwelling.[40]

According to federal court records, at each home agents found a trove of paperwork, including ledger books, fake green cards, and fake Social Security cards. Although Ibanez told agents he was himself just a day laborer who charged immigrants five hundred dollars a month to live in the homes, officials quickly learned otherwise. A total of sixty-nine illegal immigrants said in interviews that both Ibanez and Zavala were the people who had gotten them into the country. Faced with overwhelming evidence, the pair entered guilty pleas in Brooklyn federal court on November 5, 2004, to a variety of charges, including conspiracy to obtain forced labor, conspiracy to harbor forced labor, and other crimes such as dealing in false alien registration cards. At her sentencing in November 2005, Mariluz Zavala received a fifteen-year prison term, even though, while in custody, she had given birth some months earlier to her fourth child, a daughter. She and Ibanez were forced to surrender the house in Amityville (valued at about 220,000 dollars) to the federal government as well as about 30,000 dollars in cash that had been plucked from the immigrants' paychecks.[41]

The sentence meted out to Zavala was actually double what the defense and prosecuting attorneys believed was appropriate under the federal sentencing guidelines, which recommended a range of seventy to eighty-seven months. U.S. District Court Judge Sandra Feuerstein seemed especially angered by the fact that Zavala's activities had been more extensive than the plea agreement had disclosed and because she had involved her daughter in the trafficking and forced labor operations. Statements from five of Zavala's victims describing their mistreatment may also have influenced Feuerstein's decision. One woman, identified only as Carmen, said Zavala had forced her to live in a small basement room next to a room inhabited by five men. According to Carmen, one of the men had sexually abused her four-year-old daughter; but Zavala told her she would be deported if she reported the incident to police.[42]

The Zavala case revealed numerous factors about the trafficking situation in the United States. Most important it highlighted how simple it was for traffickers to use overcrowded dwellings in places like Queens and Brooklyn as stables for labor trafficking victims. Because this particular form of trafficking, exploits people through debased wages, extortion, and poor living conditions, it may continue to prevail in areas where it is cheap and easy to house migrants.

In part, officials were able to prosecute Zavala because Carmen decided to approach the local Long Island office of Catholic Charities, which directed her to the authorities. Charitable groups have played key roles in revealing other labor trafficking cases; for instance, in the Al-Jader case, the Coalition to Abolish Slavery and Trafficking helped a victim. Yet another avenue of help is victims' hope of recovering back wages through lawsuits. With the help of legal aid groups or the pro-bono advocacy of major law firms, they can negotiate the federal court system and often win substantial judgments. Consider, for example, a labor trafficking situation that involved domestic workers living in Sewell, a suburban town in western New Jersey near the Pennsylvania border.

Chandra Gedara spent much of her life in a small farming village in Sri Lanka. Then, at the age of forty-two, she was recruited to work in Lebanon as a domestic worker for Nyla Jishi, who had an extended family in the Mideast. In need of temporary work to support her family (her husband was unemployed), Gedara took the job, living with the Jishi family in Lebanon and Qatar until early 2002.[43]

Like families in other cases, the Jishis had business interests in the United States and decided to move there in 2002. They convinced Gedara to travel with them to care for some family members for a few months. They promised that her pay would amount to three hundred dollars per week, plus free room and board. Gedara accepted the deal and entered the country in April. But as soon as she stepped off the plane, she sensed that plans had changed. At the airport, Manal Jishi, wife of businessman Maher Jishi, took Gedara's passport, return ticket, and luggage. During the car ride to Sewell, Manal suddenly informed Gedara that her brief tour of duty in the United States had been extended from two years to five.[44]

At the Jishis' Sewell home, Gedara's living and working conditions fell into an all-too-familiar pattern. Her work days lasted as long as seventeen hours, with no vacations or holidays. The pay did not even reach minimum-wage levels of $5.15 per hour. The family scolded Gedera if she tried to go outside the house, once even reprimanding her when she darted out to stop their little boy from running into the road.[45]

On the night of February 21, 2004, a desk officer at the Washington Township police station suddenly found himself in a dilemma. Standing before him was a woman who was talking in a language he couldn't understand. The woman was excited, and it took a while for police to find a slip of paper she carried. On it was the Jishis' telephone number. When police called, Manal Jishi answered the phone and admitted she knew Gedara. When a cop asked how long Gedara had been living with her and why the woman might have left the house, Jishi was "unresponsive."[46]

Maher Jishi eventually showed up at the station house. After officers told him Gedara had been asking for her passport, he pulled it from his pocket, adding that he wasn't trying to keep it from her. His ensuing conversation must have confused the officers: according to a police report of the incident, he said the distraught woman had come to the United States for medical treatment but wasn't ready to go home yet. He also said her passport may have expired but did admit that Gedara was working his family. Jishi convinced Gedara to return home with him and told her in front of the police that he would send her back to Sri Lanka.[47]

A few days later police visited Jishi at his home and heard a different story. He told officers that Gedara was lazy and not a good worker but insisted that she wasn't restricted to the house. He also reiterated that she had a passport problem but that he was trying to help her get it renewed. The officers reported their conversations to federal investigators, who charged Jishi and his wife with harboring an alien for financial gain—cheap or free domestic labor. By federal court standards, the resulting plea bargain worked out well for the couple. Both pleaded guilty to harboring an alien, received probation, and were fined several thousand dollars. They could have faced up to ten years in prison. Their big penalty, however, involved Maher Jishi's agreement to pay Gedara more than 225,000 dollars in restitution to settle her federal lawsuit for breach of contract and violation of various federal laws, including the TVPA.[48]

This chapter's litany of forced labor cases shows that the crime of human trafficking is embedded in American work culture. Domestic servants, factory workers, and day laborers are all susceptible to this form of coercive migration. Given the growth in the number of immigrant households needing domestic help, coupled with the fact that factories and agricultural businesses constantly need temporary—and cheap—sources of labor, it is likely that labor trafficking cases are much more pervasive than federal enforcement actions indicate.

As I've already stated, a review of prosecutions commenced under the TVPA shows that sex cases far exceed the number of labor cases, both in terms of cases filed in the courts and percentage of convictions won. In some ways sex trafficking cases are easier for law enforcement to prosecute than labor cases are. Sex cases tend to focus on brothel and massage parlor situations, the kinds of establishments that police vice units can readily target and then report to federal officials if they find evidence of trafficking. With passage of the TVPA, officials at state and local levels have become more sensitive to the fact that prostitutes in immigrant neighborhoods might be trafficking victims and thus subjects of interest to federal investigators. But of course, as the Jishi case shows, local law enforcement must also become more sensitive to labor exploitation, a phenomenon that may happen just as often as sex trafficking cases—and maybe even more often.

A February 2005 report from the Human Rights Center at the University of California at Berkeley offers some guidance in making judgments about the labor case versus sex case dichotomy. In an effort to inspire state legislators to adopt legislation increasing prosecutions of human traffickers and those who contribute to forced labor, the center assessed forced labor in California and found a distinction between *trafficking* (defined as the movement of people across borders for exploitation) and *forced labor* (defined as "all work or service" taken from a person involuntarily under "the menace of any penalty").[49] Nevertheless, in a practical sense the terms have become interchangeable, although the migration element is crucial to trafficking.

After reviewing both media and U.S. government accounts as well as the experiences of NGOs and advocates, the Human Rights Center broke down trafficking and forced labor cases in California between 1998 and 2003. Researchers found fifty-seven total cases in the following subcategories: prostitution (47.4 percent), domestic service (33.3 percent), sweatshop labor (5.3 percent), mail-order bride (5.3 percent), sexual abuse of children or others (1.8 percent), agriculture (1.8 percent), and other or unclassified (5.3 percent). Clearly, prostitution cases amounted to the largest single category. But the other categories combined, even when factoring out the sex abuse and unclassified groupings, amounted to almost as many (45.7 percent).[50]

Critics of the Berkeley study see a flaw in its reliance on reported cases, which reflect law enforcement priorities and thus cannot reveal an unbiased perspective. But even assuming that law enforcement can more easily target sex trafficking cases, the proportion of other cases is clearly significant. California, like New York, Texas, and Florida, has a large immigrant population base, both legal and illegal. If that state's experience as an immigrant center is analogous, other high migration states might have similar rates of sex and non-sex labor trafficking cases, something that federal data do not reflect.

Unfortunately, as of 2005, both state and federal governments lack a rigorous and thorough method of compiling trafficking cases. Although the Civil Rights Division of the U.S. Department of Justice gave a me long list of pertinent cases that on the surface involved allegations of trafficking under the TVPA, several seemed idiosyncratic and certainly unrelated to immigration. For instance, a Kansas couple was convicted in November 2005 of involuntary servitude charges after a jury found they had forced mentally ill patients to perform sexually explicit acts on videotape and physical labor in the nude at a private home in the city of Newton. A case in Brooklyn led to the arrest of a New York man on charges that he had compelled a woman to take part in a sexual dominance-submission relationship, allegedly threatening her with harm if she didn't satisfy his sadomasochistic demands. Though such cases are certainly allegations of coercion, they are a far cry from the kinds of abuses that led to the passage of the TVPA. Including them in the documentation of trafficking cases confuses the matter at a time when we already lack valid research methods and a clear debate about trafficking priorities.

In short, while federal government data suggest that sex trafficking incidents make up the largest number of cases, we must view any such claim skeptically.

Nevertheless, when federal officials contend that the government should take a position against prostitution, they continue to rely on limited empirical data.[51] Between 2002 and 2005, this abolitionist perspective seemed to gain more traction, sparking controversy and criticism among those who saw it as evidence that U.S. policy on trafficking was being driven by moralistic positions that would further stigmatize and marginalize trafficking victims and prostitutes who needed assistance.

Chapter 9   Sexual Slavery

The Immigrant's Gilded Cage

As THE CADENA CASE HAD SHOWN, sex trafficking cases were filled with particular human rights abuses. They invariably involved prostitution and sex-related businesses such as nightclubs that featured topless dances. Like labor trafficking cases, they depended on coercion, sometimes with overt force to back up their intimidation. The migrants found themselves indebted to their masters, much as agricultural and domestic workers were. But sex trafficking was particularly odious because *sex* lay at the core of the economic transactions that supported the exploitation. In its worst forms sex trafficking involved rape, physical violence, and the special degradation that arises from being coerced to sell one's body for sex.

By the beginning of 2001, American law enforcement officials clearly understood that human trafficking would be a significant part of their future. The U.N. trafficking protocol and the TVPA of 2000 were a double mandate for action. Almost immediately, the FBI turned its attention to the problem. Various news accounts—in particular, stories about the sex migration in Eastern Europe—coincided with the signing of the protocol and the passage of the American legislation.[1] With so many migrants from Eastern Europe arriving in the United States, the FBI paid close attention to those immigrant communities for signs of trafficking, particularly in sex.[2]

But it became apparent that, despite a plethora of news accounts about the terrible ordeals of trafficking victims in Eastern Europe, the situation in the United States was different. According to one FBI organized crime expert, while the agency was looking for large-scale importation of European women to American cities for prostitution, agents weren't finding them. Either the cases didn't exist at the rumored level, or the alleged victims were keeping silent about their travails.[3]

The truth lay somewhere in between. As New York City's ethnic and community newspapers proved, there were plenty of massage parlors and "out-call" escort services available during that period in Eastern European immigrant communities. Women were clearly arriving in the city and engaging in sex work. But they appeared to be regular prostitutes, not trafficking victims. If they worked under duress, compulsion, or debt servitude, they did not say so—at least not to law enforcement.

For many years Asia had also been a source of sex workers in the United States, as evidenced by police arrests in large metropolitan areas with significant Asian enclaves. But the Asian sex worker culture, particularly in the Korean, Chinese, and Thai communities, showed little sign of the truly oppressive conduct illustrated in the Cadena case.

In 1999, I initiated a series of contacts with Korean prostitutes in New York City, working through private defense attorneys who had Korean women as clients. The women had been arrested on various prostitution-related charges ranging from solicitation to bribery. In my interviews with several women, they revealed details about their migration and their lives in the brothels of Flushing, Queens, which illuminated the wide variations among immigrant sex workers. Their activities were difficult to pigeonhole in the new trafficking jargon, despite the fact that many police investigators viewed them as "sex slaves," a catchphrase freely adopted by headline-hunting journalists.

The Koreans said that they often arranged passage to the United States through brokers in Korea. Frequently acting in concert with brothel owners in New York, these brokers gave the young women plane tickets, visas (often just tourist visas), and contact numbers in the States. The money such brokers advanced could amount to as much as 15,000 dollars. Some of the women traveled first to Canada, which at the time did not require visas from Korean nationals. The women said they knew they would be working for a Korean "mommy" as prostitutes. Once in New York City, the women would service clients in the brothels and earn back the fees that the brokers had advanced for their travel.[4]

The Korean system in New York could be very liberal, the women said. They were allowed to go out on their own and lived in apartments away from the brothels. Once they had paid back the money they owed the brokers (although interest had often doubled the original amount), they were free to travel anywhere they wanted.[5]

Many of the women continued to work as prostitutes, following a circuit that took them through big U.S. cities such as Philadelphia, Atlanta, Houston,

Los Angeles, and Honolulu. As Asian migrants spread into smaller cities, the women found work in those locations as well. Some sent part of their earnings back to families in Korea. Others settled in the United States and started businesses such as nail salons. Still others gambled away their earnings, which could amount to 10,000 dollars per month.[6]

Invariably, the Korean women said they knew the kind of work they were expected to perform. According to the women who managed the brothels, new arrivals surrendered their passports to the managers. Once the immigrants had earned back the money they owed, the managers returned their travel documents. One manager said some of the brokers actually dictated where the prostitutes had to live so they could be watched.[7]

Technically, some of the subtle controls placed on the Korean women—surrender of passports, debt obligations, living arrangements—fit the definition of trafficking, especially if those actions or situations coerced the women into forced labor. But in a practical sense, prosecutors would likely have had difficultly proving a trafficking violation: the women had relative freedom of movement and had joined the sex business of their own free will.

In the main, the Korean women I interviewed had a lifestyle as prostitutes that did not fit the stereotype of trafficked women that had developed from the Eastern European horror stories. What the Koreans experienced was nothing like the brutal conditions faced by the Mexican women in the Cadena case. The sex business showed some distinctions across ethnic lines; and although American laws may have labeled an immigrant woman as a victim, she may not necessarily have perceived herself as such, nor would she do anything about it.

As I've mentioned, it was also clear that in early 2001 American law enforcement was not finding nearly as many trafficking situations as certain members of Congress or anti-trafficking advocates had predicted. While critics might claim that U.S. agents just weren't looking for such situations, the law enforcement officials I interviewed said their intelligence operations within Russian organized crime syndicates were not backing up the trafficking estimates. Privately, American police officers said the same thing. In 2004 this disjuncture came to the fore in New York City, when some law enforcement officials questioned the need to create a unit to investigate trafficking because they had no clear sense of the size or significance of the problem in what was certainly the largest immigrant-destination city in the United States.[8]

But if some Asians were migrating to large cities to work in the sex industry—and frankly didn't care if their working conditions were covered by the anti-trafficking laws—others may very well have been tricked. The potent image of a deceived woman, analogous to the Victorian "white slave" stereotype of sexual servitude, outraged those who saw contemporary sex trafficking as a special brand of evil. According to this view, all the women must have been either tricked or coerced to sell their bodies; how could they make such a choice willingly? Yet this belief disregarded the fact that, for some people, prostitution was the quickest and easiest way to earn a living.

With the TVPA as a weapon, however, federal prosecutors did discover cases of fraud and coercion that gave some credence to the Victorian concept of sexual slavery. One such case was uncovered in the Northern Mariana Islands—like American Samoa, a U.S. territorial outpost. A string of tropical islands between Hawaii and the Philippines, Northern Mariana is a commonwealth in political union with the United States and governed by American laws. Its indigenous peoples are considered to be American citizens but don't vote in U.S. elections. A federal district court based in Saipan has jurisdiction over the islands.

Tourism is a big industry, along with garment production and some farming. Most of the garments produced on the islands are sent to the United States under import and quota exemptions. About 28,000 foreign workers live on the islands, in addition to about 6,000 indigenous peoples. The foreign workers are predominately Chinese, and service industries such as markets and nightclubs have developed to cater to their needs. One such establishment, located on the island of Saipan, was the Tea House Club Karaoke.

Although karaoke clubs are generally legitimate businesses, investigators said that the Tea House had another purpose. In August 2004, two Chinese businessmen, Zheng Ming Yan and Liu Chang Da, began to recruit women in Dalian, China, to come to the Northern Mariana Islands to work at legitimate jobs that would earn them seven dollars an hour plus health insurance and taxes covered by the company. The women signed contracts to seal the deal and were told they had to pay more than 5,000 dollars to cover transportation costs and the commonwealth's work-authorization fees.[9]

What happened next, according to investigators, followed a basic trafficking pattern. At least three Chinese women said the businessmen had them told that the Tea House was a legitimate karaoke nightclub that required no sex work. In fact, as investigators charged in an indictment filed in 2005 with the U.S. District Court for the Northern Mariana Islands, it was a house of prostitution. To compel the women to work as prostitutes, the defendants took their passports, forced them to perform sex work, and then required them to turn over their income from that work. If the women showed signs of complaining, they were told that their families in China would learn they had been working as prostitutes. In late 2005 a grand jury indicted Zheng and Liu on several counts, including conspiracy to commit sex trafficking, foreign transport for prostitution, and fraud. The case was pending in mid-2006.[10]

As I've discussed, places like the Northern Mariana Islands and American Samoa are so far away from the continental United States that they are tempting markets for human traffickers, who mistakenly believe they can evade law enforcement scrutiny. Because the islands are close to China, South Korea, the Philippines, and other Asian countries with a significant emigration patterns, there is no shortage of potential recruits; and traffickers do not have to struggle with long transportation routes. But traffickers have also developed Asia-based schemes using familiar tactics of deception and coercion that involve directly importing their victims to the U.S. mainland. This was the case of a well-to-do Korean couple who ran a popular bar in downtown Flushing, Queens, which has a large and vibrant Asian community.

Kyongja and Wun Hee Kang lived in Port Jefferson, a suburban community on Long Island, some thirty-five miles east of New York City. In addition to running the Renaissance Bar in Flushing, the Kangs operated a number of nail salons in the city. These establishments had proliferated as employment niches for Korean women immigrants, who used the salons as points of entry into the labor force. Sources in the Korean community told me that sometimes former prostitutes or madams owned the beauty establishments. Occasionally, the businesses also temporarily housed prostitutes newly arrived from Asia, said one knowledgeable attorney. But for the most part, the nail salons were legitimate operations popular with customers from many ethnic groups.[11]

In 2004, the Renaissance Bar was part of the Korean immigrant social scene, where many kinds of bars had become enormously popular. There were karaoke bars, small "stand" bars (just large enough to accommodate standing crowds), and larger businesses like the Renaissance where male customers sat with a woman who pushed high-priced drinks as the fee for the pleasure of her company. Tips could be very generous, and sometimes prostitution was involved.

In South Korea, Kyongja Kang had recruited a number of young women who were eager to work in the United States but didn't want to be prostitutes. Kang emphatically assured them that prostitution was out of the question. He said, however, that bar work could be very lucrative and that the women could earn up to 6,000 dollars per month from wealthy clients who were good tippers.[12]

Citing a fee of 15,000 dollars, an immigration broker in Korea gave each young woman an American tourist visa and an airline ticket to the United States. The women agreed that they would work at the Renaissance and pay back their transportation costs from their earnings. They would live in an apartment owned by the Kangs. But problems soon developed: no matter how good they were as bar hostesses, the women weren't able to earn enough money both to pay back their transportation costs and to keep anything substantial for themselves. Sensing their vulnerability, Wun Hee Kang suggested to at least two of the women that they could pay off their debts faster if they worked as prostitutes. As the women later told investigators, they refused, which was when the real trouble started.[13]

Relentlessly, Mr. Kang pressured the two women to work as prostitutes. He also began sexually abusing one of them, groping her when his wife wasn't around. Finally, the women had had enough: they filed a complaint with the local police precinct, which referred the matter to the Queens County district attorney's office. Local prosecutors filed assault and sexual abuse charges against Kang and then tipped off federal authorities. In a desperate move to stave off more trouble, he allegedly used an immigration inspector to try to compel one of the victims to go with him to Kennedy International Airport for a flight back to South Korea. Agents said that the inspector flashed his badge and told her that she was being deported for illegally working in the United States.[14]

Kang's attempt to spirit the woman back to South Korea failed after she escaped from a cab and went to police. At a local precinct in Queens, a victim told police that Mr. Kang had threatened to sell her to another business in Chinatown if she stopped working at the Renaissance. Federal officials arrested both Kangs on charges of keeping their two victims in indentured servitude. Federal peonage charges were also filed. The investigation expanded to ensnare Nisim Yushuvayev, an immigration inspector working at the airport, as well as other people who had worked with the Kangs. One source (who didn't want to be identified) told me that federal officials had uncovered numerous bank accounts that the couple had used to send money back to South Korea.

Although the Kangs wanted to fight the prosecution, luck went against them: a young woman named Myung Hee Kim agreed to cooperate with the government and detail how the couple's businesses worked. Faced with an unbeatable case, the pair pleaded guilty to human trafficking charges in 2005 and received stiff sentences reflecting the severity of the abuse they had heaped on their victims.[15]

The case of the Kangs and that of the Northern Mariana Islands defendants involved relatively small numbers of victims—at least in terms of what investigators were able to prove. But before passage of the TVPA, cases had surfaced in the Asian immigrant communities indicating that brothel operations were using large numbers of women. Could they all could be classified as victims of trafficking? In interviews between 1995 and 2001, some of those women told me they were voluntary prostitutes. Others may very well have been victims, as they stated to police and federal officials. But even after passage of the TVPA, sex migration from Asia continued; and in June 2005, Operation Gilded Cage, a federal investigation in San Francisco, showed just how extensive the sex smuggling operations remained.

The night of June 30, 2005, a combined force of federal, state, and local officials arrested twenty-seven people and raided fifty brothels and other businesses in a California-based probe of alien smuggling and sex trafficking. More than one hundred women, mostly prostitutes, were taken into custody and sent to non-detention facilities for health care and other services. During the raids officials seized more than 2 million dollars in cash, an indication of the brothels' brisk business. The aim of Operation Gilded Cage was to disrupt what officials believed was a far-flung illegal Asian immigration and sex trafficking network.[16]

In a statement released after the raids, San Francisco's U.S. attorney Kevin V. Ryan said, "In Operation Gilded Cage, we have actively sought to dismantle a wide-ranging operation with connections in the U.S., Korea, and Canada by targeting not only the alleged smuggling and trafficking of women, but also the related financial activities of the illicit operations." The indictment charged that two key defendants, Wu Sang Nah and Sung Yong Kim, had arranged with others to smuggle two Korean women across the Canadian-U.S. border, a common smuggling route because Canada doesn't require visas from visiting Koreans. They took the women first to Virginia, then to Los Angeles, and finally to a massage parlor in San Francisco. According to officials, the owners of the massage parlor paid a trafficking fee for the women, who were then indebted to them for that amount. The indictment alleged that the women were directed to work as prostitutes to pay off their debts and were kept under the owners' control until the money was paid back.[17]

Over the years I heard from sources in the Korean community in New York that limousine and taxi services were integral parts of the prostitution scene. Some of the arrests in the San Francisco case underscored that phenomenon. Among those charged were owners and operators of what prosecutors called an "underground" taxi service that shuttled prostitutes to and from airports and brothels in San Francisco. The indictment also charged the owner of a travel service with using the business to purchase airline tickets for prostitutes' interstate travel. Flights were booked to Las Vegas, Dallas, New York, and Boston, all key cities on the Asian prostitution circuit.[18]

The indictments and criminal complaints filed in the cases associated with Operation Gilded Cage charged a total of twenty-nine people with a wide range of offenses. Included in the charges were sex trafficking, money laundering, conspiracy, using interstate commerce to aid unlawful activity, and violations of the Mann Act. Of the one hundred women taken into non-punitive custody, twenty-one were designated as material witnesses on the grounds that they were in the United States illegally and had evidence useful for trial. Fifty-three were deemed non-material (unlikely to have significant evidence or uncooperative) and would either be deported or apply for political asylum.[19]

But as sometimes happens in cases with large numbers of defendants, Operation Gilded Cage lumped together large numbers of defendants who didn't bear the same responsibility for the most serious offenses. For instance, one defendant was a cab driver who did no more than drive women on two occasions to a brothel. The cases of three other defendants were dismissed entirely. By April 2006 plea bargains were underway with only fourteen defendants.[20]

I had noted in my research in New York's Asian community that the control exerted over women by the managers of sex businesses can be subtle. As allegations in the Operation Gilded Cage indictment showed, the managers took control of women's passports and travel documents to ensure that they would repay their debts. Although the law considers such an arrangement to be a form of debt bondage, many of the women had agreed to it beforehand. They saw it as a condition of employment that allowed them to migrate to the United States and tap into a potentially lucrative job.

Reports of violence against women in the Asian community did surface, but the anecdotal evidence showed that such episodes were infrequent. In other ethnic communities, however, physical force, overt physical intimidation, and other forms of coercion were more prevalent. In the former Soviet Union, women often worked as prostitutes without needing pimps or other intermediaries to secure customers and offer protection. But once they entered the illegal migration stream as a way to enter the United States and found themselves working as prostitutes or in other sex-related jobs, they risked falling prey to controllers and managers who weren't shy about using intimidation to protect their investment.

The case of Alex Babaev and Asker Mammadov came to light in Brooklyn, New York, in early 2005. Babaev had recruited a number of young women in Azerbaijan to work as prostitutes, promising that they would be able to keep half of what they earned and give the rest to him. But by looking at the two men, the women should have predicted trouble. Babaev was big with cropped hair and a beard. His arms were festooned with tattoos of gladiators and winged horses. Mammadov was a reputed wrestler and built like weightlifter, with a boxer's cauliflower ears.[21]

Although the women (there were at least three) agreed to work for Babaev and Mammadov in the sex business, they didn't count on physical abuse. According to an affidavit later submitted by a woman identified in court papers as Jane Doe 2, Babaev beat her so badly that she had black eyes and a broken nose. Instead of keeping half her daily earnings, Jane Doe 2 turned over everything to Babaev—as much as eight hundred dollars at a time. A woman identified as Jane Doe 1 also reported in her affidavit that Babaev had physically abused and raped her. Even with injuries (which weren't treated by a doctor), she was expected to service customers. "I have no words to describe how black this feels," she recalled. "You hate this and you know that two men are sitting in the next room, enjoying themselves and making money off of your suffering." She said that although she made a lot of money for Babaev and Mammadov, she kept nothing: "I worked so hard, nobody worked harder. I was a slave."[22]

The treatment that the Azerbaijani women described illustrates some of trafficking's worst abuses. One victim was seventeen years old when she arrived in Brooklyn, barely five feet tall and weighing about one hundred pounds. Yet according to officials, Babaev beat and sexually abused her. She received no money for her sex work, was stripped of her passport, and was unable to speak English. Federal investigators said the men used drugs and abuse to keep her in a state of psychological dependence.[23]

Complaints from the women in Babaev's stable of prostitutes reached Brooklyn's assistant U.S. attorney Thomas Firestone, who was a fluent Russian speaker and specialized in Russian and Eastern European organized crime cases. He had also spent about two years in Moscow on special assignment for the Department of Justice, working with Russian officials on Mafiya and trafficking problems. With the help of the FBI, Firestone put together a case in 2005 that led to the arrest of both Babaev and Mammedov on sex trafficking charges. Evidence was strong, and both defendants eventually pleaded guilty. Sentencing proceedings were pending in mid-2006.[24]

Not all of the Eastern European sex trafficking cases involved prostitution. One that was uncovered in the Detroit area involved strip clubs and thus blended sex and labor trafficking. In February 2005 two Ukrainian women contacted federal immigration officials to complain about the way they had been treated by some fellow countrymen in the United States. The women said that Michail Aronov and Alexsander Maksimenko had promised them jobs as waitresses in Virginia Beach. The men gave them money for U.S. visas. But the women told investigators that, in May 2004, when they arrived at Dulles International Airport in Washington, D.C., Aronov said there had been a change of plans: they would be working in Michigan instead. After a bus trip to Detroit, the women were met by Aronov and Maksimenko and taken to a motel, where they suddenly learned they owed the men 12,000 dollars each for travel costs, plus another 10,000 dollars each for identification documents and Social Security cards. To pay off their debts, the women were required to work as strippers at Cheetah's, a club in Detroit.[25]

For investigators, it was a familiar story. Apparently, Aronov, Maksimenko, and a third man had for a number of years operated a brokerage business that managed Eastern European women working as dancers in exotic nightclubs in the Detroit area. The business, known as Beauty Search, Inc., had associates in Ukraine and New York to help smuggle women into the United States through sham marriages or abuse of a cultural exchange visa program. The operation was similar to one used by a business confederate in Athens, Greece, where Eastern European women were also working in strip clubs. Coercion was often part of the deal, said U.S. officials: the men kept women in line by assaulting them and brandishing handguns.

With mounting debts, the women were forced to work twelve-hour shifts at Cheetah's and to turn over all of their earnings to Aronov and Maksimenko, who kept them in an apartment without a telephone. At least two other women also worked for the men at Cheetah's and had come from Ukraine specifically to work as strippers. But those women also had to turn over their earnings to the men and could only telephone their families in Ukraine when Aronov and Maksimenko allowed them to, according to investigators. Although the women didn't complain about being forced to work as prostitutes, two said that Aronov and Maksimenko threatened to have sex with them.[26]

In February 2005, after two of the women escaped from the operation and talked to federal officials, Aronov and Maksimenko were arrested on human trafficking and forced labor charges in. But that apparently didn't end the criminal conduct of the Beauty Search entrepreneurs. In custody, Maksimenko confided to Aronov that a business associate had offered money to the parents of some Beauty Search dancers to retract their allegations of abuse. That associate, said Maksimenko, then made death threats to the families who couldn't convince their daughters to retract their allegations; he also suggested offering bribes to Ukrainian law enforcement officials to increase pressure on the families. Under weight of the investigation, Maksimenko allegedly threatened to harm Aronov's wife or anyone else who caused him legal trouble.[27]

The threats didn't work. Aronov pleaded guilty in September 2005 to charges of forced labor, trafficking, and document servitude stemming from the Beauty Search operation. By doing so, he agreed to a lengthy stipulation of facts, a damning litany of trafficking actions, including forced labor and coercive behavior. The stipulation also detailed the substantial amount of money that had streamed through Beauty Search bank accounts in the United States, including deposits totaling 1.4 million dollars, and the existence of more than 500,000 dollars in cash kept in safety deposit boxes and at Maksimenko's home. As part of his plea bargain, Aronov agreed to turn over to the government more than 530,000 dollars to pay the victims and as forfeiture of his illegal proceeds. He also agreed to help federal prosecutors in their investigation, which could eventually reduce the sentence for his crime.[28]

If the Eastern European enterprises were tough, trafficking groups in Latin American communities were equally so. The stiff prison sentences meted out

to the notorious Cadena family didn't deter other crime groups from using similar tactics to victimize immigrants from South and Central America. One case
that surfaced in 2003 involved a Mexican woman, Maricela Martinez-Uresti,
who was living in Texas but traveling back and forth to Mexico, where she
secured contracts from families who agreed to let their daughters work in what
they thought would be restaurant jobs in the United States to repay 1,500 dollars each in immigration costs. But apparently the parents hadn't learned anything from the publicity that surrounded the Cadena case and didn't suspect
that the restaurant jobs were illusory—which was the case. Once the Mexican
girls, who were all under the age of eighteen, reached Austin, Texas, they were
forced to work as prostitutes to pay off the debts. Martinez-Uresti was caught
and in December 2003 was sentenced to 108 months in prison.[29]

Another Mexican sex trafficking case surfaced in California and involved
the madam of a Los Angeles brothel, who specialized in recruiting fourteen-
and fifteen-year-old girls. The investigation revealed that the girls had been
recruited in Mexico and knew they would be prostitutes for a set term of about
five months so that they could pay off the cost of immigration. But the
madam, Maria de Jesus Valle-Maldonado, crossed the line into unambiguous
trafficking conduct when she used abuse and coercion to keep the girls working in massage parlors and homes used as brothels. A federal immigration raid
uncovered one of the brothels, and Valle-Maldonado quickly pleaded guilty to
trafficking-related charges. She received a prison term of four and a half years
in November 2004.[30]

One of the most brutal allegations of trafficking to surface in the Latino
immigrant community since passage of the TVPA came to light in July 2005.
This time it involved Honduran immigrants who had settled in Union City,
New Jersey. Strictly speaking, the allegations did not involve sex trafficking
because the victims had not been forced to prostitute themselves. Rather, the
girls, who were mostly in their teens and early twenties, were compelled to
work long hours as dance-hall girls in clubs catering to immigrant men. But
as in the Kang case, club operators allegedly suggested to the girls that they
could earn more money by having sex with patrons.

The federal investigation that focused on the Union City dance halls
began in January 2005, when an agent with the Bureau of Immigration and
Customs Enforcement (successor agency to the Immigration and Naturalization
Service) who was conducting a smuggling investigation interviewed a young
Honduran woman who had been working at a bar. The woman, identified only
in court records as CI-1, said her job had been to drink with male customers and
encourage them to buy as many drinks as possible. Customers were charged ten
dollars per drink and three dollars per dance. The informant said she had to pay

off a smuggling fee of 15,000 to 20,000 dollars and had to reside at a safe house on New York Avenue in Union City. Another informant, this time a male customer at El Paisano Bar and Night Club told the agent that he had unexpectedly run into his fourteen-year-old cousin at the bar, who complained that she had originally agreed to be smuggled into the United States for a restaurant job but instead was forced to work at El Paisano to pay off her fee to the smugglers. The customer told the agent that his cousin was under extremely tight control at the nightclub; court papers report that the owner, a woman named Elvira Rosales, wouldn't even let the girl go out to lunch with him.[31]

After collecting more information from an undercover operative who had talked with another girl at the bar, federal agents raided two houses in Union City in late January 2005 and found nineteen illegal immigrant Honduran women inside. At least one of the girls was a minor, who told investigators that she had been caught by immigration agents crossing into the United States from Mexico but had been paroled. Undocumented immigrants who are caught illegally entering the country are often released with the understanding they will reappear for a deportation or asylum hearing. But many immigrants never show up for those hearings and simply melt into the U.S. population. The girl also told investigators that she had to pay 575 dollars a week from her earnings toward the smuggling fee, plus 250 dollars in rent and 60 dollars a week for food. In short, virtually all of the women's earnings were turned over to the smuggling ring, officials said.[32]

In July 2005 a federal grand jury returned a thirty-one-count indictment that accused ten people of being part of the Honduran-based smuggling ring. Federal prosecutors alleged that the young victims, all pretty and from poor rural villages in Honduras, were forced to work at bars and nightclubs to pay off their smuggling debts. The defendants viewed the girls as cash registers; and those who became pregnant were forced to terminate their pregnancies so they could continue to produce income, officials charged. They also said that one such victim took pills to have a spontaneous abortion and gave birth to a baby girl who soon died. Among those charged with forced labor and smuggling offenses were Luisa Medrano, a native of El Salvador, who owned three bars in Union City and Guttenberg. Medrano also owned the buildings where the young girls lived when they weren't working at the bars. Four alleged enforcers, who imposed work rules on the victims and collected smuggling fees, were also charged. Among them were three women between the ages of twenty-nine and thirty-seven. As of mid-2006, the case was pending in Newark's federal court.[33]

Investigators discovered that traffickers in the Mexican immigrant communities sometimes employed a form of psychological manipulation that exploited their victims' desire for love. Like many of the poor Mexican communities that fed the northward migration, the town of Tenancingo had its share of young, impressionable girls anxious to break away from their hardscrabble lives and limited futures. So when young men from the local Carreto clan promised love and marriage and talked about emigrating to the United States, the girls saw hope for the future.

In June 2001, impelled by such hope, a seventeen-year-old woman who worked in a Tenancingo pastry shop agreed to marry Josue Flores Carreto. But if Carreto had promised the woman love, he didn't show her any. Right after the wedding he took his new wife to a hotel in town and kept her locked in a room for about two weeks, allowing her out only with an escort. Finally, he brought her to the home of his mother, Consuelo Carreto.[34]

Josue Carreto forced his wife to work as a prostitute in the nearby towns of Puebla and Irapuato before deciding in 2003 to send her to New York. She crossed illegally into the United States with another girl, who was married to her husband's cousin. Once in New York, both women worked in brothels in the Corona section of Queens, servicing more than twenty men a day. The women were under tight control, were forced to turn over all of their earnings to the men, and endured beatings if they kept any cash for themselves. Pregnancy led to abortions.[35]

The pattern of forced prostitution was repeated numerous times with other young girls from Tenancingo who had the misfortune of dating and getting involved in long-term relationships or marriages with Carreto men. The family was actually a group of entrepreneurs deeply involved in the recruitment by seduction of young Mexican women. After breaking them in as prostitutes in Mexico, the family sent them to New York. Money the prostitutes earned was sent back by wire transfer to Consuelo and other Carreto family members.[36]

Eventually, rumors that the Carreto family was forcing Mexican women into prostitution reached officials at the U.S. embassy in Mexico City. Armed with leads developed with the help of Mexican law enforcement, federal investigators in New York began to watch two apartment buildings in Corona, which they believed Josue Carreto was using as living space for prostitutes smuggled from Mexico. When they recognized one of the women as an illegal alien whom Carreto had allegedly smuggled into the United States, investigators stopped her on the street. She admitted being "married" to Carreto and to working as a prostitute. She allowed the agents to enter one of the buildings and conduct a search, which ultimately revealed a supply of condoms, intercourse gel, business cards and flyers advertising prostitution services, and large sums of cash. Clearly, the federal agents had discovered a prostitution and smuggling operation, a suspicion reinforced after some men in the buildings admitted managing such operations for Josue Carreto.[37]

After rounding up four females, federal agents conducted interviews and discovered the manipulative nature of the relationships at the bottom of the business. All of the women professed having sexual or romantic relationships with the Carreto men and were aware of the fact that they would be working as prostitutes in New York. At first blush those admissions were proof of alien smuggling for prostitution and nothing more. But as investigators probed deeper, they discovered over weeks of interviews that the women's romantic inveiglement had easily led to threats, physical violence, and sexual assaults. The abuse may not have been the worst the agents had ever seen, but it was enough for the Carreto men to gain control over the women.[38]

As a result of that control, the women kept none of the money they made from prostitution. They charged twenty-five to thirty dollars for sex but gave half of those small sums to the brothel owners and passed along the rest to the Carreto men. They also were barred from contacting their families unless a Carreto family member monitored the telephone call. Interaction with other women who were working in the brothels was also prohibited.[39]

In February 2004 four Carreto men were arrested and charged with alien smuggling for prostitution: Josue Flores Carreto, Gerardo Flores Carreto, Eliu Carreto Fernandez, and Daniel Perez Alonso. The first two were brothers and sons of Consuelo. Fernandez was a cousin of the brothers, while Alonso was a close friend of the men from Tenancingo. As the women became more comfortable about cooperating with investigators, the charges against the four were upgraded to sex trafficking. Meanwhile, in Mexico, law enforcement officials raided Consuelo's home and garnered evidence such as letters, photographs, and other documents.[40]

Initially, the four Carreto defendants vowed to fight the case. They argued that the women were voluntary prostitutes and denied the abuse and coercion allegations. A trial seemed imminent; and taking the advice of another inmate at the federal jail about fighting the case, the defendants high-handedly refused the government's plea bargain offers. It was futile act of defiance fueled by misplaced machismo. At the last minute, faced with the prospect that nine women, including their wives and paramours, would testify, the Carreto defendants pleaded guilty; and in 2006, Brooklyn's federal district judge Frederic Block sentenced each to fifty years in prison, one of the longest sentences ever handed down for trafficking. Had they agreed to an initial plea offer, they would have received maximum terms of ten years.[41]

After 2000, with a relatively new influx of Mexican immigrants entering New York City, federal agents began more intensive investigations into suspected traffickers. They found not only groups such as the Carreto clan but also more intimate conspiracies using love as a means of psychological manipulation—for example, the case of Javier Cortes-Eliosa, which federal agents in Brooklyn and Queens began uncovering in early 2006.

Agents focused on Cortes-Eliosa after listening to the story of a young Mexican woman who claimed to have been his wife. The woman said she had married him in July 1999 after a brief courtship in the Mexican town of San Francisco. Almost immediately, as she revealed to federal agents, he told her to work as a prostitute to support herself and her child. Although the woman didn't want to, she did it anyway, depositing her earnings into a bank account that her husband also had access to. The story then took a familiar next step: Cortes-Eliosa arranged to have her smuggled across the Arizona border and flown to New York. Despite her months of work as a prostitute, the woman thought Cortes-Eliosa wanted her to go to the United States because he loved her and wanted to live with her as man and wife. But as she told investigators, after arriving in New York her romantic notions were vaporized when it became apparent that Cortes-Eliosa was also forcing two other women to work as prostitutes. To make matters worse, he wanted his wife to repay the money he had spent bringing her into the United States and, according to court papers, hit her when she resisted.[42]

Cortes-Eliosa's wife said she had worked as a prostitute in the United States for about six years, not only in New York City but also in brothels in Charlotte and Greensboro, North Carolina. According to federal agents, the brothel owners kept the money she made and eventually turned it over to Cortes-Eliosa, who sent it by wire transfer to his family in Mexico. In August 2005, Cortes-Eliosa returned to Mexico but not before allegedly ordering his wife to continue working as a prostitute. When he tried to return illegally to the United States in March 2006, U.S. border patrol agents stopped him. With him were three young Mexican women.[43]

Clearly, sex trafficking cases have arisen in many U.S. immigrant communities. Their number, while not large compared to the overall number of immigration prosecutions, does illustrate that prostitution, massage parlors, and hostess bars are significant economic elements of these communities. Case histories evince a fundamental pattern: female sex workers, either willingly or not, are smuggled into the United States to work as prostitutes or at related jobs; traffickers may or may not tell immigrants the true nature of their employment; once in the country, migrants are assessed thousands of dollars to repay travel expenses; traffickers control victims by taking their passports and threatening them with violence.

The prostitution operations related to these trafficking cases are assembly-line sex businesses: customer volume is high, assuring a constant flow of revenue. Because some of the women realize that the more customers they service, the quicker they will repay their debts and become free agents, they work large-scale brothel circuits and bring in lucrative incomes. Until such time as they are arrested and possibly deported, they send money to their home countries and live comfortably in the United States. These free agents tend to make uncooperative prosecution witnesses, which is why trafficking investigations sometimes run into trouble. Other women, however, are caught in a brutal vortex of debt servitude that they are psychologically unprepared for and unwilling to deal with. These are the cases best suited for TVPA prosecutions.

But as any good vice cop can attest, coercion, manipulation, and brutality are standard parts of traditional pimp-prostitute relationships in many American cities. The women involved aren't necessarily immigrants and are more likely than not to be American citizens who have been sucked into prostitution for a variety of reasons. As I examine in Chapter 10, the TVPA can also cover non-immigrant prostitution and sex work; and its maturation as a legal weapon has influenced a growing and contentious debate on prostitution.

| Chapter 10 | New Initiatives, More Controversy |

As I've noted, the TVPA gave law enforcement more legal ammunition to deal with trafficking; and almost immediately after its passage in 2000, federal officials tried to apply the statute against suspected traffickers. Some of those attempts had mixed results. But by 2003, when certain funding provisions of the act were due to expire, officials had close to three years' worth of experience with the law and could tell what did and did not work well.

In 2003 members of Congress introduced new legislation aimed at refining the law, extending appropriations, and strengthening the government's ability to combat trafficking domestically and worldwide. Some changes expanded protections for trafficking victims who had faced obstacles in getting help in the United States. But other changes contained the seeds of future controversy.

Initially, the TVPA contained a three-year funding authorization amounting to slightly less than 60 million dollars, not counting the Department of Labor's spending to help trafficking victims. In June 2003 Representative Chris Smith introduced the reauthorization bill in the House, and three co-sponsors authorized appropriations of 106 million dollars in 2004 and again in 2005 for various anti-trafficking programs.[1] The bulk of the money (about 61 million dollars) was earmarked for overseas assistance to protect trafficking victims and help foreign states meet the minimum standards of activity and policy as monitored by the state department's yearly country reports. In November Senator Sam Brownback introduced a related measure in the Senate— the Paul and Sheila Wellstone Trafficking Victims Reauthorization Act.

The name memorialized the couple, who had died in a tragic plane crash while Wellstone was campaigning for reelection in October 2002. Both had lived long enough to see the TVPA become the law of the land, but their deaths left a void not only among their staffers but also within the network of activists and NGOs who worked with trafficking victims.

The increased amount of money appropriated for overseas activity clearly indicated that the United States had recognized that its trafficking problem was intimately tied to developments abroad. The government wanted to encourage foreign powers to take concerted law enforcement and other actions to deal with trafficking. Victims of trafficking in the United States also needed help; and the 2003 legislation (known as the Trafficking Victims Protection Reauthorization Act, or TVPRA) authorized the Department of Health and Human Services to appropriate 15 million dollars for refugee assistance in 2004 and 2005, up from 10 million dollars in 2003. Additional authorizations for the Department of Justice and the Department of Labor amounted to a total of 25 million dollars for both years.[2]

Cash was a necessary part of U.S. anti-trafficking programs. Without funding, little could be done to ameliorate victims' situations. Unlike its appropriations components, the TVPA's criminal and immigration law elements had no sunset, or expiration, provisions. But after three years' worth of experience, policymakers believed the act needed changes to strengthen its protective and prosecutorial components.

One problem they wanted to address was sex tourism—traveling abroad for the purpose of having commercial sex. Another involved the personnel of U.S. contractors abroad; investigations and news reports indicated that some were complicit in trafficking offenses. Congress also had to consider refining methods for helping victims, which would require expansion of immigration benefits for victims' families and more liberal T-visa eligibility standards. The definition of racketeering needed to change to encompass trafficking offenses. Finally, policymakers needed to create a private right of action so that victims could sue their oppressors.

Smith and his co-sponsors were buoyed in September 2003 by President George W. Bush's public stance on the issue, when in an address to the U.N. General Assembly he singled out human trafficking as "a special evil in the abuse and exploitation of the most vulnerable."[3] His remarks, while unexpected, showed that his administration had made anti-trafficking part of its moral agenda and signaled that the United States was committed to using its bully pulpit to espouse its stance. His remarks also made good political sense because the issue had become important to evangelical Christians, who were eager to influence U.S. foreign policy and formed part of the Christian political base that Bush was trying to harness in his quest for reelection in 2004.

In 2002 there had been unsavory news stories about some employees of DynCorp, a company based in Reston, Virginia, but doing contract work in Bosnia and Herzegovina, who were allegedly involved in the trafficking of women who worked in local brothels. According to the allegations, American civilian contractors bought women, transported trafficked women, and were violent to them. One employee reportedly filmed the rape of a Moldovan woman whose services he had purchased from a Bosnian bar for about 740 dollars. According to Human Rights Watch, DynCorp stated that it had taken "prompt action," which included terminating anyone involved in improper behavior.[4]

The stories about DynCorp (and some were aired during the April 2002 hearings of the House Committee on International Relations) caused a furor. Human Rights Watch recommended that corporations should have "adequate safeguards in place to prevent employees from engaging in human rights abuses."[5] After the DynCorp allegations surfaced, President Bush issued National Security Presidential Directive 22, which forbade U.S. government employees and con-tractors from engaging in human trafficking. Breaking that rule meant that the company involved would risk breaching its federal contract and thus losing business.[6]

In the wake of the DynCorp incident, the TVPRA aimed at addressing cases in which U.S. government contractors might be complicit in human traf-ficking. As experience had shown, American companies sometimes operated in regions where they and their employees were unlikely to be held accountable for wrongdoing under local law. The TVPRA codified Bush's policy directive. The legislation required that companies receiving U.S. government–funded con-tracts in the area of international affairs agree that the government has the right to cancel the deal if the company or its subcontractors engages in sex trafficking or uses forced labor to carry out the contract. The provision called for a severe financial penalty if the anti-trafficking clause were violated.[7]

It was clear that foreign assistance programs, particularly SECI's, were vital to preventing trafficking. The TVPRA required the president to form foreign assistance schemes that would lead to border interdiction programs. The act would channel funding to NGOs, which would then provide transit shelters for trafficking victims at borders and help train border and immigrations offi-cials to identify such victims. The legislation specifically required agencies to call on trafficking survivors to help them identify other victims.[8]

In another provision related to foreign activity, the TVPRA sought to dis-courage U.S. citizens from taking part in sex tourism, a form of international travel in which male clients visited countries such as Thailand, which had large sex centers, or Costa Rica and other Latin American countries, which had developed a reputation for promoting child prostitution and pedophilia.[9] U.S. airlines and other carriers operating in such countries had to develop and disseminate literature alerting travelers to the fact that sex tourism was illegal under American law (18 U.S.C. 2423) and that offenders could be prosecuted. According to the TVPRA, this requirement could be tailored to specific carriers and routes to havens for sex tourism.[10]

The 2000 TVPA had a T-visa provision, which policymakers viewed as crucial for the protection of trafficking victims. As discussed, the government could issue no more than 5,000 such visas and only to victims who cooperated with American law enforcement. Although critics had claimed that the number would be either too low or too high, experience showed that during the TVPA's first five years of existence officials had issued fewer 10 percent of the allotted visas. To use up that allotment and extend protection to victims' families, the TVPRA expanded its conditions for eligibility. Formerly, in their decision to grant the special visa, officials considered only one issue: cooperation with federal law enforcement. Now, however, victims were also eligible if they had helped state and local law enforcement authorities during investigations. Because local rather than federal agencies sometimes prosecuted trafficking cases, the change was an attempt to mend a gap in the law.[11]

In its report on the TVPRA, the Committee on International Relations stated that "every effort should be made to enable a victim of trafficking to benefit from the 'T' visa provision" when the victim cooperated in good faith with law enforcement at the federal and local levels. Even if an inquiry didn't result in a formal investigation or prosecution, the committee believed that the victim's assistance should merit the endorsement of a special visa application.[12]

A second change gave family members of trafficking victims the opportunity to receive a derivative T-visa. As Smith explained during a House floor debate in November 2003, the change was designed to prevent a situation in which family members were "exploited back home because their daughter or their sister or their wife, who had been trafficked, goes into a situation of protection here." A third change in the T-visa provisions, aimed at what policymakers believed was an oversight in the original TVPA, eliminated the requirement for law enforcement cooperation if the trafficking victim were between the ages of fifteen and eighteen.[13]

In addition to granting T-visas, the TVPA included provisions allowing the Department of Health and Human Services to provide victims with public benefits. Their family members, however, were not included. The TVPRA changed that situation: if a family member entered the United States under a derivative T-visa, that person would be available for public benefits and services as well. This could prove important if a newly admitted family member was seeking a job or language skills. The new law also gave trafficking victims the right to sue in federal court for actual and punitive damages, as well as attorney fees.[14]

The TVPRA included a number of changes related to law enforcement. One of the most important was adding various trafficking offenses (peonage, slavery, involuntary servitude, forced labor, and child sex trafficking) to the list of racketeering offenses under U.S. law.[15] Known as the Racketeer Influenced and Corrupt Organizations (RICO) statute, the law required any racketeering enterprise or offender to forfeit its ill-gotten assets. It applied not only to traditional Cosa Nostra or Mafia activity but to any activity that resulted in racketeering offenses—what the law called predicate crimes, which now included human trafficking. The TVPA had beefed up prison terms for trafficking-related offenses: from twenty years to, in some cases, life. The RICO element now added severe financial penalties as well.

Congress also believed that involved agencies should integrate their anti-trafficking efforts and that foreign governments should have one source of information when comparing their own and U.S. efforts. The Interagency Task Force, which the TVPA had created in 2000, was required under the TVPRA to give various House and Senate oversight committees information about ongoing trafficking programs and initiatives. The new law also established the Senior Policy Operating Group, a team of senior officials appointed by the task force, which was responsible for coordinating activities and sharing information about trafficking policies. When assessing the anti-trafficking efforts of other nations, American officials had been frustrated by a dearth of information about trafficking arrests, prosecutions, convictions, and sentences. The TVPRA now required officials to consider such information when assessing the tier rankings of foreign governments and stated that it was up to those nations to provide such information to Washington. Failure to do so created a presumption that the foreign government wasn't vigorously engaged in fighting trafficking.[16]

The original TVPA had called for the creation of a special state department office known as the Office to Monitor and Combat Trafficking, commonly known as the Trafficking in Persons (TIP) Office, which compiled the yearly tier rankings of other countries. In 2003 its director was John Miller, a former member of the House of Representatives from Washington State and a zealous anti-trafficking advocate. Before taking over the TIP Office, Miller had for three years chaired the Seattle-based Discovery Institute, a nonpartisan organization formed by a former Reagan administration official and devoted to research on a number of issues, among them the theory of creationism known as intelligent design.[17] He had garnered the support and admiration of a number of members of Congress, including Chris Smith; and both Michael Horowitz, a Jewish senior fellow at the Hudson Institute, and Charles Colson, former counsel to President Richard Nixon (who after spending a stint in prison for his role in the Watergate scandal became an evangelical Christian leader) backed Miller for the job.[18]

The TVPRA effectively elevated Miller's status, raising his rank to ambassador-at-large. As Smith commented to his colleagues in the House, such a change in status would give the director of the TIP Office more power and influence over policy changes in Washington and abroad.[19] With influential mentors such as Horowitz and Colson, both of them well-known prostitution abolitionists who had considerable clout with President Bush's inner circle of advisors, Miller had an interest in pushing such policies and in later years used his job as a pulpit for abolitionism.

The TVPRA made yet another important change—one that provoked controversy and illustrated how politicized trafficking policy had become in the United States. According to the new law, unless an organization agreed formally that it refused to "promote, support or advocate" the legalization or practice of prostitution, it would receive no funding for anti-trafficking work. The intent of the provision, as explained in a House Committee on International Relations report, was to apply the restriction to organizations and NGOs working with prostitutes under the control of traffickers.[20]

The TVPRA also mandated a few smaller changes. It required the White House, acting in concert with agencies such as the Department of Health and Human Services, the Department of State, and the Council of Economic Advisors, to research the causes of trafficking and the effectiveness of programs designed to prevent trafficking and help its victims. It also required those entities to study the relationship between trafficking and global health risks.[21]

At the Cabinet level, some officials voiced concerns about the TVPRA, particularly about the provision that allowed NGOs to train trafficking victims, who would in turn educate and train border personnel to identify new victims. In a letter to the House Committee on the Judiciary, officials at the Department of Justice stated that such a provision was "unnecessary and would potentially undermine the ability of Federal law enforcement to conduct border interdiction." In the department's view, border security and intelligence gathering were federal law enforcement functions. Officials also believed that monitoring border interdiction wasn't the best use of money, noting it was not always clear who at the border was a trafficking victim because "a victim must be destined for an exploitive labor or commercial sexual situation in order to have been trafficked." The agency also opposed the creation of a private right of action in federal court for trafficking victims. In the view of department officials, such a provision could be accomplished instead by making a small change in the RICO law, which already gave aggrieved persons the right to bring lawsuits.[22]

Despite such reservations, the TVPRA easily passed in the House of Representatives on November 5, 2003, and on December 10 in the Senate. The version that became law added a modification addressing justice department concerns about the private right of action, stating that any civil action "shall be stayed" during any criminal action arising out of the occurrence that served as the basis for the lawsuit. The bill became public law after President Bush signed it on December 19.[23]

As discussed, many of the TVPRA's provisions simply modified and extended provisions of the 2000 TVPA. But section 7, which required organizations to state that they do not "promote, support or advocate the legalization or practice of prostitution" in order to receive funding, created considerable controversy. In essence, the provision encapsulated the developing tensions between activists who believe that women have the right to choose to perform sex work and those who want to abolish prostitution.[24]

During the drafting of the 2000 U.N. trafficking protocol, certain feminist groups had pressured diplomats to include language that would prohibit prostitution. After a number of western governments threatened to withdraw support for the protocol if it took such an overt abolitionist stance, negotiators softened the final language to condemn only sex work that had been procured by force, fraud, or duress. But by 2003 some advocates had begun to push their abolitionist views in U.S. trafficking policies. In her April 2003 testimony before a subcommittee of the Senate Foreign Relations Committee, Donna Hughes, a professor of women's studies at the University of Rhode Island, declared that activists against the sexual abuse and exploitation of women and children were applauding the Bush administration's stance on prostitution. They were pleased, she said, "that it is now U.S. policy that prostitution and related activities are considered 'inherently harmful and dehumanizing' and are recognized as 'contributing to the phenomenon of trafficking in persons' and sex tourism." In her remarks Hughes quoted from a National Security Presidential Directive news release dated February 25, 2003. The language of that directive, she said, suggested a policy that was "especially crucial in fighting trafficking in women and children because over the past decade there have been attempts to de-link trafficking from prostitution, and even to legitimize prostitution as a form of work for women." Hughes believed that it was time to "relink" trafficking to prostitution and to analyze the harm of prostitution and its role in trafficking.[25]

But why "relink" trafficking and prostitution? In essence, some rationalized that, because the trafficking phenomenon involved women who had been forced, tricked, or intimidated into working as prostitutes, then combating and eventually eradicating prostitution would extinguish that variety of trafficking and thus reduce human trafficking in general. Yet why single out prostitution instead of, say, domestic, farm, or factory work, all of them settings for labor trafficking? The answer: abolitionists and certain feminists viewed prostitution as a special evil, a violation of women's rights, and by its nature an exploitation. Because prostitution involved sexual commerce, it was laden with enormous moral and religious implications, particularly for evangelical Christians, who saw it as sin.

Opposing such an absolutist view were groups that saw a difference between people who chose to perform sex work and those who were coerced into doing so.[26] But in 2003 the abolitionist view was gaining traction with the Bush administration, particularly among advocates such as Horowitz, Caulson, and influential White House advisors. The administration manifested its opinions in a number of ways. One was the tough language in the TVPRA's section 7; another was a similar prohibition required for funding of HIV/AIDS projects. U.S. officials also began advancing the position, both domestically and internationally, that prostitution was not a legitimate form of employment for any human being.[27]

In January 2004 the human rights group Global Rights: Partners for Peace analyzed section 7 and noted that, while the U.S. anti-trafficking law of 2000 didn't require NGOs to adopt any policy on prostitution, the TVPRA appeared to require groups to adopt a policy on sex work even if the entity didn't focus on the issue. This discrepancy confused NGOs because "they do not know how they can meet the U.S. requirements when their mission statements and policies do not include the goal of working on prostitution or adopting any policies on prostitution." In other words, human rights groups were worried that they might have to answer a U.S. demand for a prostitution policy even if they did not work on the subject.[28]

According to Ann Jordan, author of the Global Rights analysis, a November 4, 2003, colloquy between representatives Tom Lantos and Chris Smith, both of them TVPRA supporters in the House, offered some guidance. Lantos said that an organization would be in compliance with U.S. law if it stated "in a grant application or in a grant agreement or both that it does not promote, support, or advocate such action since it has no policy regarding this issue." Smith agreed with Lantos, adding, "It was also my understanding that an organization can satisfy the prohibition that the gentleman [Lantos] has referred to if it states in a grant application, a grant agreement, or both that it does not promote, support, or advocate such actions since it has no policy regarding this issue."[29]

According to the Global Rights interpretation, the Lantos-Smith exchange indicated the legislative intent that many types of groups would be able to receive U.S. funding without having to adopt a policy on prostitution: "Thus, an NGO working with children trafficked into forced labor in mines will not be required to adopt a policy on prostitution in order to receive U.S. money." The organization concluded that the Lantos-Smith interpretation of the section 7 restriction was "reasonable and logical."[30]

But in practice the issue of the prostitution pledge was not resolved so easily. By early 2005, the Bush administration began requiring U.S. groups seeking federal funding for their overseas AIDS programs to sign a pledge opposing prostitution. According to a letter from Congressman Henry A. Waxman to Attorney General Alberto Gonzales in April 2005, the requirement followed the Department of Justice's changed belief in the constitutionality of such a policy in AIDS and trafficking programs. The change, Waxman wrote, was revealed in September 2004 Department of Justice correspondence to the Department of Health and Human Services, which stated that government lawyers had initially believed that the TVPRA and the "AIDS Act" restrictions applied only to foreign organizations acting overseas. But they changed their minds, said Waxman, quoting from government letters, on the basis of precedents from two U.S. Supreme Court decisions—one in 1950, another in 1987.[31]

Waxman noted that those precedents (*South Dakota v. Dole* and *American Communications Association v. Douds*), were not "persuasive legal justification for the Justice Department's about-face." He said that many public health and social service advocates were worried that any policy condemning prostitution "will both increase stigma and make it harder to work effectively with the vulnerable populations they are trying to reach.[32]

Waxman was right: public health and human rights advocates on many levels were concerned. On May 18, 2005, scores of organizations around the world as well as individual academics, directors of faith-based programs, directors of AIDS programs, and physicians sent an open letter to President Bush criticizing and opposing the prostitution restrictions. According to the signatories, the legal restrictions were contrary to "best practices in public health and will undermine efforts to stem the spread of HIV and human trafficking." They also believed that requiring domestic groups with mixed government and private funding to adopt positions consistent with U.S. policy was tantamount to compelled speech and thus an unconstitutional condition on government funding. To "insure transparency in policy making," they asked the Department of Justice to reconsider its legal interpretations and the government to consult with a broad range of experts in the area of AIDS research and trafficking before issuing directives. The latter request was an apparent reference to the alleged influence of conservative religious groups on Bush administration policies concerning AIDS and trafficking.[33]

Despite an earlier belief that NGOs wouldn't be required to take a stand against prostitution in order to get federal funds, there were strong indications to the contrary. In late August 2005, DKT International, a Washington-based NGO that had been involved for fifteen years in overseas family planning work and HIV/AIDS prevention training, filed suit to stop the United States from enforcing the requirement that groups take a position explicitly opposing prostitution and sex trafficking in order to get government funding. As DKT stated in court papers filed in the federal district court for the District of Columbia, the requirement violated the organization's First Amendment rights. In a memorandum submitted in the case, a DKT official said the organization had never taken a position either supporting or opposing prostitution. It believed, however, that taking a position against prostitution would likely have the effect of stigmatizing many of the very people it was trying to help—that is, sex workers   and limiting DKT's access to a group of AIDS-vulnerable people.[34]

In its responsive legal papers, the U.S. Agency for International Development (USAID), which administered the funding in question, said that conditions of subsidies approved by Congress do not directly restrain speech and are not subject to strict scrutiny under the First Amendment. Under the U.S. Leadership against HIV/AIDS, Tuberculosis, and Malaria Act of 2003 (commonly known as the Leadership Act), any organization was free to make any statement or adopt any policy the First Amendment contemplated but not with government funds. Congress may impose restrictions designed to advance the overall policy goals of the United States, particularly in connection with attempts to fight the HIV/AIDS pandemic. The agency argued that, because Congress had concluded that prostitution and sex trafficking are "causes of and factors in the spread of the HIV/AIDS epidemic," eradication of those practices was necessary in any plan to fight those diseases.[35]

In reply, DTK said its legal action did not attempt to challenge the right of the federal government to attack HIV/AIDS, eliminate sex trafficking, or attempt to eradicate prostitution. The NGO acknowledged that the federal government has the ability under the law to make sure that federal funding is not used to advocate or support prostitution. Instead, DTK argued that the federal government cannot legally inhibit an organization's First Amendment rights or dictate what it does with private funding. DTK won a preliminary injunction in May 2006, and the battle was expected to result in continued legal action.[36]

The fight over prostitution as it related to sex trafficking and, by extension, HIV/AIDS programs, had become a moral battle. President Bush's position, enunciated in his National Security Presidential Directive, that prostitution was demeaning and dehumanizing was mirrored in the 2003 Leadership Act, which authorized spending 15 billion dollars worldwide to fight HIV/AIDS. The act stated that prostitution and sex trafficking contributed to the spread of HIV/AIDS and that Congress had found prostitution to be "degrading to women and children." Under the evolved standards of the Bush administration, prostitution could not be a job choice for women or even men. It had to be eradicated.

That stance was also embodied in a Department of State fact sheet dated November 24, 2004. Titled "The Link Between Prostitution and Sex Trafficking," the document stated that "where prostitution is legalized or tolerated, there is a greater demand for human trafficking victims and nearly always an increase in the number of women and children trafficked into commercial sex slavery." It also argued that legalized prostitution created a market for traffickers and that prostitution was inherently unsafe. "State attempts to regulate prostitution by introducing medical check-ups or licenses don't address the core problem: the routine abuse and violence that form the prostitution experience and brutally victimize those caught in its netherworld. Prostitution leaves women and children physically, mentally, emotionally, and spiritually devastated. Recovery takes years, even decades—often, the damage can never be undone."[37]

In April 2005, a group of human rights activists, lawyers, and researchers challenged the state department document. In an open letter to Ambassador Miller, the group said that the statements in the fact sheet made assertions of fact about prostitution and trafficking that were "unsupported or unproven by valid research methods and data." The writers were concerned that such statements might damage ongoing efforts to prevent trafficking and protect the rights of trafficked persons. In their view, the government's single-issue focus on prostitution rather than all forms of labor trafficking was skewing U.S. actions.[38]

Specifically, advocates challenged the statement that "80 percent of victims are women and 50 percent are children" as well as estimates claiming that 600,000 to 800,000 people are trafficked across international borders each year. According to these critics, in some countries no data exist on the trafficking of men because local definitions of trafficking deal only with women or sometimes only with women involved in prostitution. They also found no support for the assertion that "where prostitution is legalized or tolerated, there is a greater demand for human trafficking victims."[39]

In response, Miller agreed to disagree. He said it was obvious to his officials that, "as stated in the fact sheet, . . . prostitution 'fuels' the increase in sex trafficking. Where prostitution thrives, so does sex trafficking!" That belief underpinned the National Security Presidential Directive 22, which asserted that prostitution is connected to trafficking. While Miller cited no research linking trafficking and prostitution, he said that the fact sheet's estimates also appeared in a 2004 U.S. government report published according to TVPRA requirements; and he stood by its methodology. In Miller's opinion, critics risked ignoring the fact that people were being used and abused for prostitution. It would be wrong to wait for more studies before addressing their plight.[40]

Miller's letter squarely framed the administration's policy on prostitution: sex work caused sex trafficking; thus, eliminating one would eliminate the other. Abolitionists did not believe that most people chose prostitution of their own free will. Even if they did, the job was morally offensive, risky, and demeaning to women and children. This policy approach was a dramatic shift from the U.N. protocol's position, which did not condemn prostitution. Rather, it condemned the coercion or deceit used to inveigle and compel a person to do a job, which may or may not be prostitution.

U.S. officials, both publicly and privately, began turning to Sweden, which had taken an approach to the issue that Miller believed was "intriguing and worthy of close review."[41] According to Swedish policy, purchasing sex equaled male violence against women; there was no such thing as voluntary prostitution. Swedish authorities targeted the sex industry by criminalizing clients' purchase of sex.[42] By this logic, if attacks on consumers destabilized the sex market, then prostitution would dry up. U.S. officials promoted this policy in many forums. During a diplomatic reception in Bucharest, one official from the Department of State even told Iana Matei that the Swedish approach was useful.[43]

Norway's Ministry of Justice and Police compiled a comparison between Sweden's policy and that of the Netherlands, which allowed voluntary prostitution but prosecuted trafficking and child sex work. Published in December 2004, the study noted that "the social phenomenon that one dislikes and that [one] wants to do something about can be defined politically in different ways." The Swedish approach saw prostitution as an issue of gender *inequality*. The Dutch approach saw the "voluntary sale of sexual services . . . as a job of work"—in other words, as a matter of gender *equality*, as in equal rights to "good working conditions, safety and security." The report also pointed out that the Dutch penal code dealt with criminal activities such as trafficking, illegal immigrants, and minors who worked in prostitution.[44]

According to the Norwegian study, Swedes widely supported the law against the purchase of sex, citing a 2001 poll in which 81 percent of respondents viewed it favorably. But while the law was in effect, there were problems with enforcement, both practically and legally. Because of shrinking funds, Swedish police had reduced their focus on sex clients in favor of people involved in human trafficking. One police official cited in the report said that investigative agencies had to prioritize resources and thus could not concentrate on the purchase of sex, an activity that was more or less equivalent to petty theft.[45]

The enforcement that did take place focused on street prostitution, obviously the easiest realm to target; Norwegian researchers found no evidence that anyone working on the "indoor market" had been charged. Legal issues had also arisen, stemming from "unclear wording" in legal texts and strict rules of evidence. As the study noted, "if both parties deny everything, then a great deal will be needed to show that a deal has been made and that sexual service [has] been given." In other words, from an evidentiary point of view, unless the prostitute and the client were caught in the act and the entire transaction recorded, prosecutors would have difficulty making a case.[46]

In contrast, as the Norwegian inquiry found, the Dutch decriminalization of prostitution made its regulation a municipal administrative matter, with licensing requirements and mandated health checkups for sex workers. Some sex clients agreed so thoroughly with the legalization regime that they were alerting police to any suspicions of human trafficking or child prostitution.[47]

How effective was the Swedish law? Had it reduced prostitution and changed Swedish attitudes about the purchase of sex? The Norwegian study found that enforcement of the statute "had not achieved all its intended effects" and that the law was weakly enforced. While street prostitution was reduced by 41 percent in some areas, authorities had no idea about how much of the sex trade had moved indoors, a change made easier by Internet and cell phone access. Police in Sweden told the researchers that they were having difficulty investigating cases of human trafficking because prostitution was no longer openly practiced on the streets.[48]

In regard to its influence on attitudes about prostitution, however, the Swedish law was successful. The Norwegian study cited the finding that 81 percent of the public was "positive towards the law." But even that finding was ambiguous. Do those results mean that the public agreed with the enforcement potential of the law? Or with the normative aspect? In the Netherlands the legalization process had not been uniformly successful because of differences in relationships between brothel owners and the municipalities. But in the words of the study, "our impression is that what the municipalities have offered in the way of health, safety, fire provisions etc. have worked well in relation to the prostitutes."[49]

The Norwegian study made an interesting finding about the effect of legalization on human trafficking, which policymakers elsewhere could certainly take into account. Under the Dutch scheme, brothels must prove that employees have work or residence permits and are not there under coercive conditions.

Thus, the sex establishments "serve as a brake on illegal prostitution." According to the researchers, sex workers in legal prostitution zones often reported underage women to police or social workers. So, while critics such as Ambassador Miller believe that prostitution and human trafficking have a cause-and-effect relationship, the Norwegian study indicates that legal prostitution may actually work against trafficking.[50]

In 2005, abolitionist tendencies among U.S. policymakers influenced federal legislative proposals that attempted to emulate the Swedish initiative. The proposals, presented in both the Senate and the House, targeted a reduction in the demand for commercial sex in an effort to stem human trafficking. Senator John Cornyn of Texas, a key supporter of President Bush and a Republican member of the Senate Judiciary Committee, introduced the Senate version on April 28, 2005.[51] On the same day, Representative Deborah Pryce of Ohio introduced a companions bill in the House.

Essentially, the proposals asked the federal government, through the Department of Justice, to award 45 million dollars between 2005 and 2007 in grants to "states and their political subdivisions to establish model law enforcement programs that promote the effective prosecution of purchasers, exploiters, and sex traffickers and to assist victims of a commercial sex act." As mentioned, the aim was to reduce demand for commercial sex and thus the demand for prostitutes, thereby reducing sex trafficking.[52] But just how many prostitutes in the United States have been trafficked? As I've made clear throughout this book, some of them are indeed trafficking victims. But anecdotal evidence suggests that, among sex workers, their number is relatively small. In an interview, a representative of the Urban Justice Center in New York City told me that fewer than 25 percent of the immigrant women served by the center's sex workers project fit the criteria for being labeled a trafficked person.[53]

Apparently, abolitionists also don't take into account the stratification that exists in the sex industry. At one end are street and indoor prostitutes, who may or may not be trafficked and who offer relatively low-priced sexual services. When anti-trafficking advocates describe "trafficking victims," they often refer to these particular sex workers. But at the other end of the spectrum are international call girls, often high-priced fashion models and pornographic film stars who work on a global circuit with women from many countries. In this segment of the business, a individual can earn 50,000 dollars plus expenses for a weekend of sex work in a major city such as New York. This was true for several women who worked for a Manhattan-based business run by a Ukrainian immigrant woman convicted in 2005 in a federal prostitution investigation involving the Mann Act.[54] Are such high-priced women prostitutes? Yes. Can they be considered trafficked persons under the law? No. Are they victims of exploitation? When they look at their bank balances, they most likely don't consider such a question.

Supporters of the sex demand legislation either missed or ignored those nuances. They justified the bills' passage by relying on statements from Miller's TIP Office asserting that "prostitution and related activities, including pimping and patronizing or maintaining brothels, fuel the growth of modern-day slavery by providing a facade behind which sex traffickers operate."[55] The preamble to the legislation also harkened back to President Bush's National Security Presidential Directive 22, which stated that prostitution was dehumanizing and contributed to the trafficking phenomenon.[56] The sex purchaser bills were referred to individual judiciary committees in both houses of Congress. Although they cited as support those controversial TIP Office assertions that had been criticized for having no basis in research, they clearly garnered interest in Congress. Senator Cornyn submitted several letters to the Senate from various religious groups and supporters, including some who worked with sexually exploited children, all of whom agreed that cutting demand for prostitution would reduce sex trafficking.[57]

Nevertheless, some organizations that worked with trafficking victims were concerned about features in the bills. In an open letter to Representative Pryce, they pointed out that statements in the preamble were unsupported or unproven by valid research methods: "We are deeply concerned that Congress might pass this legislation based on inaccuracies that do not reflect the true experience of trafficked persons in the United States." They were also dismayed that two-thirds of the proposed funding was docketed for law enforcement activity and only one-third for services aimed at preventing people from being trafficked or involved in the "unlawful commercial sex sector." Critics found the bills' language unclear; terms such as "commercial sexual activities" were undefined, and there were no criteria for determining which NGOs would be "qualified" to receive funding. These critics believed that NGOs should compete for funding based on expertise. This last point reflected a concern among some human rights experts and NGOs that funding under the TVPA and TVPRA was being disbursed to groups that supported the Bush administration's view of trafficking and prostitution.[58]

The federal government had thrown its weight behind an abolitionist stance in hopes of reducing one form of human trafficking. This simplistic approach is reminiscent of the way in which Prohibitionists advanced a ban on alcoholic beverages as a way to cure social ills, a notion that culminated in the 1920 Volstead Act enforcing the Eighteenth Amendment.[59] The Bush administration believed that eradicating prostitution would stop the evil of sex trafficking—though it would have no effect on other forms of trafficking.

In January 2006, the commercial sex legislation became the law of the land; but its effects, as shown by its modest authorization proposal of 45 million dollars over two years, will necessarily be mostly symbolic, aimed at influencing public attitudes about prostitution. In most states prostitution and related offenses such as solicitation are already a crime. Enforcement of those laws is by and large a local law enforcement priority that must compete with high-profile issues such as terrorism, narcotics, and serious felonies. Even if all of the proposed funding is authorized, it will be unlikely to significantly affect U.S. prostitution.

Chapter 11   The Bully Pulpit

THROUGHOUT ITS HISTORY the United States has not been shy about behaving like a moral leader and using its clout and dollars to set an agenda. After passing the TVPA, the U.S. government used its bully pulpit to influence other nations' efforts at dealing appropriately with trafficking. The U.N. protocol included provisions requiring signatory countries to pass domestic trafficking laws. But while the language of some of its provisions was mandatory (particularly those dealing with assistance to victims), others had what Ann Jordan of the Washington-based NGO Global Rights called "weaker terms, such as 'in appropriate cases' and 'to the extent possible.'"[1]

The American legislation was designed as an incentive for other nations. It had an interrelated system of minimum standards, reviews of compliance with those standards, and a framework of possible sanctions for any nation that failed to measure up. Section 108 of the TVPA outlined its minimum standards and applied specific terms to nations with a "significant number of victims of severe forms of trafficking." The TVPA had three key expectations: countries should prohibit severe forms of trafficking; such acts should be appropriately punished under the law; and countries should make serious, sustained efforts to eliminate severe forms of trafficking. Section 108 also listed a number of indicators for the U.S. government to use when determining whether or not a country was doing enough to eliminate trafficking. Among the criteria were vigorous prosecution of offenders, extradition of suspects when appropriate, protection of victims, education of the public and potential victims, cooperation with international efforts to stop trafficking, and prosecution of public officials who participate or facilitate trafficking.

In a major reporting provision, section 110 required the secretary of state to prepare and distribute to Congress an annual report on trafficking that listed countries and whether or not they were meeting the minimum standards set forth in section 108. This report was controversial because some poorly ranked countries were U.S. allies and protested their characterization. Moreover, a poor ranking could lead the president to decide to wield the Big Stick—that is, to withhold certain kinds of non-humanitarian aid and assistance.

The first trafficking report was compiled in 2001 and released in July— about five weeks later than planned, primarily because the state department had never done such a project before and had dedicated too few people to it. Relying on input from U.S. embassy staffs around the world, the department reviewed data to see if countries had enough trafficking victims to merit inclusion in the report. For the most part, embassy staff had to rely on law enforcement intelligence gleaned from foreign government reports and liaison officers. Only countries with cases "in the hundreds or higher" were included.[2]

American officials admitted that, in some countries, official corruption and complicity might hide trafficking cases and keep them underreported. Nevertheless, countries with a clear record of numerous incidents were ranked according to a tier system. Tier 1 countries had "fully complied" with the TVPA's minimum standards for eliminating trafficking. Tier 2 nations didn't fully meet the minimum standards but were making "significant efforts to bring themselves into compliance." Tier 3 countries weren't in compliance with the standards and weren't making any effort to comply.

In the 2001 report, the tier 1 list included twelve countries: Austria, Belgium, Canada, Colombia, Germany, Hong Kong, Italy, the Netherlands, Spain, Switzerland, Taiwan, and the United Kingdom. All were U.S. allies and were either places where trafficking victims had originated (such Colombia, Taiwan, and Hong Kong) or destinations for them.[3]

Tier 2, which was by far the largest list, contained forty-seven countries from all over the world, representing Asia, Latin America, Europe, and Africa. As articulated in the TVPA, this ranking meant that, while the countries didn't comply with U.S. minimum standards, they were "making significant efforts" to do so. The report noted, "Some are strong in the prosecution of traffickers, but provide little or no assistance to victims. Others work to assist victims and punish traffickers, but have not yet taken any significant steps to prevent trafficking." And some were just beginning to address trafficking but had taken key steps.[4]

Notable among the tier 2 countries were several Balkan states. Although the region was an important source of trafficking victims as well as a transit zone and a final destination, some countries had made significant strides. One was Moldova, a source country; others were notorious destination zones such as Macedonia and Bulgaria. African nations such as Ghana, Sierra Leone,

South Africa, and Uganda had large pools of economic migrants whom traffickers could easily exploit; yet the state department believed these countries
were making noteworthy efforts to stop such practices.[5]

Twenty-three nations were listed in tier 3, and more than a half-dozen
were significant U.S. allies: Greece, Israel, Romania, Saudi Arabia, South
Korea, Turkey, and the United Arab Emirates. In addition to Romania, other
Eastern European nations also made the list, among them Albania, Belarus,
Bosnia-Herzegovina, and Russia.[6] The rationale for the tier 3 rank centered, in
some cases, on the lack of specific anti-trafficking laws and, in others, a failure
to enforce laws that did exist. Regarding some countries, the state department
report noted the existence of corruption and the involvement of government
officials and police in trafficking. Where authorities were able to enforce labor
laws, prostitution laws, or other measures that indirectly attacked trafficking,
the victims either were deported or did not receive any assistance.

A number of nations, including South Korea, Israel, and Saudi Arabia,
complained publicly about their tier 3 rank. Although the full report received
extensive news coverage, some human rights activists criticized it as a mixed
bag. For example, some believed that the report concentrated on sex trafficking but not on other forms of forced labor. Others pointed out that it failed to
include certain countries. Human Rights Watch, for example, believed that Costa
Rica, Japan, Moldova, and Nigeria should have received tier 3 rankings.[7]

Yet the report's existence showed that the United States was committed
to dealing with trafficking as Congress had intended when it passed the TVPA.
According to the report, evidence showed "that most government are in fact
taking steps to curb this horrific practice, and to help the hundreds of thousands of men, women, and children who are its victims."[8] The tier listings
were not intended to criticize or penalize countries but to mobilize international efforts to deal with the problem.

With a year's experience behind them, officials at the state department
published a second report on June 5, 2002, virtually on time. They included
eighty-nine countries, up from eighty-two in 2001. The new report's overview
reprinted its 2001 estimates of both worldwide trafficking (700,000 to 4 million people) and the number trafficked to the United States (50,000 people, a
figure dating from 1997).[9]

The report noted that, in addition to disseminating these country rankings, the U.S. government had enhanced its own efforts to monitor and combat trafficking. One notable step was the creation of the President's Interagency
Task Force to Monitor and Combat Trafficking in Persons, a body chaired by
the secretary of state and made up of several cabinet-level officials, including
the attorney general, as well as the director of the Office of Management and

Budget. The government had also supported more than one hundred anti-trafficking programs in nearly fifty countries to help tier 2 and 3 countries improve their standings.[10]

The 2002 report listed eighteen tier 1 countries, up from twelve in 2001. A noteworthy addition was South Korea, which had moved up from tier 3. Poland, Macedonia, Lithuania, France, and the Czech Republic had all moved up from tier 2. According to U.S. officials, South Korea's standing increased dramatically because it had set up a trafficking task force, coordinated more than 1,000 prosecutions of traffickers, took active steps to protect victims, and carried out a wide public education campaign. In 2001, Seoul officials had complained about its tier 3 rank, arguing that the country was just beginning to implement its anti-trafficking programs. By 2002, South Korea's significant elevation in status showed that the trafficking report had been an incentive for action.

The tier 2 level in the second report included fifty-three countries, up from forty-seven in 2001. Albania, Romania, and the Federal Republic of Yugoslavia all rose from tier 3. Romania, for example, had passed an anti-trafficking law in December 2001, coordinated investigations (through SECI) with other countries, and allocated shelter space for trafficking victims. Although Yugoslavia still didn't have a specific anti-trafficking law, it was prosecuting suspects under various kidnapping, slavery, and prostitution laws; and its federal government had set up a special board to coordinate trafficking policy. One of the republic's states, Montenegro, was an intelligence clearing-house for Kosovo (which is under U.N. administration) and Albania. Albania itself moved up to tier 2 because of its efforts to prosecute traffickers. While the report noted that Albanian prosecutors had a relatively low conviction rate for trafficking arrests (just 13 percent) because of a lack of evidence and allegations of police corruption, police no longer viewed trafficking victims as criminals but referred them to NGOs and other agencies for help.

In 2002, nineteen countries received tier 3 rankings, down from twenty-three in 2001. Nevertheless, several key U.S. allies maintained their low status: Saudi Arabia, Turkey, the United Arab Emirates, Greece, Bahrain, and Russia. Russia's problem was its lack of an anti-trafficking law, although its national legislature (the Duma) had asked for U.S. help in drafting one. Police rarely arrested traffickers under available laws and had received no training on trafficking issues. Saudi Arabia had apparently made minimal efforts to deal with trafficking, instead referring such problems to labor courts. Greece had no anti-trafficking law, which made prosecutions difficult and kept penalties minimal. Greek officials had changed policies to allow trafficking victims to remain in the country; but the government did not have shelters to help them, and

NGOs had limited capabilities. Turkey also had no trafficking law, although it was developing one, and did not offer assistance to victims. Turkish officials often detained and deported trafficking victims but sometimes allowed them to remain in the country for investigations.

Like the 2001 report, the 2002 document drew criticism in the United States, primarily from conservative religious elements who disagreed with the tier 1 rankings of some western countries. Among the most critical was Concerned Women for America (CWA), a political action group that defined itself as a public policy women's organization that tried to bring biblical principles into American public policy. According to the CWA, the 2002 report was a "severe disappointment to many activist groups" that had worked to pass the TVPA in 2000. Its main criticism was that the United States had given tier 1 status to Germany and the Netherlands, "two countries that have recently legalized prostitution, increasing the demand for women and child prostitutes." Without revealing its source of information, the CWA asserted that "sex trafficking is a major means of supplying women and child prostitutes" to work in legal brothels in these countries. The group cited statistics claiming that, in Germany, 75 percent of the estimated 400,000 women prostitutes were foreign and, in the Netherlands, there were between 4,000 and 15,000 child prostitutes. Even without documentary support, the implication was clear: legal prostitution caused sex trafficking of women and children. The CWA also criticized the 2002 repetition of certain tier 2 rankings. According to the group, if those tier 2 countries had done nothing to improve their anti-trafficking efforts, they should have been bumped down to tier 3. The CWA was particularly critical of the tier 2 status of India, Nepal, Thailand, and Vietnam, saying that such a rank was equivalent to a "passing grade" from the state department.[11]

With staff at the state department's TIP Office now dedicated to report preparation and data collection, the 2003 version was a professional-looking document with color pictures and sections that went beyond tier rankings and country narratives. The report listed a total of twenty-six nations in tier 1, up from eighteen. Tier 2 countries expanded from fifty-three to seventy-five, and tier 3 countries decreased from nineteen to fifteen.[12]

Under the TVPA, countries listed in tier 3 in 2003 risked being denied certain kinds of non-humanitarian aid in fiscal year 2004 (which began on October 1, 2003). Thus, the 2003 report had the distinction of being the administration's source of information when deciding which nations might lose U.S. aid. Ostensibly, all fifteen countries ranked as tier 3 qualified for those sanctions. But as I will discuss, the government gave several last-minute reprieves that raised questions about whether or not Washington was playing politics.

Notable changes were the United Arab Emirates' move from tier 3 to tier 1 and Canada's relegation from tier 1 to tier 2. According to the report, the United Arab Emirates had taken assertive steps to deal with a specific child trafficking problem: coercing children to work as camel jockeys, a form of labor abuse. Among those steps were criminalization of the use of child jockeys and DNA testing to ascertain the parentage of children used in such labor. Country officials also implemented victim-friendly policies such as a refusal to deport trafficking victims and the establishment of crime-victims' programs pertinent to trafficking. The country also reached out to foreign embassies and NGOs to assist victims.

The report criticized Canada for uneven enforcement of its trafficking laws and the practice of deporting victims, which undercut efforts to carry out prosecutions. Although Canadian law allowed some trafficking victims to apply for refugee status, the government in fact often deported them. When I compared the 2002 and 2003 narratives' for Canada, I found them to be similar. Apparently, the Department of State had subjective reasons for giving Canada a lower rank in 2003.

In 2003, Saudi Arabia, Qatar, Russia, Lebanon, Indonesia, and Tajikistan all moved up to tier 2. According to the report, while these countries did not yet fully comply with U.S. minimum standards, each seemed determined to make significant efforts to comply. But other countries dropped from tier 2 to tier 3—notably, the Dominican Republic and Georgia. The report said that new information had allowed state department analysts to make more refined assessments about the nations' lack of compliance.

On September 9, 2003, about three months after the report's release, President Bush released a memorandum in which he justified aid sanctions against certain tier 3 nations while rationalizing his decision to avoid similar actions against others. Five nations would not receive U.S. non-humanitarian funding: Burma, Cuba, Liberia, North Korea, and Sudan. But ten countries would qualify for aid because, as the president explained, they had made last minute-adjustments in trafficking policies: Belize, Bosnia-Herzegovina, the Dominican Republic, Georgia, Greece, Haiti, Kazakhstan, Suriname, Turkey, and Uzbekistan.[13]

Of the five sanctioned countries, Cuba, North Korea, and Burma were not receiving any direct U.S. aid anyway; so they lost nothing. The Bush determination allowed the flow of money to NGOs to continue in those countries. In the case of Sudan and Liberia, U.S. concerns stemmed from ongoing civil wars. But in both countries peace negotiations (which had taken place after the report's release) gave Washington grounds for optimism that responsible governments might emerge. While sanctions would prevent Sudanese and Liberian government officials from participating in U.S.-funded educational and cultural exchange programs, the United States would still support programs intended to implement effective governance.[14]

If the 2003 report was the first to involve sanctions, the 2004 report was the first to include a watch list—a form of probationary status added during a legislative retuning of the TVPA. Countries in this new category had tier 2 status, but state department officials could not find evidence of any increasing effort to address trafficking issues. At first glance, such an assessment seems contradictory: if a nation is making significant efforts to combat trafficking, how can it not be increasing its efforts? But the watch list rank was meant to be a signal, reminding countries that they were in danger of slipping down to tier 3 if they did not show progress.[15]

The 2004 report ranked the anti-trafficking efforts of 127 countries. Twenty-five were ranked as tier 1, fifty-four as tier 2, forty-two as tier 2 watch list, and ten as tier 3. According to the state department, Canada was reclassified as tier 1 based on a higher level of government coordination and reportage on its anti-trafficking policy. Senior Canadian officials spoke out more often on the issue, the country had devoted additional resources to border control, and the Royal Canadian Mounted Police had created an anti-trafficking task force.

In 2003, fifteen nations had received tier 3 ranking, thus facing the threat of losing aid unless they showed improvement. With the new watch list category, state department analysts now had a way to help nations avoid the stigma and possible financial penalties associated with tier 3 status. The following U.S. allies now appeared on the watch list: Belize, Georgia, Greece, Suriname, the Dominican Republic, Kazakhstan, and Turkey. Bosnia-Herzegovina and Uzbekistan, both ranked as tier 3 in 2003, improved to tier 2.

The 2004 report gave tier 3 rankings to nominal U.S. allies Venezuela and Ecuador along with North Korea and Cuba. U.S. analysts found that Ecuador's law enforcement agencies had failed to make significant efforts to directly combat trafficking in 2003; in addition, the country lacked an anti-trafficking law enforcement strategy and had not conducted any arrests, prosecutions, or sentencing of traffickers. Venezuela's political situation had prevented the government from devoting serious attention or resources to trafficking in persons, which was a growing regional problem. The government also had no anti-trafficking law enforcement and no victim-protection policy.

The 2004 report drew some complaints. Countries such as the Philippines and Greece, which had received watch list status, said the U.S. government had not adequately taken into account efforts such as the passage of new laws and (in Greece's case) disbursement of funding to NGOs.[16]

But at a press briefing on June 4, 2004, TIP Office head John Miller said the country reports were prodding governments to do something about the trafficking problem: "For example, 24 countries this past year have new, comprehensive anti-trafficking laws. There have been almost 8,000 prosecutions of traffickers worldwide and almost 3,000 convictions." He mentioned that, from the United Kingdom to Macedonia, governments had jailed major organized crime figures associated with human trafficking.[17]

By this time, the state department's trafficking reports had become glossy, high-quality documents with plenty of photographs and graphics. But as some critics noted, they seemed to dwell on sex rather than labor trafficking cases. In response, the TIP Office adjusted the 2005 report to show a noticeable increase in the mention of labor trafficking cases, including those in Thailand's fishing industry and those involving young boys used as camel jockeys in the Middle East. According to the report, the Department of State intended to focus more attention on "involuntary servitude and its related manifestations." And for the first time, a nation's failure to address trafficking for forced labor would earn it a tier 3 rating.

With the release of the June 2005 report, the TIP Office had issued a total of five trafficking reports. The nations covered in the assessments had increased from 82 in 2001 to 142 in 2005, a jump of 73 percent made possible by the ability of the state department's staff as well as U.S. embassy and law enforcement personnel to gather useful data. Despite their polished surface, the documents were sometimes skimpy on details. Nevertheless, they came to serve an important carrot-and-stick role in U.S. foreign policy on trafficking: positive reinforcement for countries whose anti-trafficking efforts met U.S. standards, and source of embarrassment for those who didn't measure up. Sanctions were the ultimate penalty but, as I've noted, were rarely imposed. By September 2005, it seemed clear that Washington would always find a way to keep tier 3 nations from suffering aid cuts, as long as those countries weren't otherwise considered outlaw nations.

Although the TIP reports did indeed spur governments to take action on trafficking, experts sensed that some of those actions were hastily conceived and poorly executed. At a Council on Foreign Relations' symposium on trafficking, held in New York in May 2006, Joyti Sanghera, an advisor on trafficking for the U.N. Office of the High Commission for Human Rights, said that draconian laws rushed into force to counter poor TIP ratings are actually counterproductive in terms of punishing traffickers: "In some countries the punitive measures in their legislation for trafficking have been hiked up to life imprisonment and sometimes even to capital punishment. This has led the criminal justice system in those countries—and I would mention Bangladesh as one of those—to be reticent in meting out such harsh punishments because the evidentiary processes are weak and trafficking is a very hard crime to . . . lay charges on. Evidence is very, very difficult to correct." According to Sanghera, the result may be few prosecuted cases, which may send the message that a country has no serious enforcement of trafficking laws. She also pointed out an opposite reaction: zeal to counter U.S. criticism may lead some nations to imprison people without adequate investigation of their alleged offenses. In addition, tougher border restrictions can actually have the effect of driving would-be migrants to use the services of smugglers and trafficker. "If there's one thing we do know," Sanghera said, "that is that while opening up borders may not address the problem of trafficking, closing borders also does not address the problem of trafficking, in fact, it might contribute to it."[18]

Critics were also concerned that foreign governments, sometimes in response to the U.S. tier system, were primarily focusing on law enforcement and the criminalization of trafficking rather than the needs of victims. As Ann Jordan explained at the May 2006 symposium, "so many governments think if they pass a law to criminalize, then that's all they need to do. And there is no safety, no protections for victims." Jordan, who has traveled extensively to study trafficking policies, also believed that hastily drafted laws do not give prosecutors much guidance about what constitutes a trafficking offense. These same countries may also see victims as disposable and thus not give them safety nets that will help them take control of their lives and live without fear.[19]

But not every nation has the capability to develop safety nets or victims' programs. Although appropriating tens of millions of dollars to help victims is small change in the United States, other countries are not as fiscally blessed. Several representatives of foreign NGOs pointed out this discrepancy to me during a 2005 briefing in New York held under the auspices of the Department of State. According to the foreign visitors, countries such as Indonesia, Pakistan, and Malaysia feel the tier system forces them to initiate programs that they simply can't afford or implement. In this sense, U.S. bullying has been counterproductive.

Another problem has confronted countries who may want to meet U.S. standards: they lack the necessary political will power or legislative mechanisms. This difficulty was underscored in 2005 when a U.N. diplomatic body known as the Conference of the Parties assessed how well the world community had complied with the letter and the spirit of the 2000 protocol on human trafficking. The assessment relied on answers to detailed questionnaires that the Conference sent to governments that had signed the protocol, had adopted it through legislation, or hadn't signed it but were interested in doing so at some point.[20]

About 43 percent of the countries that had signed the protocol responded to the questionnaire. In the main their responses showed that most had some legislation that covered the offense of human trafficking. But a number had inconsistent laws, and details of the statutes varied from nation to nation. At least two countries, Mauritania and Jamaica, reported they didn't have any laws dealing with trafficking, with Jamaica claiming that trafficking didn't exist within its borders. Specifically, however, the Conference report revealed that some countries were hampered by systemic political problems that prevented the passage of laws conforming to the protocol. These issues included government administrative problems, lack of experienced government staff, and lack of any commitment to deal with trafficking. Some countries also said they needed a great deal of technical assistance for every aspect of compliance—from actually drafting legislation to training law enforcement personnel, judges, and victim-protection specialists. As the report clearly indicated, while most states had undertaken action to conform to the protocol, a number needed a great deal of help, particularly "developing countries and countries with economies in transition," to build the capacity to strengthen their anti-trafficking laws and programs.[21] In so many words, the Conference was mirroring the concerns that NGOs had voiced: their countries were unable, in the face of U.S. approbation, to quickly create credible responses to trafficking.

Chapter 12   Measuring Effectiveness

SINCE PASSAGE OF THE TVPA, the federal government has spent tens of millions of dollars on various anti-trafficking programs, commenced scores of criminal prosecutions, and undertaken numerous international initiatives. How effective have these actions been? As I will show, this question is not easy to answer.

Because it spells out the components of U.S. trafficking policy, the TVPA can also frame an analysis of that policy. The Clinton administration had designed its original policy around the Three Ps: prosecution, protection, and prevention. The Bush administration essentially stayed with those ideals, fitting its abolitionist aims into the prevention category.

Of the Three Ps, prosecution results are easiest to quantify because the federal government keeps extensive records of the Department of Justice's criminal case load and regularly makes them available to the public. Researchers can ascertain prosecution outcomes and analyze results using criteria such as conviction rates and sentencing. Protection and prevention are more difficult to measure, however, because they deal abstractly with criminal conduct. It's easy to say that granting T-visas and other federal benefits protects victims from both traffickers and the circumstances that initially led them to migrate illegally. But what about undiscovered victims? What protection have they received? And how many prospective victims exist who have not been protected?

The prevention category has similar problems of measurement and assessment. Trafficking thrives in a conspiratorial and secret world. This creates two related problems involving measurement of conduct. First, how do we measure conduct that has occurred? Second, how do we measure conduct that has been prevented by various government strategies? In both cases it is nearly impossible to establish baselines from which to begin measuring.

Because the TVPA calls for the establishment of certain government programs and practices, it is easy to see whether or not the government has undertaken actions to meet those requirements. Federal agencies have increased their volume of reporting on such programs, which has made it simpler to analyze the effects of U.S. policy on human trafficking. Not only does the bill require the Department of State to produce its annual country reports, but it also mandates the government to assess its own prosecution, protection, and prevention work. Currently, various cabinet agencies have produced three years' worth of assessments on U.S. government anti-trafficking activities, covering the period between 2003 and 2005. But such self-analysis has an inherent problem: how well can any executive branch objectively and fairly appraise its own actions? As of this writing, no independent agency has undertaken any analysis of the subject, other than the Government Accountability Office (GAO)'s projected 2006 report on the federal government's response to trafficking and small notices in audits of other activities.[1]

Although existing government reports on domestic activity remain useful for analysis, especially in terms of factual material, they have their weaknesses. We know, for instance, that the government has successfully prosecuted traffickers and protected victims. But have its policies and practices done anything to deter trafficking? The criminal cases prosecuted thus far indicate that sex trafficking continues to exist. But the government's emphasis on sex cases obscures the fact that labor cases may be just as rampant, and its continued focus on sex trafficking and the abolition of prostitution has become divisive.

Using federal fiscal years (which begin on October 1) as its relevant reporting periods, the government has documented a steady rise in trafficking investigations and indictments since the TVPA's passage: federal prosecutors have initiated more investigations, charged more defendants, and reported more total convictions. These statistics include cases prosecuted under both the TVPA and other relevant federal statutes (see table 12.1).

As I have noted, most of these cases involve sex trafficking: between fiscal years 2003 and 2004, there was a notable increase in investigations started, cases filed, and defendants charged. At the time, fourteen key FBI field offices were focusing on the problem of forced prostitution of children, which partly explains the increase.[2] Unfortunately, we cannot calculate an accurate conviction rate from the statistics because cases indicted in one fiscal year may not be resolved in the same year. In other words, there is no correlation between raw indictment numbers reported in one year and the conviction numbers reported in that same year.

Table 12.1
Number of Trafficking Investigations and Prosecutions, Fiscal Years
2001–2004

	2001	*2002*	*2003*	*2004*
Investigations started	63	65	82	130
Criminal cases filed				
Total	10	10	13	29
Sex cases	4	7	10	26
Defendants charged				
Total	38	41	32	59
Sex cases	26	27	26	52
Convictions				
Total	23	28	26	43
Sex cases	15	23	21	40

SOURCE: U.S. Department of Justice, "Report to Congress from Attorney General Alberto R. Gonzalez on U.S. Government Effort to Combat Trafficking in Persons in Fiscal Year 2004," July 2005.

Though the numbers of prosecutions have risen since enactment of the TVPA, trafficking cases represent only a small percentage of the total criminal investigative workload dealing with immigration. In a May 2005 audit report, the GAO studied federal alien smuggling operations, focusing on investigative efforts in fiscal year 2004 and part of fiscal year 2005. It determined that, for the new federal Bureau of Immigration and Customs Enforcement (ICE), human trafficking was one element within a broad area of concentration. Reviewing ICE's 10 million investigative hours spent on various enforcement programs, the GAO found that the agency had spent 71 percent of its time on drug, financial, and criminal alien investigations and related probes. Alien smuggling encompassed 7 percent of its time—that is, nearly 715,000 hours of investigative work. Human trafficking accounted for just 2 percent, or about 200,000 hours. The GAO voiced no opinion on whether or not the amount of time spent on human smuggling was sufficient.[3] But the percentage split showed that, in the post–September 11 environment, law enforcement had many competing, pressing, and more politically popular areas of concern, including terrorism, the activity of drug cartels, and illegal immigration generally.

Sentencing is a critical component of any criminal justice strategy. But because of how federal court statistics are compiled, it is impossible to determine average or median sentences in all trafficking prosecutions because cases that commence as trafficking prosecutions may wind up with convictions for nontrafficking offenses. Thus, researchers cannot use court data bases to compare case outcomes meaningfully. But according to a 2005 Department of Justice report, among fourteen defendants sentenced for trafficking crimes in fiscal year 2004, the average term was eighty-six months in prison.[4] This was a sharp decrease from an average of 127 months in prison for ten defendants sentenced in fiscal year 2003.[5] Does the change mean that courts are taking trafficking less seriously? Not necessarily. First, in situations involving small numbers of cases, using an average sentence as a benchmark means that the final number can change dramatically in response to an unusually high or low sentence. Analysts could iron out such swings by using the median sentence as a basis for comparison. Second, there is no way of telling if or how the defendants sentenced in fiscal year 2003 differed from those sentenced in fiscal year 2004 in terms of criminal history and other variables.

Fortunately, there is a way to assess federal investigative work that doesn't rely on the limited reporting data in the Department of Justice reports: the Transactional Records Access Clearinghouse, which I've already discussed in this book. I used TRAC data to analyze how federal criminal laws were applied to human trafficking offenses between fiscal years 2000 and 2004, a total of five fiscal years. For certain offenses I also analyzed data from the first eleven months of fiscal year 2005. But before discussing the results, I want to offer a couple of caveats. First, primarily for security reasons, federal agencies have withheld a small fraction of data from TRAC. As a result, some information about criminal matters is not included in what TRAC receives for analysis. Second, because my subject is human trafficking, I used the TVPA as my basic framework for analysis. But although the TVPA developed some new criminal categories and revised other definitions, the statute is not the only way in which prosecutors can attack the offense. They have the option of bringing cases under the Mann Act (interstate transportation for prostitution) as well as laws covering foreign transportation for prostitution, kidnapping, alien smuggling, harboring of aliens, use of false documents for immigration, money laundering, and conspiracy. The TVPA is broken into discrete sections that relate to defined trafficking and sex trafficking offenses, making it easy to analyze data by referring to those particular sections. Analysis is less simple with other statutes because they can apply to circumstances that don't fit the definition of trafficking. For example, money laundering offenses can involve drug trafficking, alien smuggling, and racketeering offenses such as extortion—none of which necessarily involves human trafficking. So without knowing the factual details of an individual case of money laundering or alien smuggling, a researcher can't tell if trafficking was involved. Therefore, I did not use data from those cases even though people involved in trafficking were prosecuted.

Given the limitations just discussed, I used TRAC data to analyze trafficking cases, relying on the following sections of the U.S. criminal code as outlined in the TVPA:

- 18 U.S.C. 1584 (sale into involuntary servitude)
- 18 U.S.C. 1989 (forced labor)
- 18 U.S.C. 1590 (trafficking with respect to peonage, slavery, forced labor)
- 18 U.S. C. 1591 (sex trafficking of children, or by force, fraud, or coercion)

My analysis also included the Mann Act—specifically, 18 U.S.C. 2421 (interstate transportation for prostitution) and 18 U.S.C. 2422 (coercion and enticement to travel for prostitution)—which prosecutors have used in trafficking cases.

TRAC officials note that the federal prosecutorial data base contains a number of specific definitions that researchers use to analyze cases. Federal law enforcement agencies frequently investigate possible cases of wrongdoing, referring those that may be adequate for prosecution to the Department of Justice, which ultimately decides if a prosecution is warranted and which law applies. According to TRAC, federal prosecutors classify such referrals into two categories: referrals that are immediately declined (also called "immediate declinations") and matters that are pursued further. These latter cases may or may not become prosecutions. "A large number of referrals accepted as 'matters' are ultimately declined," explained TRAC officials. But those that survive the process become cases that lead to actual prosecutions by either grand-jury indictment or a criminal complaint.[6]

As TRAC experts have noted, the situation can get confusing: sometimes different federal prosecutors use different terminology to describe referrals that progress to the prosecution stage: "If the U.S. Attorney's office decides to prosecute through regular court action, the 'matter' becomes a 'case.'" But if a federal magistrate-judge (who is not an article 3 judge under the U.S. Constitution) handles a case, then the proceeding is categorized as a matter even if it is handled in the very same courthouse. Because less information is entered about matters than about cases, it is sometimes impossible to learn if a prosecutor has actually taken a matter to a magistrate's court until the prosecution is finished, a state of affairs that may lead to missing data.[7]

When analyzing referrals using the TRAC data, a researcher can determine not only how many referrals were declined for prosecution but also the reason why those decisions didn't proceed further. The researcher can then track prosecuted cases to learn how many led to convictions and then to prison sentences as well as the median length of those sentences. See tables 12.2 and 12.3 for a breakdown of trafficking referrals and prosecutions under the TVPA and the Mann Act.

Table 12.2

Analysis of Trafficking Investigations, Fiscal Years 2000–2004

	2000	2001	2002	2003	2004	Total	Percent
Total referrals	8	13	32	41	50	144	100.0
Type of disposition							
Declination	6	10	21	20	27	84	58.3
Dismissed without prejudice	—	—	—	—	1	1	0.7
Guilty	—	—	5	12	16	33	22.9
Immediate declination	2	3	6	6	5	22	15.3
New filing	—	—	—	—	1	1	0.7
Not guilty	—	—	—	2	—	2	1.4
Transfer	—	—	—	1	—	1	0.7

SOURCE: TRAC assessment of Department of Justice data.

Table 12.3

Disposition of Mann Act Referrals (under 18 U.S.C. 2421, 22, 23), Fiscal Years 2001–2005

	2001	2002	2003	2004	2005
Total referrals	236	185	197	241	145
Referrals disposed*	279	376	289	297	216
Referrals declined	153	193	130	148	80
Referrals convicted	113	157	138	122	119
Referrals found not guilty	13	26	21	27	17

SOURCE: TRAC analysis of Department of Justice data.
NOTE: Mann Act cases may or may not be related to the crime of human trafficking.
* Referrals may be from prior fiscal year.

My analysis of the TVPA data shows that more than half the referrals made by agencies such as the FBI and the Immigration and Naturalization Service (now ICE) were declined as viable prosecutions. Including the immediate declinations, those total dispositions amounted to 73.6 percent of all referrals (see table 12.2); and over five years, they numbered 106 of 144 dispositions. Of the remainder, thirty-three (22.9 percent) resulted in guilty findings by either plea or jury trial. Clearly, then, if prosecutors do not decline a referral, there is a strong likelihood that the resulting prosecution will lead to a conviction: of the thirty-eight referrals that did survive an initial review, 87 percent resulted in a conviction, a result comparable to the national conviction rate of all referrals that led to charges in fiscal year 2004.

Table 12.4
Referral Dispositions, Fiscal Year 2005

	Total	Percent
Total referrals	89	100.0
Declined prosecution	74	83.1
Guilty	2	2.2
Immediate declination	12	13.5
New filing	1	1.1

SOURCE: TRAC analysis of Department of Justice data.

But it is also clear that referrals from investigative agencies are weeded out at a high rate (see table 12.4). Although the data displayed in table 12.4 covers only fiscal year 2005, it shows that, of the eighty-nine matters reported in justice department statistics, prosecutors immediately declined twelve (13.5 percent) of the cases that investigative agencies had referred to them. Seventy-four (83.1 percent) were declined after longer review. This left two matters that proceeded to conviction (guilty pleas) and one that apparently resulted in either an indictment or the filing of criminal information. In sum, based on justice department data supplied to TRAC for analysis, prosecutors declined to bring criminal charges in 96.6 percent of the matters.

Why do trafficking cases seem so hard to bring to prosecution? A more detailed review showed that prosecutors in all federal court districts declined to proceed to criminal charges for reasons that seemed constant from year to year: lack of evidence of criminal intent, weak or insufficient admissible evidence, "office policy" (which was not defined), problems with jurisdiction or court venue, no evidence of a federal offense, "minimal" interest of prosecutors because a prosecution wouldn't have deterrent value, and problems with witnesses. According to experienced prosecutors, this last reason makes trafficking cases particularly hard to pursue. One federal prosecutor in New York City, who asked not to be identified, said that victims are often unable to identify the traffickers, who may be removed by distance and time from the place of exploitation. Fear is also a factor: while appreciating help and rescue, victims may not want to go further in trying to apprehend the traffickers. Moreover, they may not remember everything that happened; and in cases involving single victims, prosecutors find it extremely difficult to corroborate their statements.[8]

After a case is successfully prosecuted in federal court and a conviction is secured, the defendant must be sentenced. Under the federal court system, sentences can range from probation to penalties such as fines, restitution, or confinement. Usually confinement involves a prison facility, although some defendants receive a term of home confinement that involves electronic monitoring. Until a 2005 U.S. Supreme Court ruling essentially struck down the mandatory sentencing guidelines, federal judges were hemmed in by complex sentencing calculations. Now, however, they use the guidelines only as advice and can adjust prison terms as they see fit. In its self-assessments on trafficking cases for fiscal year 2004, the Department of Justice reported that, of a total of eighteen defendants who were convicted of TVPA offenses, fourteen received prison sentences. The average prison sentence was eighty-six months (slightly more than seven years), with terms ranging from 27 to 168 months at a point when the sentencing guidelines were still mandatory.[9] A TRAC analysis of thirteen convictions for "slavery and involuntary servitude" revealed that twelve defendants received prison sentences with a median time of sixty-three months and an average time of sixty-nine months, somewhat less than the justice department had reported but still longer than five years.[10]

How do trafficking and involuntary servitude sentences compare from year to year? A TRAC analysis of prosecutions between fiscal years 1995 and 2004 looked at cases in the civil rights division of the Department of Justice, a category that includes crimes of slavery and involuntary servitude (see table 12.5). The data show that, since passage of the TVPA, both median and average prison terms have generally increased, although not steadily. For example, in fiscal year 2002 the median prison term was twenty-six months; in fiscal year 2004 it was sixty-three months. In 2002 the average prison term was forty-one months, and by 2004 it had increased to sixty-nine months.

Table 12.5
Sentencing in Slavery and Involuntary Servitude Cases

Fiscal Year	Convictions	Prison Sentences	Median Prison Term (months)	Average Prison Term (months)
All	63	57	36	50
1995	0	0	—	—
1996	1	1	57	57
1997	0	0	—	—
1998	0	0	—	—
1999	13	11	24	33
2000	8	8	44	53
2001	5	5	33	33
2002	8	6	26	41
2003	15	14	43	55
2004	13	12	63	69

SOURCE: TRAC analysis of Department of Justice data.

Why do TRAC and justice department data differ in their record of average prison terms? The likely explanation is that the Department of Justice report includes cases involving not only the Mann Act and the TVPA but also cases not filed under the headings of slavery and involuntary servitude as well as crimes that predate the TVPA.

At this point I want to point out that a purely statistical approach to reporting trafficking enforcement activity obscures the fact that state and local law enforcement are cooperating with federal investigators in meaningful ways. In fact, local officials are often in the best position to monitor trafficking complaints in their neighborhoods and immigrant communities. This local-federal nexus was important in the 2004 Carreto case (already discussed in this book), when a special trafficking unit of the New York City Police Department (NYPD) received crucial information about Mexican immigrant women living in the Corona section of Queens. Police discovered the women working as prostitutes in a number of locations. Since the officers had regular contact with federal investigators at ICE, their information led to a wider probe. NYPD and ICE investigators determined that as many as five of the women, possibly more, had fraudulently entered the United States and had been compelled to work in brothels around New York City. Federal officials at the Brooklyn U.S. attorney's office charged four men, all members of the Carreto clan, on sex trafficking charges.[11]

The Carreto case required close coordination among local and federal agencies as well as delicate handling of the victims, some of whom were married or had personal relationships with the suspects. Because the Carreto family was notorious in southern Mexico for exporting women to the United States, investigators also contacted officials in Mexico, who made arrests there. The defendants in the case were on the verge of accepting a plea bargain, which would have given them prison terms of up to ten years. But at the last minute, allegedly because of bad advice from jailhouse lawyers, the defendants rejected the plea. Angry federal prosecutors took the deal off the table. Finally, the defendants realized they had no viable defense and decided to plead guilty. In April 2006 two were sentenced to fifty-year terms, while a third received twenty-five years in prison.[12]

Some of the women in the case were eligible for T-visas and other immigration benefits; and at this writing, federal officials were processing their cases. As discussed, the T-visa is a key benefit for victims under the TVPA but is available only if they cooperate with law enforcement. For two years the government has reported statistics related to T-visa applications and grants; and while hundreds of victims have received the benefit, their number has not been close to reaching the TVPA's maximum allotment of 5,000 per year. Certainly, there is no

Table 12.6
T-Visa Applications, Fiscal Years 2004 and 2003

	2004	2003
Received	520	601
Granted	136	297
Denied	292	30
Pending	92	274

SOURCE: U.S. Department of Justice, "Report to Congress from Attorney General Alberto R. Gonzalez on U.S. Government Effort to Combat Trafficking in Persons in Fiscal Year 2004," July 2005.

sign that the program is being abused. Table 12.6 records T-visa processing, based on data available through September 30, 2004.

The relatively low number of T-visa applicants compared with the yearly allotment raises questions. Is the total number of trafficking victims in the United States smaller than estimated? Are victims unaware of the T-visa benefit and therefore not applying? Are trafficking victims electing not to cooperate with law enforcement and thus not qualifying for the benefit?

There is no way to answer the question of total number because criminal activity is difficult to gauge and measure, although the issue continues to vex human rights activists, journalists, and government officials. Regarding the second question, victims are unlikely to remain ignorant of the benefit. The number of U.S. government organizations and NGOs working with trafficking victims has increased, and experts and lawyers involved with those groups do make appropriate visa applications. Regarding the third question, however, many victims probably choose not to cooperate with law enforcement, despite the reward of a coveted T-visa—hence, the relatively low number of applicants who meet the visa criteria. Other victims or alleged victims may cooperate but don't want to stay in the United States. Such reluctance was evident in Operation Gilded Gage, the 2005 California federal investigation that broke up a suspected Asian prostitution trafficking network. Although the government determined that twenty-one people, mostly women, were material witnesses and held them in custody, all of them (as well as fifty-four other women who apparently decided not to cooperate) subsequently went into deportation proceedings.[13]

Another federal statistic also shows that relatively few trafficking victims cooperate with investigations. Under the TVPA, the Department of Health and Human Services' Office of Refugee Resettlement (ORR) is permitted to issue certificates to adult and child trafficking victims. These certificates allow victims to access federally funded or administered benefits and services similar to those available to refugees, including food stamps and Medicaid as well as housing, education, and legal assistance. Adult victims have to meet statutory requirements, which include a willingness to help law enforcement agencies investigate cases of trafficking. By September 30, 2004, ORR had granted 611 certificates of eligibility: 198 in fiscal year 2001, 99 in fiscal year 2002, 151 in fiscal year 2003, and 163 in fiscal year 2004. Those numbers include both adult and child victims, but women were the primary recipients (65 percent in fiscal year 2004, 80 percent in fiscal year 2002). Still, the figure is very small, considering that Congress expected thousands of trafficking victims to apply each year for such special benefits.[14]

Trafficking victims who are identified and do seek help have found a growing number of service providers. The federal government assists refugees through the Department of Health and Human Services. As supplement to that aid, the department in turn offers grants to organizations that are active in helping victims of trafficking. Agencies such as the Department of Justice's Office for Victims of Crime (OVC), the Department of Labor, the Legal Services Corporation, and the Department of Agriculture also provide services.

Because the federal government didn't start reporting its actions on trafficking until 2003, it is difficult to prepare a consistent breakdown of all expenditures across the various federal agencies. The justice department's assessment reports vary in terms of depth of information, but generally the reports for 2003–5 offer some details for comparison.

By fiscal year 2004, ORR had awarded 8.1 million dollars to create a network of organizations that worked with trafficking victims, including those that provided temporary housing, transportation, legal assistance, and other needs: 1.25 million dollars in fiscal year 2001, 3.37 million dollars in fiscal year 2002, and 3.48 million dollars in fiscal year 2003. For fiscal year 2004 the awards reached 3.37 million dollars, with an additional 3.48 million dollars in continuation grants, making a grand total to date of 14.95 million dollars.[15]

The Department of Justice's OVC also began offering grants to assist trafficking victims. In January 2003 it awarded NGOs twelve grants totaling more than 9.5 million dollars to support victims' services such as housing. The money granted that year assisted two hundred victims. Through 2004, OVC-funded program grantees helped an additional 357 victims, but the assessment did not disclose the dollar amount provided. In 2004 the Department of Justice also gave funding to twenty-one local communities so they could form law enforcement task forces to address ways of dealing with trafficking and rescue victims. According to a department assessment, the amount totaled 9.7 million dollars.[16]

In support of domestic trafficking programs, the Department of Labor provides job search assistance, occupational training, and career counseling through local service providers. It does not, however, collect information about the proportion of those services provided specifically to trafficking victims, so no data on funding or persons helped are available. Likewise, the Legal Services Corporation, a nonprofit unit established by Congress to fund legal programs for the poor, helps trafficking victims; but data on funding spent specifically on trafficking victims are not available. Overall, the corporation helped 81 victims nationwide in fiscal year 2003 and 170 in fiscal year 2004.[17]

As federal self-reports illustrate, various agencies were becoming aware of the concrete need to address human trafficking. Prosecutorial agencies were commencing cases and, for the most part, getting convictions that led to substantial prison terms. Other agencies were spending money on various victims' protection services, and the government had initiated a number of domestic campaigns aimed at increasing public awareness of trafficking and thereby helping the prosecutorial and protection functions. A Department of Health and Human Services' program known as "Look Beneath the Surface" had 5 million dollars to spend between fiscal years 2003 and 2005. Public service announcements were part of a strategy to reach trafficking victims or people who knew about them and involved targeted displays in ethnic media, religious media networks, and other appropriate outlets. Since passage of the TVPA, the government has also set up two telephone hotlines. The Department of Health and Human Services line is designed to deal with victims who are reluctant to approach law enforcement but need counseling or help. The Department of Justice's complaint line handles callers who are willing to cooperate with law enforcement.[18]

History shows that trafficking is an international problem and that even domestic U.S. trafficking has a foreign component. In an effort to look comprehensively at trafficking, alien smuggling, and terrorism, the federal government created the Human Smuggling and Trafficking Center in December 2000. Its main role was to disseminate intelligence and coordinate activity "needed to support effective enforcement, diplomatic, and other actions to counter smugglers and traffickers." The center was designed to have a "strong foreign focus" to help American law enforcement work with foreign governments and, in the process, help officials determine how much assistance should go to certain countries or regions. With the nation's increased attention to terrorism, the center had the potential to become a useful as a law enforcement device.[19]

But according to the 2005 GAO report, the center was not reaching its potential. By March 2005 staffing was only about half of what it was supposed to be. The events of September 11 had diverted resources and staff and prevented the center from becoming operational until July 2004, nearly four years after a White House directive had established it.[20]

The center's slow start didn't prevent the United States from funding foreign NGO programs or cooperating on trafficking with foreign law enforcement agencies. SECI activity in Romania as well as the creation of SECI-style organizations in the Republic of Georgia, Azerbaijan, and other areas of South Asia showed that Washington was taking action. Other indications were the participation of U.S. law enforcement personnel in training foreign police and prosecutors to deal with trafficking as well as assistance in drafting model trafficking laws and enabling foreign agencies to prosecute traffickers and free victims. But the center's slow start may have prevented law enforcement from exploiting trafficking intelligence in a timely manner and on a larger scale.

Although the Department of Justice's 2005 assessment of U.S. anti-trafficking efforts lists the many accomplishments of various federal agencies, it includes virtually no appraisal or actual assessment about whether or not strategies were viable or what was being done right or wrong. It concludes by stating that "the U.S. government is committed to combating this moral evil with all the resources available to it" and that "fighting against trafficking and modern-day slavery is one of our highest priorities for ensuring justice in the United States and around the world." It remained for the GAO to say in a July 2006 audit report that the United States had developed neither a coordinated strategy for combating trafficking abroad nor ways to gauge results. The GAO audit also said the individual country reports prepared by the TIP Office were incomplete and inconsistent, lessening their credibility as a diplomatic tool. The GAO planned more studies of trafficking prosecutions and other domestic efforts.[21]

In September 2005, the IOM released a document showing that, five years after passage of the U.N. protocol and the TVPA, trafficking was still an intractable problem in parts of the world where the U.S. had focused considerable effort and attention. Researchers found that victims in Eastern Europe were increasingly being trafficked for forced labor, begging, and delinquency. Though the number of victims assisted in the region appeared to remain stable (an average of 1,270), the IOM analysis stressed that there was a wide gap between the number of assisted victims and the total number of trafficked persons, which the organization estimated to be greater.[22]

According to the report, most victims assisted had been involved in sex trafficking; but significant numbers had also been trafficked for labor, begging, adoption, and other criminal conduct. In countries such as Albania, trafficking victims were predominately men involved in labor and begging. Traffickers had adapted their tactics to law enforcement pressure, and the region still suffered from a lack of specialized assistance for victims.[23]

Read alongside the broad aspirations in the Department of Justice's 2005 assessment, the IOM study indicates that trafficking is a complex phenomenon undergoing continuous change and is not easily addressed by slogans and statements of moral resolve. While economics is often the root cause of trafficking, the IOM study noted that a "striking number" of victims were from well off families, "signaling that economics alone is an insufficient explanation for trafficking."[24]

Chapter 13   Final Thoughts

W HEN I VISITED Eastern Europe in the summer of 2000, the subject of human trafficking had begun to captivate journalists everywhere. Lurid stories about sex slaves and forced prostitution were ideal fodder for the tabloid press, even making the occasional chewy story in broadsheet newspapers such as the *New York Times* and the *Washington Post*. After politicians took over the situation, the result was significant legislation that has helped to spawn a new federal bureaucracy, pumping tens of millions of dollars abroad and nearly as much into domestic programs. Putting aside the fact that it is difficult to figure out just how big a problem human trafficking is, we can safely say that hundreds of victims have been helped by U.S. actions, and others have been deterred from falling prey to traffickers.

But I wanted this book to be more than another recitation of the horrors faced by trafficking victims: I wanted to appraise U.S. policy and its direction. Clearly, the United States has been at the forefront in addressing the trafficking issue and putting it on the international agenda as both a human rights issue and a law enforcement priority. A combination of legislative initiatives, diplomatic jawboning, and the related work of human rights advocates and NGOs has forced government organizations and private businesses to confront the uncomfortable reality that their operatives and employees have sometimes been responsible for the plight of trafficked persons.

For example, the Department of Defense took steps in 2004 to prevent military personnel from procuring the services of traffickedw persons as well as of prostitutes generally. One measure was a zero tolerance policy on trafficking, which required military commanders to help law enforcement pursue investigations. The Pentagon also developed and distributed to American forces worldwide a training program to make military personnel aware of trafficking. To push the Bush administration's claim that a demand for prostitution drives trafficking, the military implemented new sections of the Uniform Code of Military Justice, making it an offense to patronize prostitutes.[1]

After a series of discussions that began in 2003, the North Atlantic Treaty Organization (NATO) adopted its 2004 zero tolerance policy on trafficking, which leaders of all NATO nations endorsed, including the United States. Under the terms of the policy, the allies agreed that all personnel, both military and civilian, who take part in NATO operations should "receive appropriate training to make them aware of the problem and how this modern day slavery trade impacts on human rights, stability and security." Using the U.N. protocol as a model for action, NATO allies also agreed that they should make national efforts to meet the obligations spelled out in the protocol.[2]

The TVPRA requires U.S. government contractors not to employ or exploit trafficked persons. It remains to be seen if those provisions can or will be enforced, although there are plenty of NGOs ready to monitor compliance. But the mere fact that a bureaucracy has implemented policies that theoretically penalize the exploitation of trafficked persons is a crucial step.

At this writing, Senator Paul Wellstone has been dead for nearly four years. But had he survived, he would undoubtedly have been satisfied by some of the accomplishments brought about by the TVPA. The law focused attention and effort on a problem he thought was a terrible crime, one result of globalization of the world economy. But according to a former staffer who worked closely with him on the trafficking issue, Wellstone was puzzled by the way in which sex trafficking preoccupied some of his congressional colleagues; and it's probably fair to say that he would be troubled by how the goal of protection for trafficking victims has been supplanted by a moral agenda determined to abolish prostitution. Such an approach breeds false hopes and can repel some activists who are working to help victims. In Romania, for instance, Iana Matei will not take any money from the U.S. government because of its abolitionist stance.[3] She continues to resist, even though the TIP Office's 2006 country assessment report has highlighted her Reaching Out program as one of the most meritorious efforts ever made to combat trafficking.

Any reader has personal feelings about the idea of a sibling or a child engaging in prostitution. But like it or not, it's a livelihood for many people. During the 2006 trafficking symposium in New York City, a debate was broached over the question of whether or not prostitution is work, discussion that involved a number of experts, journalists, lawyers, and human rights advocates. One participant, Neha Misra, affiliated with the Solidarity Center, a unit of the

AFL-CIO, put it best when she said that there is too much time wasted on the question. While she was neutral on the issue, she pointedly reminded people that sex work "is what women are doing in order to make a living. So if you don't want that to be work and it's not work, give women real options for work, give them real options to make a living for their families and then we can stop the debate."[4]

In other words, if women turn to sex work as a livelihood, then it may be a better strategy to protect those that choose to work in the business and thus create a sense of empowerment. As an example, migration experts point to an association of sex workers in Calcutta. The association has a membership of 60,000 prostitutes and others types of workers who, through what's known as the Sonagachi Project, self-police the brothel areas to detect and stop trafficking, particularly of minors. Any victims found are taken to a hostel or a halfway house for reunion with their families or job training.[5]

Some U.S. government efforts abroad have been designed to help women and other potential trafficking victims develop useful skills and employment alternatives so that they can find jobs. Other U.S. efforts abroad have gone toward much more modest ventures, such as conferences, seminars, creation of websites, social worker training, and information campaigns publicizing the dangers of trafficking. USAID money has gone to education and literacy projects as well as job training. Nevertheless, given the geographic spread of all such efforts, the funding devoted to job training is quite small and may have little significant impact. Anecdotally, I heard of one case in Eastern Europe where U.S. funding was used to set up a hostel for trafficked women. But because they lacked any meaningful job training or employment, the women started returning to work as prostitutes, this time out of the hostel that was supposed to be sheltering them.

Sometimes NGOs are in the best position to create employment opportunities for those who are susceptible to trafficking. In Romania, for instance, Matei founded a tailoring and sewing facility near Pitesti, which allowed the women in the Reaching Out program to learn embroidery skills. In a more ambitious program in 2006, she raised local funding to start a hotel with a restaurant in a mountain area north of Pitesti. The plan was to capitalize on the tourist traffic and use profits from the venture to fund other Reaching Out programs that assisted trafficked women.[6]

As I have stated time and again in this book, trafficking is not just about sex. It is fundamentally about labor and the abuse of people who want to sell their labor. The TVPA allows those who are exploited by traffickers to escape from their poisonous and exploitative relationships and seek refuge. Realistically, creating havens for the exploited and hope for their future is the best focus for U.S. policy.

A protective policy for trafficking victims does not mean overlooking other components of U.S. policy, such as prosecution and prevention. Keeping up law enforcement pressure on traffickers, both domestically and internationally, actively deters criminal entrepreneurs and at the very least raises the risks and costs of doing business. But as we've seen in drug trafficking, such deterrence has not eliminated narcotics smuggling. Another important component, prevention of trafficking, can be accomplished through long-term attitudinal changes in source and destination countries about trafficking and the exploitation of trafficked persons. Such changes in attitude will require a long campaign of public education programs as well as adjustments in values to make citizens aware that trafficked people are exploited and victims of crime. So, in a sense, emphasizing the culpability of willing consumers of the services of trafficked persons may serve a useful purpose. That is the aim of certain anti-prostitution laws in Scandinavia and more modest efforts in New York State, where a proposed anti-trafficking law would increase the penalty for using the services of a prostitute from fifteen days in jail to one year. (The measure died in legislative committee.) But it seems fundamentally unfair, and unacceptable under U.S. legal standards, to make these "Johns" liable for procuring the services of a prostitute whom they have no reason to believe has been trafficked. It also is likely to have no practical effect on the market for prostitution, which is already illegal in virtually every U.S. state and locale, particularly since anecdotal evidence indicates that the number of trafficked prostitutes in the United States is a relatively small portion of the sex worker population.

The sex urge is great; and as the proliferation of pornography has shown, interest in buying sex in whatever form is hard to quell by fiat. Following the logic of the abolitionists, it might be more productive to ban or more closely regulate domestic work settings, agriculture, and certain factory jobs that experience has shown are occupations with large numbers of trafficked victims. In fact, the success of homegrown worker-protection organizations such as the one I've discussed in Florida is a testament to the helping power of such assertive groups.[7] Might not this same kind of empowerment, instead of criminalization and abolition of sex work, also be as effective in assuring protection to those who work in such jobs?

In a sense, arguing about whether prostitution fuels a demand for trafficking is like arguing about how many angels can dance on the head of a pin. The question assumes that substantial portions of sex workers are trafficked, but that fact is unverifiable. It also assumes that all prostitution activity is the same everywhere. Tales of child prostitution in Nepal and other Asian countries involving girls as young as twelve or thirteen years of age are clearly repugnant to anyone who cares about children. Most people also have little tolerance for

cases in which women are beaten and forced to have sex with multiple partners. But as I've noted, there are international prostitution operations in
which women can earn up to 50,000 dollars per weekend. They may be prostitutes and may be breaking the law, but they are not trafficked persons; and
their situations are much different from that of child prostitutes in Asia and
sex slaves in Eastern Europe. It's best to stop worrying about abolishing prostitution and focus instead on labor policies and economic realities that make
systemic changes and increase work options while protecting those in disfa-
vored occupations such as sex work.

Migrants around the world seek economic improvement in their lives
because conditions at home are unacceptable to them or hold limited potential. Drawn by images of affluence on satellite television and the Internet,
they will make deals with the devil—the traffickers and smugglers—to travel
to places in search of jobs. If the economic conditions at home were better,
some victims would never enter the migration stream. But economic development requires programs and policies that work over the long term. Until such
development occurs, people will place their misguided trust in traffickers and
subject themselves to all sorts of abusive situations. The protective policies of
the TVPA's hallmark legislation give those victims a chance to escape and
make decisions in relative safety that can help them extricate themselves and
their families permanently from the economic deprivations and dangers that
got them into trouble in the first place. As any mariner in a storm knows, it is
always good to have a safe harbor nearby.

Appendix

ACCORDING TO THE U.S. DEPARTMENT OF STATE, the following countries do not meet minimum standards for eliminating human trafficking and are not making significant efforts to do so. As a result they are ranked as tier 3 nations. Countries that meet the minimum standards or are making significant efforts to do so are rated as tier 1 or tier 2 nations. The state department publishes these rankings annually in its "Trafficking in Persons Report."

A tier 3 nation may be subject to certain U.S. sanctions, such as the withholding of non-humanitarian, non-trade–related assistance. It may also face U.S. opposition to certain assistance from international institutions such as the World Bank and the International Monetary Fund.

Tier 3 Countries in 2001
Albania
Bahrain
Belarus
Bosnia-Herzegovina
Burma
Democratic Republic of Congo
Federal Republic of Yugoslavia
Gabon
Greece
Indonesia
Israel
Kazakhstan

Lebanon
Malaysia
Pakistan
Qatar
Romania
Russia
Saudi Arabia
South Korea
Sudan
Turkey
United Arab Emirates

Tier 3 Countries in 2002

Afghanistan
Armenia
Bahrain
Belarus
Bosnia-Herzegovina
Burma
Cambodia
Greece
Indonesia
Iran
Kyrgyz Republic
Lebanon
Qatar
Russia
Saudi Arabia
Sudan
Tajikistan
Turkey
United Arab Emirates

Tier 3 Countries in 2003

Belize
Bosnia-Herzegovina
Burma
Cuba
Dominican Republic
Georgia

Greece
Haiti
Kazakhstan
Liberia
North Korea
Sudan
Suriname
Turkey
Uzbekistan

Tier 3 Countries in 2004

Bangladesh
Burma
Cuba
Ecuador
Equatorial Guinea
Guyana
North Korea
Sierra Leone
Sudan
Venezuela

Tier 3 Countries in 2005

Bolivia
Burma
Cambodia
Cuba
Ecuador
Jamaica
Kuwait
North Korea
Qatar
Saudi Arabia
Sudan
Togo
United Arab Emirates
Venezuela

Notes

Introduction

1. Anette Brunovskis and Guri Tyldum "Describing the Unobserved: Methodological Challenge in Empirical Studies on Human Trafficking," *http://www.blackwell-synergy.com/doi/pdf/10.1111/j.0020-7985.2005.00310.x?cookieSet=1*.

2. Global Commission on International Migration, "Migration in an Interconnected World: New Direction for Action," October 5, 2005.

3. Donna M. Hughes, "Trafficking of Women and Children in East Asia and Beyond: A Review of U.S. Policy," remarks to the U.S. Senate Foreign Relations Committee, Subcommittee on East Asian and Pacific Affairs, April 9, 2003.

4. Author's interview with defense attorney involved in federal prosecution in Manhattan, 2005.

5. Gretchen Soderlund and Emma Grant, "Girls (Forced to) Dance Naked! The Politics and Presumptions of Anti-Trafficking Laws," *Bad Subjects* 40 (October 1998), *http://eserver.org/bs/40/soderlund-grant.html*.

6. U.S. Department of Justice, Federal Bureau of Investigation, "Anatomy of an International Trafficking Case, Part 1: Kil Soo Lee and the Case of the Samoan Sweatshop," July 16, 2004, *http://www.fbi.gov/page2/july04/kisoolee071904.htm* (hereafter cited as FBI, "Anatomy, Part 1").

7. *U.S. v. Mariluz Zavala et al.*, 04-MJ-00857, U.S. District Court, Eastern District of New York (Central Islip), case file.

8. *U.S. v. Michail Aronov et al.*, 05-CR-80187, U.S. District Court, Eastern District of Michigan, case file.

9. *U.S. v. Kong Sun Hernandez*, 04-CR-80, U.S. District Court, Western District of Washington, case file.

10. *U.S. v. Nam Young Lee*, 05-CR-00395, U.S. District Court, Northern District of California, San Francisco Division, case file.

11. *U.S. v. Wun Kang et al.*, 04-CR-00087, U.S. District Court, Eastern District of New York, case file.

12. *U.S. v. Joseph Djoumessi et al.*, 05-CR-80110, U.S. District Court, Eastern District of Michigan, case file.

13. U.S. Department of Justice, "Woman Found Guilty of Conspiracy, Harboring a Domestic Worker for Financial Gain," November 19, 2004, *http://www.usdoj.gov/opa/pr/2004/November/04_crt_759.htm*.

14. *U.S. v. Johannes Du Preez et al.*, 04-CR-008, U.S. District Court, Northern District of Georgia, Newman Division, case file.

15. Ibid.

16. Christopher Booker, *The Seven Basic Plots: Why We Tell Stories* (New York: Continuum, 2005).

Chapter 1   **The Barrio Girls**

1. Sean Gardiner, "Choices Made of Fear and Pressure," [New York] *Newsday*, March 12, 2001, p. A3.
2. Sean Gardiner and Geoffrey Mohan, "The Sex Slaves from Mexico: Teenagers Tell of Forced Prostitution," [New York] *Newsday*, March 12, 2001, p. A3.
3. Ibid.
4. Florida State University Center for the Advancement of Human Rights, "Florida Responds to Human Trafficking," 2003, *http://www.cahr.fsu.edu*.
5. Gardiner and Mohan, "Sex Slaves from Mexico," A16.
6. Ibid.
7. Ibid., A15.
8. Ibid., A16.
9. Ibid.
10. *U.S. v. Hugo Cadena-Sosa et al.*, 98-CR-14015, U.S. District Court of Southern Florida, case file.
11. Ibid.
12. Rudolph W. Giuliani, speech, "Immigration: The Progress We've Made and the Road Ahead," March 31, 1998, Washington, D.C., *http://www.nyc.gov.html.rwg*; and author's personal recollection of 1997 events.
13. Giuliani, speech; author's personal recollection of 1997 events.
14. Ibid.
15. Giuliani, speech; American Civil Liberties Union (ACLU) News Wire, "While Bosses Face Justice, Deaf Immigrants Face Limbo," March 30, 1998, *http://www.archive.aclu.org*.
16. Author's interview, confidential law enforcement source, 2004.

Chapter 2   **The Emerging Issue**

1. *U.S. v. Zheng Ming Yan et al.*, 05-00027, U.S. District Court for the Northern Mariana Islands, case file.
2. Annie Sweeney, "Surviving Chicago's Sex Slave Trade," *Chicago Sun Times*, August 7, 2005, *http://www.ipsn.org/organized_crime/prostitution/surviving_chicago.htm*.
3. *U.S. v. Zheng Ming Yan et al.*
4. Sweeney, "Surviving Chicago's Sex Slave Trade."
5. Sheila Wellstone, remarks, 2001, copy provided by Wellstone Action, a nonprofit civic-action group in St. Paul, Minnesota.
6. Author's personal recollection.
7. Brunovskis and Tyldum, "Describing the Unobserved."
8. Tara McKelvey, "Of Human Bondage: A Coalition against Human Trafficking Worked Well until a Prostitution Litmus Test Was Imposed," *American Prospect*, November 2, 2004, *www.prospect.org/web*.
9. Frank Laczko and Marco Gramegna, "Developing Better Indicators of Human Trafficking," *Brown Journal of World Affairs* 1, no. 1 (2003).
10. Amy O'Neill Richard, "International Trafficking in Women to the United States: A Contemporary Manifestation of Slavery and Organized Crime," monograph prepared for the Center for the Study of Intelligence, Central Intelligence Agency, Washington, D.C., April 2000.
11. Ibid.
12. U.N. Educational, Scientific, and Cultural Organization (UNESCO) Trafficking Project, "Data Comparison Sheet #1: Worldwide Trafficking Estimates by Organizations," *http://www.unescobkk.org/culture/trafficking*.

13. Ibid.
14. Paul Wellstone, *The Conscience of a Liberal: Reclaiming the Compassionate Agenda* (New York: Random House, 2001), 29–31.
15. Ibid., 3–4; Sheila Wellstone, remarks.
16. Sheila Wellstone, remarks.
17. Paul Wellstone, floor statement denouncing international sex trafficking, U.S. Senate, March 10, 1998, *http://wellstone.senate.gov/sextrffl.htm*.
18. Ibid.
19. Paul Wellstone, "Wellstone Denounces International Sex Trafficking: Introduces Resolution Condemning Human Rights Violations against Women," news release, March 10, 1998, *http://wellstone.senate.gov/sextraf.html*.
20. Paul Wellstone, remarks denouncing international sex trafficking on the floor of the Senate, S. Con. Res. 82, 105th Cong., 2d sess., March 10, 1998, *Congressional Record*, S1703–4.
21. Ibid.

Chapter 3   The Global Response

1. Luigi Lauriola, "Address by Ambassador Luigi Lauriola, Chairman of the Ad Hoc Committee on the Elaboration of a Convention against Transnational Organized Crime," U.N. General Assembly, November 15, 2000, *http://www.unodc.org/pdf/crime/convention/crime_cicp_convention_lauriola.pdf*.
2. Author's interview with confidential source.
3. Ibid.
4. Lauriola, "Address."
5. Ibid.
6. Henry Campbell Black, ed., *Black's Law Dictionary*, rev. 4th ed. (St. Paul, Minn., West, 1968), 401.
7. United Nations, "Informal Group of the 'Friends of the Chair' of the Ad Hoc Committee on the Elaboration of the Convention against Transnational Organized Crime," U.N. General Assembly, A/AC.254/2, December 15, 1998, p. 2.
8. U.N. Commission on Crime Prevention and Criminal Justice, "Trafficking in Persons: the New Protocol," *http://www.unodc.org/unodc/en/traffficking_protocol_background.html*; author's interviews, 2004–5.
9. Author's interviews, 2004–5.
10. Author's interviews with confidential diplomatic sources, 2005.
11. Ibid.
12. Ibid.
13. United Nations, "Revised Draft Protocol to Prevent, Suppress and Punish Trafficking in Women and Children, Supplementing the United Nations Convention against Transnational Organized Crime," U.N. General Assembly, A/AC.254/4/Add.3/Rev.1, February 22, 1999, pp. 1–10.
14. Ibid.
15. Ibid., 1.
16. Author's interviews with confidential law enforcement sources, 2004.
17. United Nations, "Draft Protocol to Combat International Trafficking in Women and Children Supplementary to the United Nations Convention on Transnational Organized Crime" [U.S. proposal], U.N. General Assembly, A/AC.254/4/Add.3, November 25, 1998, pp. 1–10.
18. United Nations, "Revised Draft Protocol to Prevent, Suppress and Punish Trafficking in Persons, especially Women and Children, Supplementing the

United Nations Convention against Transnational Organized Crime," U.N. General Assembly, A/AC.254/4/add.3/Rev.2, May 18, 1999, p. 3.

19. Ibid.
20. Ibid., 4.
21. Ibid.
22. Gardiner and Mohan, "Sex Slaves from Mexico," 15–16.
23. United Nations, "Draft Proposal," May 18, 1999, p. 5.
24. Ibid., 5–6.
25. Ibid., 6.
26. Ibid.
27. United Nations, "United Nations Convention against Organized Crime," U.N. General Assembly, A/RES/55/25, annex 3, January 8, 2001.
28. Josh Friedman and Anthony M. DeStefano, "Their Cargo Is Human," [New York] *Newsday*, June 12, 1994, p. 4.
29. Chin, "Safe House or Hell House?" in *Human Smuggling: Chinese Migrant Trafficking and the Challenge to America's Immigration Tradition*, ed. Paul J. Smith (Washington, D.C.: Center for Strategic and International Studies, 1997), 176.
30. Friedman and DeStefano, "Their Cargo Is Human," 4.
31. Anthony M. DeStefano. "Immigrant Smuggling through Central America and the Caribbean," in *Human Smuggling: Chinese Migrant Trafficking and the Challenge to America's Immigration Tradition*, ed. Paul J. Smith (Washington, D.C.: Center for Strategic and International Studies, 1997), 143–49.
32. United Nations, "Convention against Organized Crime," January 8, 2001, pp. 35–36.
33. The Clinton administration widely broadcast the concept of the Three Ps.
34. United Nations, "Revised Draft Protocol to Prevent, Suppress and Punish Trafficking in Women and Children," February 22, 1999, pp. 8–9.
35. Ibid., 10.
36. United Nations, "Informal Note by the United Nations High Commissioner for Human Rights," U.N. General Assembly, A/AC.254/16, June 1, 1999, pp. 1–6.
37. Ibid., 4–5.
38. Ibid., 5.
39. Ibid., 2–3.
40. Author's interview with confidential diplomatic source, 2005.
41. Author's interviews with confidential diplomatic source, 2004; Ann Jordan, ed., *Annotated Guide to the Complete UN Trafficking Protocol* (Washington, D.C.: Global Rights: Partners for Justice, 2003), 4–5.
42. United Nations, "Revised Draft Protocol to Prevent, Suppress and Punish Trafficking in Women and Children," February 22, 1999, pp. 3–4.
43. Author's interview with confidential diplomatic source, 2004; also see Jordan, *Annotated Guide*, 4–5.
44. United Nations, "Protocol to Prevent, Suppress and Punish Trafficking in Persons, Especially Women and Children, Supplementing the United Nations Convention against Transnational Organized Crime," U.N. General Assembly, 2000.
45. United Nations, "Report of the Ad Hoc Committee on the Elaboration of a Convention against Transnational Organized Crime on the Work of Its First to Eleventh Sessions," U.N. General Assembly, A/55/383/Add.1, November 3, 2000, p. 12.
46. Mae Cheng, "Unfinished Story: Shipwreck Survivors, 5 Years after Vessel Ran Aground in Struggle for Asylum," [New York] *Newsday*, May 31, 1998, p. A4.
47. Author's interview with confidential diplomatic source, 2005.

48. Ibid.
49. Ibid.
50. United Nations, "Protocol to Prevent, Suppress and Punish Trafficking in Persons, Especially Women and Children," 4–5.
51. Lauriola, "Address," 3.
52. Frank Loy, "Text: Under Secretary Loy's Speech to Transnational Crime Conference," Palermo, Italy, December 13, 2000, pp. 2–3, *http://www.usembassy.it/ file2000.*
53. United Nations, "More Than 120 Nations Sign New UN Convention on Organized Crime, As High-Level Meeting Concludes in Palermo," L/PMO/12, December 15, 2000.
54. International Organization for Migration (hereafter cited as IOM), "Trafficking in Migrants," December 28, 2003, p. 1.

Chapter 4 *"We Need This Bill"*

1. *U.S. v. Nur Alamin et al.*, 00-CR-01001, U.S. District Court for the Central District of California, case file and docket sheet; Arthur Jones, "Global Slave Trade Prospers," *National Catholic Reporter—Online*, May 25, 2001, *http:// www.natcath.com/NCR_Online/archives/052501/052501a.htm;* Asian Pacific American Legal Center, "Asian American and South Asian Organizations Applaud Sentencing in Bangladeshi Slavery Case in Los Angeles," May 15, 2001, *http://apalc.org/pressr_may_15_2001wr.htm;* U.S. Department of Labor, Office of the Inspector General, "Semiannual Report to the Congress: April 1 to September 30, 2001," p. 56, *http://www.oig.dol.gov/public/semiannuals/46.pdf.*
2. *U.S. v. Nur Alamin et al.*
3. Ibid.
4. *U.S. v. Michael Allen Lee*, 00-CR-14065, U.S. District Court for the Southern District of Florida, case file and docket sheet; U.S. Department of Justice, "Labor Contractor Admits He Enslaved African-American Farm Worker in Florida, Pleads Guilty to Federal Charges," February 15, 2001, *www.usdoj.gov/opa/pr/ 2001/February/069crt.htm;* Kay Buck, "Human Trafficking and Slavery: Tools for an Effective Response," presentation prepared for Coalition to Abolish Slavery and Trafficking, *http://www.acjrca.org/ppt06/10.humantraffikincalif.ppt#1.*
5. *U.S. v. Michael Allen Lee.*
6. International Trafficking of Women and Children Victim Protection Act of 1999, S.600, 106th Cong., 1st sess., March 11, 1999, *http://thomas.loc.gov/cgi-bin/ query/C?c106:./temp//~c106SBfndB.*
7. Richard, "International Trafficking in Women to the United States," 1–46.
8. U.S. Department of Justice, "Assessment of U.S. Activities to Combat Trafficking in Persons, 2004," p. 7, *http://www.usdoj.gov/trafficking.htm.*
9. Richard, "International Trafficking in Women to the United States," 45.
10. Ibid., 45, 46.
11. Wellstone, *Conscience of a Liberal*, 189.
12. Paul Wellstone, floor statement introducing the Trafficking Victims Protection Act of 2000 to the Senate, S.2414, 106th Cong., 2d sess., April 12, 2000, *Congressional Record*, S2630–32.
13. Ibid.
14. Ibid., S2631.
15. "International Trafficking of Women and Children Victim Protection Act of 1999," S600.
16. Wellstone, floor statement, April 12, 2000, S2631.

17. Ibid.
18. Ibid.
19. Frank Loy, prepared remarks at hearings before the Subcommittee on Near Eastern and South Asian Affairs concerning international trafficking in women and children, 106th Cong., 2d sess., February 22, 2000, p. 15.
20. Ibid.
21. Comprehensive Antitrafficking in Persons Act of 1999, S.1842, 106th Cong., 1st sess., November 2, 1999, pp. 4–15, *http://thomas.loc.gov/cgi-bin/query/C?c106:./temp/~c1065ktnpy*.
22. Ibid., 11, 12.
23. Bill summary of H.R. 3244, Trafficking Victims Protection Act of 2000, 106th Cong., 1st sess., p. 1, at *http://thomas.loc.gov/cgi-bin/bdquery/z?d106:HR03244:@@@D&summ2=0&*.
24. Ibid., 5.
25. Ibid., 3.
26. White House Office of Management and Budget, remarks on H.R. 3244, Trafficking Victims Protection Act of 2000, May 9, 2000, *http://www.whitehouse.gov/omb/legislative/sap/106-2/print/HR3244-h.html*.
27. Author's confidential interview with former Wellstone staff member, 2004.
28. U.S. Senate Committee on Foreign Relations, hearings before the Subcommittee on Near Eastern and South Asian Affairs concerning international trafficking in women and children, 106th Cong., 2d sess., February 22, 2000, pp. 19–21.
29. Soderlund and Grant, "Girls (Forced to) Dance Naked!"
30. Ibid.
31. Paul Wellstone, press release, March 10, 1998.
32. U.S. Senate Committee on Foreign Relations, hearing, 30–31.
33. Ibid.
34. Ibid., 30.
35. Ibid., 31.
36. Ibid., 26
37. Ibid.
38. Ibid., 26–27.
39. Ibid., 28.
40. Ibid., 27.
41. Ibid., 29.
42. U.S. House of Representatives, remarks on appointment of conferees on H.R. 322, Trafficking Victims Protection Act of 2000, 106th Cong., 2d sess., September 14, 2000, *Congressional Record*, H7628–29.
43. Ibid.
44. Ibid.
45. U.S. House of Representatives, "Joint Explanatory Statement of the Committee of Conference," H.R. 3244, 106th Cong., 2d sess., October 5, 2000, *Congressional Record*, H8877.
46. Ibid., H8879–80.
47. Ibid., H8879.
48. Ibid., H8880.
49. Ibid.
50. Ibid., H8881.
51. Wellstone, *Conscience of a Liberal*, 193.
52. Ibid., 194.
53. U.S. House of Representatives and U.S. Senate, roll call votes, 106th Cong., 2d sess., *http://thomas.loc.gov*.

54. Jordan, *Annotated Guide*.
55. Author's interview with confidential source, 2004.

Chapter 5   The Learning Curve

1. Graham Rayman, "Stripped of Their Dignity: Czech Women Lured to Work at NYC Sex Clubs," [New York] *Newsday*, March 13, 2001, p. A6.
2. Author's interviews with FBI officials, 2001.
3. Ibid.
4. Ibid.
5. U.S. Department of Justice, "Assessment of U.S. Activity to Combat Trafficking in Persons, 2004," 7–8.
6. Ibid.
7. Anthony M. DeStefano, "Three Plead Guilty to Visa Fraud: Were Charged under Sex Smuggling Law," [New York] *Newsday*, June 23, 2001, *http.//www.protectionproject.org*.
8. Ibid.
9. U.S. Department of State, "Alaska Man Sentenced to 30 Months for Immigration Fraud and Transporting Minors from Russia to Dance in an Anchorage Strip Club," August 31, 2001, *http://canberra.usembassy.gov/hyper/2001/0831/epf505.htm*; letter to author from U.S. Department of Justice, Civil Rights Division, listing results of trafficking prosecutions from 2001 through 2004.
10. DeStefano, "Three Plead Guilty to Visa Fraud."
11. *U.S. v. Charles Floyd Pipkins et al.*, 378 F.3d 1281.
12. U.S. Department of Justice, "Maryland Couple Convicted of Enslaving Teenage Cameroonian Girl in Their Home," December 20, 2001, *http://www.usdoj.gov/opa/pr/2001/December/01_crt_661.htm*.
13. U.S. Department of Justice, "Report to Congress from Attorney General Alberto R. Gonzalez on U.S. Government Effort to Combat Trafficking in Persons in Fiscal Year 2004," July 2005, p. 16.
14. Letter to author from David Burham, co-director, Transactional Records Analysis Center (TRAC), Syracuse University.
15. Ibid.
16. Author review of appropriation bills, 2001.
17. U.S. Government Accountability Office (GAO), "Combating Alien Smuggling: Opportunities Exist to Improve the Federal Response," May 2005, p. 44.

Chapter 6   The Lady from Pitesti

1. Anthony M. DeStefano, "Reaching Out to the Victims: Romanian Program Offers Shelter, Skills, Hope," [New York] *Newsday*, March 13, 2001, p. A6; and author's interview with Iana Matei in conjunction with article, January 2001.
2. Ibid.
3. Ibid.
4. Ibid.
5. Ibid.
6. IOM, "Victims of Trafficking in the Balkans: A Study of Trafficking in Women and Children for Sexual Exploitation to, through and from the Balkan Region," 2001, pp. 9, xii, 3, 6.
7. Ibid., 14, 32.
8. Ibid., 13.

9. IOM, "Victims of Trafficking in the Balkans," 60; author's interview with Matei, September 2000.
10. IOM, "Victims of Trafficking in the Balkans," 59.
11. Author's interviews with Matei, July and September 2000.
12. Richard Schifter, interactive television interview for the U.S. Department of State, September 22, 2000 [transcript], 1–2, *http://www.usembassy.it/file2000_09/alia/a0092215.htm.*
13. Author's interview with Richard Schifter, November 2004.
14. Schifter, television interview, 2.
15. Ibid.
16. SECI website, *http://www.secicenter.org.*
17. Schifter, television interview, 2.
18. Author's interview with confidential law enforcement sources, 2001.
19. Author's interview with SECI officials, September 2001.
20. Author's interview with Schifter, November 2004.
21. Ibid.
22. Author's interview with confidential law enforcement source, September 2000.
23. Author's interview with Matei, September 2000.
24. Author's interviews with Matei, 2001.
25. Ibid.
26. Adrian Nastase, "Opening Remarks by H.E. Mr. Adrian Nastase, Prime Minister of Romania, to the Regional Conference on Trafficking in Human Beings and Illegal Immigration," Bucharest, May 21, 2001, *http://www.roembus.org/english/journal/seci/address_Nastase.htm.*
27. Ibid.
28. Louis Freeh, remarks to the Regional Conference on Trafficking in Human Beings and Illegal Immigration, reported by BBC News Online, "FBI Urges Human Trafficking Co-operation," May 21, 2001, *http://www.news.bbc.co.uk/1/low/world/europe/1342537.stem.*
29. Ibid.
30. Author's interviews with U.S. and Romanian diplomats, 2003, 2005.
31. Ibid.

Chapter 7 **Finding Leku**

1. Author's interviews in Bucharest, September 14, 2001.
2. Ibid.
3. Ibid.
4. Anna Matveeva, with Duncan Hiscock, Wolf-Christian Paes, and Hans Risser, "Macedonia: Guns, Policing and Ethnic Division" (Bonn: Safeworld and Bonn International Center for Conversion), October 2003, p. 13.
5. Preston Mendenhall, "A Balkan Kingpin Defends His Lair," MSNBC report, January 2, 2003, *http://www.protectionproject.org/daily_news/2003/ne211.htm.*
6. Matveeva et al., "Macedonia," 9.
7. Mendenhall, "Balkan Kingpin."
8. Author's interview with confidential law enforcement source.
9. Author's interview with Matei, 2005.
10. Ibid.
11. "Shadowy Ethnic Albanian Group Claims Responsibility for Blast in Macedonia," *Associated Press,* February 21, 2003, *http://www.balkanpeace.org/hed/archive/feb03/hed5488.shtml.*
12. Ibid.

13. Author's interview with Matei, 2005.
14. International Crisis Group, "Macedonia: No Room for Complacency," *Europe Report*, October 23, 2003, p. 15, *http://unpan1.un.org/intradoc/groups/public/documents/UNTC/UNPAN015070.pdf*.
15. IOM Skopje, "Romanian Girl Testified against Valeshta Pimp Dilaver Bojku, aka Leku," March 6, 2003, *http://www.iomskopje.org.mk/CT/news/news_030603.html*.
16. "Macedonian Guilty of Slavery Charges," *New York Times*, December 7, 2003; IOM Skopje, "Dilaver Bojku Transferred to Struga Prison," April 7, 2003, *http://www.iomskopje.org.mk/CT/news/news_040703_2.html*.
17. Author's interview with U.S. diplomatic official who asked not to be identified, 2003.
18. Author's interview with Matei, 2005.
19. IOM Skopje, "Dilvar Bojku-Leku Escapes," June 21, 2003, *http://www.iomskopje.org.mk/CT/news/news_062103.html*.
20. Vasko Popetrevski, "Macedonia: 'Obvious Mishaps'—Ethnic Albanian Slaver Escapes Prison," *Reality Macedonia*, June 23, 2003, *http://www.reality-macedonia.org.mk/web/news_page.asp?nid=2634*.
21. Author's interview with U.S. diplomatic official who asked not to be identified, 2005.
22. IOM Skopje, "U.S. Offers $10,000 Reward for Bojku Leku," July 6, 2003, *http://www.iomskopje.org.mk/CT/news/news_070603.html*.
23. IOM Skopje, "Bojku-Leku Caught; Brought to Skopje," July 7, 2003, *http://www.iomskopje.org.mk/CT/news/news_070703.html*.
24. Author's interview with U.S. diplomat who asked not to be identified, 2005.
25. Ibid.
26. Ibid.; SECI, "In Europe Sex Slavery Is Thriving," news release, October 7, 2002.
27. Author's interview with U.S. diplomat who asked not to be identified, 2005; SECI, evaluation report, Operation Mirage.
28. SECI, evaluation report, Operation Mirage.
29. Ibid.
30. Ibid.
31. IOM, "Changing Patterns and Trends of Trafficking in Persons in the Balkan Region, July 2004, pp. 8–14.
32. Ibid., 9.
33. Ibid., 15.
34. SECI assessment provided to author by confidential U.S. diplomatic source, 2005.
35. Ibid.
36. Author's interview with confidential law enforcement source, 2006.

Chapter 8　*Sweat, Toil, and Tears*

1. Brad Wong, "Chapter 1: Servitude in American Samoa," *Seattle Post-Intelligencer*, November 17, 2003, *http://seattlepi.nwsource.com/specials/madeinmisery/148325_day1main17.html*.
2. Ibid.
3. Ibid.
4. Ibid.; FBI, "Anatomy, Part 1."
5. FBI, "Anatomy, Part 1."
6. Ibid.
7. U.S. Department of Justice, Federal Bureau of Investigation, "Anatomy of an International Human Trafficking Case, Part 2: Kil Soo Lee and the Case of

the Samoan Sweatshop," July 19, 2004, *http://www.fbi.gov/page2/july04/kisoolee 071904.htm*.

8. Debra Barayuga, "Owner Imprisoned in 'Slavery' Case," *Honolulu Star-Bulletin*, June 23, 2005, *http://starbulletin.com/prnt/?fr=/2005/06/23/news/story6.html*; U.S. Department of Justice, "Statement by U.S. Attorney Ed Kubo on the Sentencing of Kil Soo Lee Today before the Honorable District Judge Susan Oki Mollway," June 22, 2005, *http://www.usdoj.gov/usao/hi/pr/2003/0506kilsoolee.html*.

9. U.S. Department of Justice, "Statement by U.S. Attorney Ed Kubo."

10. *U.S. v. Johannes Du Preez et al.*

11. Ibid.

12. Ibid.

13. Ibid.

14. Ibid.

15. Ibid.

16. *U.S. v. Maria Garcia et al.*, 02-CR-00110, U.S. District Court for the Western District of New York, case file.

17. Ibid.

18. Ibid.

19. Ibid.

20. Ibid.

21. U.S. Department of Justice, "Three Florida Men Sentenced in Conspiracy to Detain Workers in Conditions of Involuntary Servitude," November 20, 2002, *http://www.usdoj.gov/opa/pr/2002.November/02_crt_687.htm*.

22. Ibid.

23. Ibid.

24. *U.S. v. Michael Allen Lee*.

25. Ibid.

26. *U.S. v. Hana Al Jader*, 05-CR-10085, U.S. District Court for the District of Massachusetts, case file.

27. Ibid.

28. Ibid.

29. Ibid.

30. *U.S. v. Homaiden Al-Turki et al.*, 05-CR-00280, U.S. District Court for the District of Colorado, case file; *U.S. v. Homaiden Al-Turki et al.*, 05-CV-02445, U.S. District Court for the District of Colorado, case file.

31. *U.S. v. Homaiden Al-Turki et al.*

32. Ibid.

33. *U.S. v. Joseph Djoumessi et al.*

34. Ibid.

35. *U.S. v. Mariluz Zavala et al.*

36. Ibid.

37. Ibid.

38. Ibid.

39. Ibid.

40. Ibid.

41. Ibid.

42. Ibid.

43. *U.S. v. Maner Jishi et al.*, 04-CR-00697, U.S. District Court District of New Jersey, case file; *Chandra Bulathwatte v. Maner Jishi et al.*, 04-CV-05032, U.S. District Court District of New Jersey, case file.

44. *U.S. v. Maner Jishi et al.*; *Chandra Bulathwatte v. Maner Jishi et al.*

45. Ibid.

46. Ibid.
47. Ibid.
48. Ibid.
49. Human Rights Center, "Executive Summary: Freedom Denied: Forced Labor in California" (Berkeley: University of California), February 2005, p. 3.
50. Ibid.
51. Author's interviews with government officials, 2005.

Chapter 9　**Sexual Slavery**

1. Rayman, "Stripped of Their Dignity," A6.
2. Author's interviews with FBI officials, 2001.
3. Author's interview with FBI organized crime expert, May 2000.
4. Anthony M. DeStefano, "The Brothels of Queens: Ex-Owner of Korean Massage Parlors in Flushing Discloses How They Worked," [New York] *Newsday*, March 11, 2001, p. A5.
5. Ibid.
6. Ibid.
7. Ibid.
8. Author's interviews with New York Police Department detective, 2004.
9. *U.S. v. Zheng Ming Yan et al.*
10. Ibid.
11. *U.S. v. Kyongja Kang et al.*, 04-CR-00087, U.S. District Court, Eastern District of New York, case file.
12. Ibid.
13. Ibid.
14. Ibid.
15. Ibid.
16. *U.S. v. Nam Young Lee et al.*
17. Ibid.
18. Ibid
19. Ibid.
20. Ibid.
21. *U.S. v. Alex Babaev et al.*, 05-CR-00417, U.S. District Court, Eastern District of New York, case file.
22. Ibid.
23. Ibid.
24. Ibid.
25. *U.S. v. Michail Aronov et al.*
26. Ibid.
27. Ibid.
28. Ibid.
29. U.S. Department of Justice, "Mexican Nationals Operating a Brothel Sentenced for Human Trafficking," December 19, 2003, *http://www.usdoj.gov/usao.txw/index.html*.
30. U.S. Department of Justice, "Operator of Brothel Where Immigrant Minors Worked As Prostitutes Sentenced to 4.5 Years in Federal Prison," November 1, 2004, *http://www.usdoj.gov/usao/cac/pr2004/139.html*.
31. *U.S. v. Luisa Medrano et al.*, 05-CR-148, U.S. District Court District of New Jersey, case file; U.S. Department of Justice, "10 Indicted in International Human Smuggling Ring; Young Honduran Women Forced to Work in Hudson County Bars," July 21, 2005, *http://www.njusao.org/break.html*.

32. Ibid.
33. Ibid.
34. *U.S. v. Josue Flores Carreto et al.*, 04-CR-140, U.S. District Court, Eastern District of New York, case file.
35. Ibid.
36. Ibid.
37. Ibid.
38. Ibid.
39. Ibid.
40. Ibid.
41. Ibid.
42. *U.S. v. Javier Cortes-Eliosa*, 06-M-251, U.S. District Court, Eastern District of New York, case file.
43. Ibid.

Chapter 10   New Initiatives, More Controversy

1. Chris Smith, remarks on H.R. 2620, Trafficking Victims Protection Reauthorization Act of 2003, 108th Cong., 1st sess., November 4, 2003, *Congressional Record*, pp. H10284–88.
2. Ibid.
3. Ibid., H10285.
4. "SFOR Contractor Involvement," *Human Rights Watch* 14, no. 9 (November 2002): 62–68.
5. Ibid.
6. White House, press release: "Trafficking in Persons National Security Presidential Directive," February 25, 2003, *http://www.whitehouse.gov/news/releases/2003/02/20030225.html*.
7. Smith, remarks on H.R. 2620, p. H10285.
8. Ibid.
9. Ibid., H10286.
10. Ibid., H10285.
11. Ibid.
12. U.S. Congress, House of Representatives, Committee on the Judiciary, "Report on Trafficking Victims Protection Reauthorization Act of 2003," no. 108-264, 108th Cong., 2d sess., September 29, 2003, p. 15, *http://thomas.loc.gov/cgi-bin/cpquery/T?&report=hr264p1&dbname=cp108&*.
13. Smith, remarks on H.R. 2620, p. H10285.
14. Ibid.
15. Ibid.
16. Summary of H.R. 2620, 108th Cong., 1st sess., *http://thomas.loc.gov*.
17. See listing for Discovery Institute at *http://www.sourcewatch.org/index.php?title=Discovery_Institute.*; and John Miller biography at *http://www.discovery.org*.
18. McKelvey, "Of Human Bondage."
19. Smith, remarks on H.R. 2620, p. H10285.
20. U.S. Congress, House of Representatives, Committee on International Relations, "Report on Trafficking Victims Protection Reauthorization Act of 2003," 17–18.
21. Summary of H.R. 2620, *http://thomas.loc.gov*.
22. U.S. Department of Justice, Office of Legislative Affairs, letter, September 24, 2003, reprinted in U.S. Congress, House of Representatives, Committee on the Judiciary, "Report on Trafficking Victims Protection Reauthorization Act of 2003," 10–11.

23. Summary of H.R. 2620; Public Law 108–193, sec. 4.

24. Public Law 108–193, sec. 7.

25. Donna M. Hughes, remarks to the Senate Foreign Relations Committee, Subcommittee of East Asian and Pacific Affairs: "Trafficking of Women and Children in East Asia and Beyond: A Review of U.S. Policy," April 9, 2003.

26. Sealing Cheng, "Good Intentions Can Do Harm," *Korean Times*, December 13, 2004, *http://times.hankooki.com/service/print.*

27. Ann Jordan, open letter, January 7, 2004.

28. Ibid.

29. Ibid.

30. Ibid.

31. Henry A. Waxman, letter to U.S. Attorney General Alberto Gonzales, April 13, 2005.

32. Ibid.

33. ACT UP East Bay et al., open letter to President George W. Bush, May 18, 2005.

34. *DKT International, Inc., v. United States Agency for International Development et al.*, 05-CV-01604, U.S. District Court, District of Columbia, complaint, request for a preliminary injunction, responsive papers.

35. Ibid.

36. Ibid.

37. U.S. Department of State, fact sheet: "The Link Between Prostitution and Sex Trafficking," November 24, 2004, *http://www.state.gov/r/pa/ei/rls/38790.htm.*

38. Ann Jordan et al., open letter to Ambassador John Miller, April 21, 2005.

39. Ibid.

40. John Miller, letter to Ann Jordan et al., no date.

41. Ibid.

42. U.S. Department of State, fact sheet.

43. Author's interview with Iana Matei, 2004.

44. Norwegian Ministry of Justice and the Police, "Purchasing Sexual Services in Sweden and the Netherlands: Legal Regulation and Experience," abbreviated English version, October 8, 2004, *http://odin.dep.no/filarkiv/232216/Purchasing_Sexual_Services_in_Sweden_and_The_Nederlands.pdf.*

45. Ibid.

46. Ibid.

47. Ibid.

48. Ibid.

49. Ibid.

50. Ibid.

51. John Cornyn, remarks on the introduction of S. 937, "The End Demand for Sex Trafficking Act of 2005," 109th Cong., 1st sess., April 28, 2005, *Congressional Record*, pp. S4553–56.

52. Ibid., S4554.

53. Author's interview with Juhu Thukral, 2006.

54. Ibid.

55. U.S. Department of State, fact sheet.

56. U.S. Senate, "End Demand For Sex Trafficking Act of 2005," S. 937, 109th Cong., 1st sess., April 28, 2005, *http://thomas.loc.gov/cgi-bin/thomas.*

57. Cornyn, remarks on S. 937, pp. S4554–56.

58. Ann Jordan et al., open letter to Senator John Cornyn, April 22, 2005.

59. Definition of "Prohibition," *http://www.eyewitnesstohistory.com.*

Chapter 11   **The Bully Pulpit**

1. Jordan, *Annotated Guide*.
2. U.S. Department of State, "Trafficking in Persons Report," July 2001.
3. Ibid.
4. Ibid.
5. Ibid.
6. Ibid.
7. Human Rights Watch, press release, "U.S. State Department Trafficking Report a 'Mixed Bag,'" July 12, 2001.
8. U.S. Department of State, "Trafficking in Persons Report," July 2001.
9. U.S. Department of State, "Trafficking in Persons Report," June 2002.
10. Ibid.
11. Concerned Women for America, news release, "The 2002 Trafficking in Persons (TIP) Report: Analysis of the Congressional Hearing," July 25, 2002.
12. U.S. Department of State, "Trafficking in Persons Report," June 2003.
13. U.S. Department of State, "Presidential Determination with Respect to Foreign Governments' Efforts Regarding Trafficking in Persons," September 9, 2003, *http://www.state.gov/g/tip/rls/rpt/25017.htm*.
14. Ibid.
15. U.S. Department of State, "Trafficking in Persons Report," June 2004.
16. Ibid.
17. John Miller, "On-The-Record Briefing: On the Rollout of the 2004 Trafficking in Persons Annual Report," U.S. Department of State, June 14, 2004.
18. Jyoti Sanghera, remarks, Symposium on Human Trafficking, Council on Foreign Relation, New York, May 3, 2006, transcript by Federal News Service; author's notes.
19. Ann Jordan, remarks, Symposium on Human Trafficking, Council on Foreign Relations, New York, May 3, 2006, transcript by Federal News Service; author's notes.
20. United Nations, Conference of the Parties to the U.N. Convention against Transnational Organized Crime, analytical report on the implementation of the Protocol to Prevent, Suppress, and Punish Trafficking in Persons, Especially Women and Children, supplementing the United Nations Convention against Transnational Organized Crime," CTOC/COP/2005/3, September 14, 2005, pp. 42–43.
21. Ibid.

Chapter 12   **Measuring Effectiveness**

1. Author's interview with GAO officials, May 2006. The GAO was scheduled to release part of its study in the summer of 2006.
2. U.S. Department of Justice, "Report to Congress," p. 16.
3. GAO, "Combating Alien Smuggling: Opportunities Exist to Improve the Federal Response," May 2005, p. 24.
4. U.S. Department of Justice, "Report to Congress," 23.
5. U.S. Department of Justice, "Assessment of U.S. Activities to Combat Trafficking in Persons, 2004," June 2004, pp. 33–34.
6. TRAC, "About the Data: Understanding the Terminology Which Agencies Use," *http://tracfed.syr.edu/data/jus/data Terminology.html*.
7. Ibid.

8. Author's interview with member of U.S. Attorney's Office for the Eastern District of New York, March 2006.
9. U.S. Department of Justice, "Assessment of U.S. Activities."
10. Data provided to author by TRAC, December 2005.
11. *U.S. v. Josue Flores Carreto et al.*
12. Author's personal observations of court proceedings; author's interviews with law enforcement officials in the Brooklyn U.S. Attorney's Office, 2005.
13. *U.S. v. Nam Young Lee.*
14. U.S. Department of Justice, "Report to Congress," 7–9.
15. Ibid., 10–11; U.S. Department of Justice, "Assessment of U.S. Activities," 14–16.
16. U.S. Department of Justice, "Assessment of U.S. Activities," 18–19; U.S. Department of Justice, "Report to Congress," 12–13.
17. U.S. Department of Justice "Assessment of U.S. Activities," 20; U.S. Department of Justice, "Report to Congress," 14.
18. U.S. Department of Justice, "Assessment of U.S. Activities," 41, 40.
19. GAO, "Combating Alien Smuggling," 59–60.
20. Ibid., 59.
21. U.S. Department of Justice, "Report to Congress," 53 ; GAO, "Human Trafficking: Better Data, Strategy, and Reporting Needed to Enhance U.S. Antitrafficking Efforts Abroad," July 2006, highlights section, www.gao.gov/cgi-bin/getrept?GAO-06825.
22. IOM, "The Second Annual Report on Victims of Trafficking in South Eastern Europe," September 16, 2005, p. 12, http://www.iom.int/en/news/pr884_en.shtml.
23. Ibid., 12–14.
24. Ibid., 13.

Chapter 13   **Final Thoughts**

1. American Forces Information Service, "DoD Fights Human Trafficking with Training, Awareness," September 21, 2004, http://www.defenselink.mil.
2. North Atlantic Treaty Organization, "NATO Policy on Combating Trafficking in Human Beings," June 29, 2004, http://www.nato.int.
3. Author's interview with Matei, May 2006.
4. Neha Misra, remarks, Symposium on Human Trafficking, Council on Foreign Relation, New York, May 3, 2006, transcript by Federal News Service; author's notes.
5. Sanghera, remarks, Symposium on Human Trafficking.
6. Author's interview with Matei, 2006.
7. Jordan, remarks, Symposium on Human Trafficking.

Index

About the Author

ANTHONY M. DESTEFANO is a staff reporter covering New York City legal affairs and criminal justice for *Newsday* newspaper. He was part of a team of *Newsday* reporters who won the 1992 Pulitzer Prize for spot news while covering the crash of a subway train at Union Square. Since joining *Newsday* in 1986, he also has covered immigration and organized crime for the newspaper's city edition, including the trials of subway gunman Bernhard Goetz, Gambino crime boss John Gotti, Bonanno crime boss Joseph Massino, and "Mafia cops" Louis Eppolito and Stephen Caracappa. Before joining *Newsday*, he was a staff reporter at the *Wall Street Journal* and *Fairchild News Service*.

DeStefano received a bachelor of science degree from Ithaca College, a master of arts from Michigan State University, and a juris doctor from New York Law School. He is an attorney and member of the New York State bar.

DeStefano is the author of *Gloria Estefan: The Pop Superstar from Tragedy to Triumph* (Dutton, 1997), *Latino Folk Medicine: Healing Herbal Remedies from Ancient Traditions* (Ballantine, 2001), and *The Last Godfather: Joseph Massino and the Fall of the Bonnano Crime Family* (Citadel, 2006). He lives in New Jersey.

CPSIA information can be obtained at www.ICGtesting.com
Printed in the USA
BVOW07s0612250714

360461BV00003B/153/P